# The Vital Realities
# for 2020 and Beyond

*Writings on Water Wars, Nuclear Devastation,
Endless War, Economic Revolution,
and Surveillance Versus Freedom*

# The Vital Realities for 2020 and Beyond

*Writings on Water Wars, Nuclear Devastation, Endless War, Economic Revolution, and Surveillance Versus Freedom*

## Roger Armbrust

Parkhurst Brothers Publishers
MARION, MICHIGAN

© Principal text copyright 2019 by Roger Armbrust. All rights reserved under the laws and treaties of the United States of America and all international copyright conventions and treaties. No part of this book may be reproduced in any form, except for brief passages quoted within news, blogs, reviews, or similar works, without the express prior written consent of Permissions Director, Parkhurst Brothers Publishers. The Publisher manages world rights to this work and retains the Susan Schulman Literary Agency of New York City, New York, U.S.A. to execute all rights transactions.

**www.parkhurstbrothers.com**

Consumers may order Parkhurst Brothers books from their favorite online or bricks-and-mortar booksellers, expecting prompt delivery. Parkhurst Brothers books are distributed to the trade through the Chicago Distribution Center. Trade and library orders may be placed through Ingram Book Company, Baker & Taylor, Follett Library Resources and other book industry wholesalers. To order from Chicago Distribution Center, phone 1-800-621-2736 or fax to 800-621-8476. Copies of this and other Parkhurst Brothers Publishers titles are available to organizations and corporations for purchase in quantity by contacting Special Sales Department at our home office location, listed on our web site. Manuscript submission guidelines for this publishing company are available at our web site.

**First Edition, November 2019**

Printing history: 2019  2020  2021  2022      8 7 6 5 4 3 2 1

Library Cataloging Data
    1. Author—Roger Armbrust, journalist and commentator
    2. Subject—Social and Political CommentaryPresidential
    3. Subject—2020 Presidential and Congressional Elections
    4. Subject—Water Rights
2019-November  trade paperback and e-book

ISBN: Trade Paperback    978162491-144-6
ISBN: e-book    978162491-145-3

Parkhurst Brothers Publishers believes that the free and open exchange of ideas is essential for the maintenance of our freedoms. We support the First Amendment of the United States Constitution and encourage all citizens to study all sides of public policy questions, making up their own minds.

Cover and interior design by    Susan Harring Design
Acquired for Parkhurst Brothers Publishers by    Ted Parkhurst

*This collection is dedicated to my friend*

*Leonard Jacobs*

*whose courage and foresight led to creation and nurturing of*

**The Clyde Fitch Report**

*where most of these columns first appeared.*

# Table of Contents

## The Vital Realities
Five Realities the Convention Speakers Wouldn't Reveal .............................. 12
Prepare to Fight Fascism: 2017 and Beyond ................................................. 18
Simplifying Trump and Seeing His Future ..................................................... 23

## Water Wars
Water Supply: Efforts to Act Locally and Globally .......................................... 28
Water Supply: State of the World .................................................................. 31
The Rising Specter of Privatizing Our Water .................................................. 37
The World's Water: More Precious than Gold and Oil ..................................... 42
UN and US Water Concerns Increase ............................................................ 47
Water as a Weapon of Bloody and Financial War .......................................... 51
The World's Chief Global Risk? Water Supply ................................................ 56
Water: Reports Point to Worldwide Problems ................................................ 61
Your Wallet and Life Crave Water and Air ..................................................... 67
In 2017, Water Had Better Become Your Top Concern .................................. 70

## Nuclear Destruction
A Return to a Cold...or Hot...War for You and Your Children ......................... 75
U.S. Activates Trillion-Dollar Nuke Buildup .................................................... 78
China, the U.S. and Looming War .................................................................. 83
NukeBuild: This Will Not End Well ................................................................. 88
Ban Nuclear Weapons, Despite Washington .................................................. 92

## Endless War and World War
Op-Ed: Obama, Congress and Our Afghan Reality ......................................... 96
Libya, the Invasion Continuum, and Us ........................................................ 100
Memorial Day: Recalling and Caring for Our Constant Brave ....................... 104
Ferencz Condemns Drone Attacks: "A Crime Against Humanity" ................. 112
Drone Control: Secret Killings Take Center Stage ........................................ 119
"Mali? Why?" We'll Whisper ........................................................................ 123
Syria: Symbol of Our Government's Endless-War Addiction ........................ 128
Obama the Invader: Tightening His Own Noose ........................................... 131
The Coming Conflict over Santa's Home ...................................................... 134
Confronting (Encouraging?) War in 2014 ..................................................... 138
How Do World Wars Ignite? .......................................................................... 142
Wannabe Gov Opposes Nat'l Guard Invading Foreign Nations ..................... 147
Will World War III Be a "Dollar" Conflict? ..................................................... 153
A Bush Insider Cites War Crimes Against His President, VP ........................ 157
Is War a Racket? An Honored Marine General Said "Yes!" .......................... 162
Hurtling Toward World War III ..................................................................... 165
Six Films Link Warmongers' Warped Mind .................................................. 170
Ron Paul: Washington's Peacenik Nemesis .................................................. 176
Paul Craig Roberts: Economic Peace Monger ............................................... 181
"Apocalypse: WWI" Will Teach Your Children Well ...................................... 186
Memorial Day: Reflecting on Our Nation's Father and Ike ........................... 189
Global Hot Spots: Both Climate and Military Conflict ................................... 194
World War III: The Heat Rises ...................................................................... 198
Will U.S.-Russia Syria Pact Avoid World War? .............................................. 203
A War Criminal Slow Jams the "News" ........................................................ 207
After Chilcot Report: Will ICC Try Blair, Bush? ............................................. 209

Obama Widens Carter's, Bush's Global-Rule Policies ............................ 214
Saudis Wage Violent/Economic Global Wars ...................................... 219
In Vietnam and U.S., Millions Still Affected by Agent Orange .................. 224
Vet Colonel Scathes Gulf Military Policy, Prez Hopefuls ....................... 228

## Economic Revolution
Solving the Decade of Our Discontent ........................................... 235
PBS "Frontline": Yeoman's Effort at Solving Financial Crisis Puzzle ............ 240
Congress, Finance Law and Your Personal Economic Future ........................ 243
Iceland Lets Banks Fail, Sees Economy Blossom .................................. 248
Will UK Finally Jail Banksters? US Next? ....................................... 251
Austerity as Failure and Killer ................................................ 254
A Journalist's Concern about the Clintons ...................................... 258
Russia, China Forsake the Dollar, Pressing U.S., EU ............................ 263
Economic Meltdown Zombies: They're Baaaack! .................................... 267
BRICS Forms Funds, Defying U.S., IMF, and World Bank ........................... 272
Economic Meltdown Zombies II ................................................... 276
The Sanctions Mess, Energy and You ............................................. 281
Geneva Warns of Greater Global Economic Crisis ................................. 286
As U.S. Austerity Deepens, Prepare for Revolution .............................. 289
China Tightens Bonds with Russia, India ........................................ 293
Greece's Debt Battle: What's the Real Story? ................................... 297
Greece, Others Falling to Predator Creditors ................................... 300
Unsustainable: Debt Rising for Students, Individuals ........................... 304
Oligarchs, Central Banks and Our Sinking Economy ............................... 308
This is the Economic Plan All Candidates Need .................................. 312
How Hillary Must Change, for Us ................................................ 315
At Davos & UN, Xi Firms China's Global-Leader Status ........................... 319

## Surveillance Versus Freedom
Will the U.S. Indict the Wikileaks Leader? ..................................... 325
Forming America: John Adams' Thoughts on Government ............................ 330
Homeland Security Aims at Internet Control ..................................... 334
July 4: Our Independence Versus Today's Emergency Powers ....................... 338
Obama Expands His Power over Internet, Media ................................... 343
Senate Bill Supports President's Effort to Control the Internet ................ 346
Why Ecuador REALLY Gave Assange Asylum ......................................... 350
In a Free Country, We Can Protest Conventions .................................. 354
Who Won the Presidential Debate? Edward Bernays! ............................... 357
Big Brother (Homeland Security) Keeps Going Local .............................. 361
What's Left of Human Rights? ................................................... 365
Our Government's Abusive, Selective Rule of Law ................................ 369
Senate Scraps CISPA...But Watch Your Back ...................................... 374
None's Well That's Orwell ...................................................... 378
American Majority Finally Opposes NSA Surveillance ............................. 385
Bradley Manning: Within the Torture, Signs of Victory .......................... 390
Whistleblowers, Activists Call on Intelligence Peers to Step Forward ........... 393
National Security Depends on Press Freedom ..................................... 398
Oligarchy's Sibling Rivals: the U.S. and Russia ................................ 404
Following Paris, Police States Grow as Economies Shrink ........................ 407
Your Freedoms and the TPP, TTIP, and RCEP ...................................... 413
Time for U.S. "Third" Parties to Rise .......................................... 417
Why Fascists Fear the Arts...and You ........................................... 422

Water Wars = Climate change's war with water and its disappearance, the war over privatization of water, and water as a tool of bloody war.

Nuclear Devastation = Political leaders expanding the threat of final war through build up of nuclear arsenals, destruction of nuclear treaties, and technology's vulnerabilities making nuclear war more possible.

Endless War = America's decades of conniving to maintain the Military-Industrial Complex and regional war as a racket, dissolving the nation's psyche for the profit of a few.

Economic Revolution = The decade of cancerous revolution which has been happening to you whether you realize it or not. Wall Street's wolves conning the entire economy; subprime loans (homes, cars, student loans, credit cards, small business loans), and credit leading to the deepest global public and private debt in history. Also, creditor nations abusing debtor nations with austerity demands, costing people's lives and countries' natural resources.

Surveillance Versus Freedom = The continuum of government-corporate efforts to stifle sustainable economic revolution, and our press-and-public pushback.

# Foreword

The journalist's job is to observe, record, analyze, connect the dots, and inform the public.

The politician's job is to succumb to a constituency in order to get and stay elected. The politician doesn't want the public to connect the dots and be informed. Nor does the military-industrial complex, which needs endless war to continue to exist. Nor does the major corporation or bank, whose goal is not public service, but to encourage consumption. Their vital realities are not your vital realities.

These columns cover political and economic issues from 2010 to 2017, most published in my "Peculiar Progressive" columns for *The Clyde Fitch Report* out of New York. They are issues still vital today. Many are concerns which politicians want to avoid or distort. But they will matter when you vote in 2020 and beyond. The columns trace the recent history of politics and the economy in these areas which deeply affect you. Hopefully these writings will help you better understand the reality when candidates work to twist your emotion and attitude toward them.

In one column I quote the country songwriter Tom T. Hall who, when asked to write a song about ecology, responded, "You can't write a song about ecology. You have to write a song about an empty beer can." Meaning it's hard to grasp a concrete image of ecology. But you can see and hold a beer can, and see them cast on the roadside.

It's the same for climate change, in my view. All the effects of climate change come down to one thing: water. Humans, who are 60-70 percent water, must have clean water to survive. Without it, none of the other issues will matter because we won't be here to deal with them.

So this book's first section deals with water.

The next major deterrent to your and my life on earth: nuclear devastation. So that's the book's second segment.

The third book unit concerns endless war. Our younger generations have grown up surrounded by it and expecting life to be that way. It doesn't have to be. But you have to understand what causes it if you're going to do anything about it.

The fourth section: economic revolution. It directly affects you every day. I try to clarify it with concrete examples of how it has evolved over nearly the last decade.

Lastly, surveillance versus freedom. The younger generations have grown up with surveillance, thinking it's necessary for freedom, when it's just the opposite.

# The Vital Realities

# Five Realities the Convention Speakers Wouldn't Reveal

**Roger Armbrust,** September 9, 2012

Politicians are kind of like poets: It's not what they say; it's what they don't say. The difference is this: Poets will give you a concrete image or a specific, and invite you to apply it to the universe and reality, the good and the bad. The universal shines through the particular, Aristotle believed. The country songwriter Tom T. Hall said you can't write a song about ecology; you have to write about an empty beer can.

> Politicians, however, will ply you with their alleged
> good specifics and the opponents' bad to evil ones.
> They want you to apply that to the universe. And they
> don't want you to *even think* about reality.

Through two weeks of Republican and Democratic propaganda, no one spoke of how they have failed us, or their low esteem in the polls. Only the possible worst of them, George W. Bush, suddenly and briefly became a decent politician: he didn't show up at the Republican soiree, recognizing and silently signaling his failure through his absence. If only the others had joined him.

Here are five specific issues, five vital realities, they wouldn't dare discuss *concretely* in their droning words. We should consider these in questioning whether America needs either of these men as president, or if you should keep your current Congressmember and senators in office. Also, there are two solutions for taking back control of your country, maybe.

You've heard of all these issues before, but have you considered them all together? They all are linked, both in this column and in reality. Each of these specific areas seems to be growing dire. So, if you care, you'll see a lot of red links to click and read. If you don't care, then just accept what you get in the coming four years.

First the five realities you'll surely be facing with the next president and Congress:

## 1. Water

Humans are made up of 60 percent water. The number of humans on earth is increasing, now at 7.04 billion, and projected to grow.

The earth's fresh water is decreasing. The world's aquifers are being diminished faster than nature can refill them.

The earth's water is 97 percent ocean, salt water. China is looking at investing as much as $31 billion in desalination. America has invested $1 trillion in foreign military invasions but trails in desalination efforts. That needs to change.

## 2. Food

Eighty percent of the nation's fresh water is used for agriculture, both crops and livestock. If population is growing and fresh water is diminishing, then logically humans will have less food to eat. We're seeing this now in a worldwide drought the pols try not to talk about. Did you hear Obama or Romney talk about solutions for this?

Scientists said last month the world should look to a future as vegetarians, since there won't be enough water and crops to supply food for livestock and humans both. (I'll have a No. 5

veggie burger with fries, please...No, make that a No. 3 veggie burger.)

But there's a problem with veggies: Genetically modified organisms (GMOs), i.e. the recombining of a plant's DNA. Controversies abound over GMOs and food.

European countries and China have outlawed Monsanto's and other firms' GMOs in food. India and Latin America are seeing a battle between traditional farming and corporate proliferation, including Monsanto's GMOs in corn and soybeans, patenting of seeds and purchase of seed companies. Farmers in the U.S. have legally battled alleged intimidation by Monsanto.

The United States government, since at least George H.W. Bush, has catered to Monsanto and GMOs. In fact, Obama appointed former Monsanto VP Michael Taylor as America's food czar, who is supposed to be our protector.

But an effort has begun in the U.S. to at least find out if GMOs are in our food. California's November ballot includes a proposition requiring labeling of foods to show any GMO contents. Monsanto and other corporations are spending millions in opposing the proposal. What does that tell you about the safety of GMO food?

**3. Energy**
The world-meaning humans' homes, governments and businesses-operates on energy. Oil, natural gas, vehicular gas. Electricity from water (yes, water again), solar and wind, and nuclear.

America daily consumes as much oil as the industrial world's next five largest countries*COMBINED*.

The American military accounts for 93 percent of the U.S. government's energy consumption, mostly through invading foreign countries to control oil and gas resources, though our government calls it expanding democracy.

We've seen deadly problems with nuclear accidents: Russia's Chernobyl in 1986 and Japan's Fukushima Daini disaster in March 2011. Scientists are still researching environmental problems resulting from both.

U.S. nuclear-energy plants continue to age, bringing growing environmental concerns. The Great Lakes' shores alone are encircled by 37 aging nuclear power plants. Others operate near major metropolitan areas like New York City.

**4. Military-industrial complex**
War hero and Republican President Dwight Eisenhower was the caring leader who warned us about the military-industrial complex. We've seen deadly, torturous specifics of its proliferation under Bush, more under Obama and you can expect more under Romney. Neither Obama nor Romney touched these in their speeches. Surprised? These will include:

   a. Continuing of endless war, war profiteering and weapons sales, and drones. Leon Pinetta, our Secretary of Defense, hopes to expand this.
   b. Further eliminating of Human Rights – Killing without trial, spying without warrant, secret prisons, private prisons, quelling government whistle blowers.
   c. Expandng police state-massive surveillance, quelling protests, controlling cyberspace and society.

**5. Personal and Economic Health**
You can't really separate these since one affects the other. Candidates tell you they want to turn the depressed economy around. But they don't want to truly regulate the big banks, or separate the commercial and investment banks as Congress did under the Glass-Steagall Act in the '30s. In fact, Congress overturned it in the '90s, leading to the 2008 economic meltdown and today's depression.

And they don't want to discuss with you dissolution of the middle class, America's nearly trillion-dollar credit card debt,

Roger Armbrust

America's trillion-dollar student loan debt, or American homeowners who were supposed to get relief from the bailout, but didn't.

**Two Solutions**

How can YOU solve this? You'll have to get organized, get educated, and get active so you can implement these:

**1. Take back Congress:**
You must take control of your Congressional delegation. Why? Because Congress controls the federal government's purse strings. Without money, a president can't invade foreign countries or support the military-industrial complex or growing police state. How do you fight the multi-national corporations and their Washington lobbyists? You vote, and you convince others in your Congressional district to vote with you.

Actually, Ralph Nader explained it about as simply as one can in a 2007 speech:
Each of you lives in a Congressional district. Each of you has two senators and a Congress member who you pay to serve you.

The average Congressional district consists of about 600,000 Americans. Research shows that, of those 600,000 Americans, about 2,000 truly affect your legislators' votes on funding, laws and regulations. **YOU** need to be one of those 2,000.
You can do that, can't you? Sure you can. Your future and your children's future depend on it.

**2. Constitutional right of petition:**
If you don't replace your senators and Congressmember, or if they won't serve you but keep serving the president and military-industrial behemoth, you will need to exercise your right of petition to pass or change laws. This link is a look at that process. It's slow and arduous. But the Vietnam, Iraq and Afghanistan invasions have been too.

If Solutions 1 and 2 don't work, history shows you'll see the securing of totalitarianism, or violent revolution. And we know where that leads by looking at Russia a century ago and currently in the Middle East.

Can't happen in America? That depends on whether you get organized, get educated, and get active.

# Prepare to Fight Fascism: 2017 and Beyond

**Roger Armbrust,** November 14, 2016

When Donald Trump takes the presidency next year – bringing with him the likes of Rudolph Giuliani and Chris Christie – you'll need to protect yourself against efforts to turn our oligarchic state into a fascist state.

First, here's why. And lastly, here's how.

**Why**

Merriam-Webster's dictionary defines Fascism:

*...a political philosophy, movement, or regime (as that of the Fascisti) that exalts nation and often race above the individual and that stands for a centralized autocratic government headed by a dictatorial leader, severe economic and social regimentation, and forcible suppression of opposition.*

This, of course, also defines Donald Trump, his professed philosophy, actions and where he plans to take us. Voters seem to think they elected (via the electoral college, not the popular vote, which he lost) a populist, garrulous, successful entrepreneur — a powerful corporate leader opposed to the establishment. That's a media illusion developed through a decade on his "reality" TV show. It's a corporate media that, first, loved him because of his TV ratings, then, second, began to attack him when they realized they had helped him become a viable candidate.

## The Vital Realities for 2020 and Beyond

So, now, he is about to take command of the most powerful, war-aggressive military in world history, massive government spy apparatus and abusive federal legal system.

Trump, in his youth, was weaned by a real-estate father to be a business "killer" (his father's term), and a winner and not a loser, according to *PBS Frontline*. In young adulthood, he was trained by the notorious lawyer Roy Cohn. Cohn made his name as a legal henchman for Sen. Joseph McCarthy, the notorious '50s "Red-Scare" politician. Cohn represented Trump in business for years, pushing him to (1) never admit to anything negative, (2) propagandize every negative into a positive and (3) if anybody sues you, countersue. That's not what you would call an honest life, but it is a way to help protect yourself legally.

You can get a clear view of Trump's history, as well as Hillary Clinton's — the formation of their thinking, philosophy, speech and actions — in the powerful *PBS Frontline* documentary "The Choice 2016".

Trump has applied those three Cohn dictums in his aggressive business and political behavior for decades. And he will apply them as president. He's let no one stand in his way. When he personally made millions off his failed Taj Mahal Casino in Atlantic City, he sloughed off the millions of dollars stockholders lost, saying they should have monitored their investments better, according to *Frontline*.

When the Trump Taj Mahal and other Trump-titled assets began to fail in the '90s, banks kept from busting him, deciding they'd lose all their loan money if they took his name off the buildings. He's gone to school on that, no longer starting new hotel projects, but selling his name worldwide while others actually own and develop the businesses. He may say he's doing the constructing, but he's not. That, and his illusive TV persona, carry him to this day.

Can't you just see Trump turning into a Vladimir Putin, secretly making billions off of others' businesses when he's president? He's been groomed for it. And if anyone gets in his way, now he can implement presidential power to overrun them. Look for him to operate with policymakers globally, publicly pushing American nationalism, but in private saying, "Let's you and I make a deal. What's in it for me?"

**The Constitution**
So you'll have to, first, be prepared to defend your Constitution of the United States and its Bill of Rights.

Think immediately of the First Amendment, and particularly the freedom of the press and freedom of speech. Recall that Trump, during his presidential campaign often ostracized members of the press — refusing to let them into his campaign functions — if he didn't like their questions or articles about him.

President Barack Obama took great pains to control the press. His Federal Bureau of Investigation (FBI) tapped the *Associated Press*'s emails. We included this in our column "None's Well That's Orwell". And Obama's Justice Department also tried to intimidate *all* reporters by going after Pulitzer Prize-winning *New York Times* reporter James Risen, threatening him with jail if he didn't reveal the name of a whistle-blowing source. We wrote about this in detail in our column "National Security Depends on Press Freedom".

Trump will be ready to put all the government power available to him to carry Obama's press intimidation program even farther. How far will a fascist dictator go? Just research Turkey currently under its democratically-elected president-turned-dictator Recep Tayyip Erdogan.

Trump has also shown abusive disdain for minorities, immigrants, women and public protesters. And you can bet he'll find ways to intimidate and jail them. And if he can't pass a law to do it, he'll simply sign a presidential executive order, and it will come into play before the public even realizes it.

Also, Congress has given the president broad emergency powers if he decides to declare a national emergency. These powers allow dictatorial control over the nation when the chief executive declares a national emergency. We wrote about the overwhelming emergency presidential powers in our column "July 4: Our Independence Versus Today's Emergency Powers".

**Austerity and Police Power**
Following the U.S. national midterm elections in 2014, we wrote the column "As U.S. Austerity Deepens, Prepare for Revolution".

We saw the Millionaire Congress begin implementing its austerity, fighting health care, limiting unemployment compensation, caring little about hundreds of thousands returning military veterans from our endless wars with Traumatic Brain Injury (TBI) and Post Traumatic Stress Syndrome (PTSD), leading to daily suicides.

As the new Millionaire Congress (Republicans and Democrats) further ramp up austerity, and Trump supports it, look for the nation to move even closer to revolution. Hopefully peaceful revolution, but probably not.

During his campaign, Trump preached for more police control of the public, not less. Fear of revolution prompted the federal government under Obama to supply military hardware to local police forces. He reluctantly claimed to stop it late in his second term due to the public outcry. But expect Trump, flashing his mantle as Commander in Chief, to encourage greater militarizing of police nationwide.

**Privatization**
Internationally, American and European oligarchs have looked for chances to move into debt-torn countries and swallow up their public assets and natural resources at dirt-cheap prices, turning public services into private corporate operations. Washington has colluded with private corporations to do that, particularly in South America, as we wrote about in our column "Why Ecuador REALLY Gave Assange Asylum".

Roger Armbrust

That would be right up Trump's alley. His top priority has always been "making a deal", i.e. making money. And as president he'll have national and global opportunities to secretly do that.

Cohorts will encourage it. Giuliani as mayor of New York pushed to both censor and privatize the arts, and keep the public from investigating budgets, but was stalled by federal court rulings. After his mayoral effort, he tried to privately control millions in a fund for families of 9/11 victims — until a group of police widows threatened to file suit. Christie, as governor of New Jersey, has moved water supplyservices from public control to the private sector.

These are the first issues to consider and respond to as Trump works to consolidate his power. We'll be looking more at these and other issues — ranging from domestic to foreign affairs — as we move forward.

**How**
How can you defend yourself and your fellow citizens from the coming fascist onslaught? *Peculiar Progressive* for years has encouraged you to get organized (you can't do it alone), get educated to each issue's specifics and get active in bringing about change. It's now going to take a massive effort to defend yourself, your children and your Constitution. It's doubtful you'll get much help from the Millionaire Congress — who could refuse to fund Trump efforts, but won't — or from a conservative U.S. Supreme Court he's about to make more conservative by appointing a ninth judge.

History shows that dictators move into power unexpectedly during economic downturns, coups d'etat, revolutions or states of emergency.

So, to your marks, get set, go.

# Simplifying Trump and Seeing His Future
**Roger Armbrust,** February 20, 2017

Following the November presidential elections, we offered you our column "Prepare to Fight Fascism: 2017 and Beyond". Within it, we gave you Donald Trump's modus operandi throughout his decades of business life:

> *Trump, in his youth, was weaned by a real-estate father to be a business "killer" (his father's term), and a winner and not a loser, according to PBS Frontline. In young adulthood, he was trained by the notorious lawyer Roy Cohn. Cohn made his name as a legal henchman for Sen. Joseph McCarthy, the notorious '50s "Red-Scare"politician. Cohn represented Trump in business for years, pushing him to (1) never admit to anything negative, (2) propagandize every negative into a positive, and (3) if anybody sues you, countersue. That's not what you would call an honest life, but it is a way to help protect yourself legally.*

During his brief presidency, you've seen Trump stay with these three Cohn Core Principles. Let's look at how he's done this with two of the major issues he's faced in his first weeks:

- From his court-failed, seven-Muslim-country immigration ban to the in-out dash of National Security

Advisor Michael Flynn, Trump continues, and will continue, to see no fault or flaw in his own choices or actions. He never admits to anything negative.

- He immediately propagandized both the legally failed immigration ban and Flynn's departure. Rather than admitting to a Constitutional problem with the ban, he blamed the federal judge for ineptness, referring to him as "this so-called judge". In his rambling, ego-filled press conference last week, he refused to say Flynn lied to Vice-President Pence and the FBI about his contacts with Russia. Trump said, "Mike Flynn is a fine person...What he did wasn't wrong — what he did in terms of the information he saw. What was wrong was the way that other people, including yourselves [the press] in this room, were given that information, because that was classified information that was given illegally. That's the real problem.
- "So, you see, this is Trump's way of "countersuing". When the federal judge says your presidential order is at fault, Trump responds: Well, you're not even really a judge; you're a "so-called judge". When his national security advisor lies, he's not a bad guy. It's the fault of whoever leaked the info, and the press for revealing it.

You will see him stay with the Cohn Core Principles – the denial of truth and propagandizing of untruths — throughout his presidency, however long that may be, because they have helped him get whatever he's wanted for decades.

**The Bill Clinton Future Keys**
Bill Clinton, when governor of Arkansas, gave us the three keys to simplifying Trump's future as president.

Clinton would sometimes start a speech by telling this joke: He had just moved into the governor's office, replacing David Pryor, who had been elected to the U.S. Senate. Clinton discovered in his desk three sealed letters which Pryor had written him. Attached was a note advising him to open one letter whenever he really ran into trouble. Clinton explained he did just that at three different trouble spots:

The first letter read, "Dear Bill: Blame it on the legislature." The second letter said, "Dear Bill: Blame it on the press." The third letter advised, "Dear Bill: Write three letters."

Trump hasn't really sent any significant legislation to Congress in these first weeks, so he has yet to fume at the lawmakers. But he will. After he's eased his volley of presidential executive orders.

Trump instead has concentrated on warring with the press, which worked for him during his presidential campaign. It's a propaganda onslaught based on – as most of his arguments are – generalities with no specific data to back them up. He believes repeating terms like "fake news" and journalistic "lies" – verbalized over and over and over – will lead the public to believe him and not the press. Same with the federal courts: hammer away that they are incompetent judges while he is the competent president.

Of course, Trump's supporters – the 46 percent of voters who checked his name – already believe him. The question: How many will continue to when they see that his approach works for political campaigns, but not for governing.

The press and the courts will not go away. He'll try to make them. So, now more than ever, the citizens of the United States need to follow President Dwight D. Eisenhower's charge:

> *Only an alert and knowledgeable citizenry can compel the proper meshing of the huge industrial and military machinery of defense with our peaceful methods and goals, so that security and liberty may prosper together.*

"Only an alert and knowledgeable citizenry" can protect the nation and world from a president who refuses to acknowledge

Roger Armbrust

accountability, relies on propaganda rather than truth, and who practices "countersuing" rather than cooperation and compromise.

Only an alert and knowledgeable citizenry can force a person in power to honor the Constitution; or else open that third letter, and then write three letters of his own...or maybe just three tweets.

# Water Wars

# Water Supply: Efforts to Act Locally and Globally
**Roger Armbrust,** March 11, 2013

This evening, Lanya Ross is talking at the Andover (MN) Senior Center about "Water Supply Sustainability in the North Metro." The League of Women Voters is hosting the program.

Ross is principal environmental scientist with the Metropolitan Council, the regional planning agency of the Twin Cities metropolitan area. Andover's a suburb. Ross is explaining the council's regional analysis of the cumulative and long-term impacts of the seven-county metropolitan area's water-use choices.

This is good. Water use is a subject local communities should be examining worldwide. Why?

*Peculiar Progressive* explained in a *CFR* column last year how water is one of the five vital issues presidential candidates wouldn't touch during their national conventions. But the public IS touching it, with vigor.

In Hawaii last week, conservationists, biologists and volunteers trekked the Walanae Mountains to reintroduce the rain forests to native plants, and help preserve the area's fresh water.

In San Francisco, the nonprofit group SPUR recently issued a report on how to meet the bay area's water-supply needs in the 21st century.

Two telling global analyses came out recently:

First, The World Economic Forum released its *Global Risks 2013*, listing its top five risks by likelihood and impact and 50 overall risks. Water supply crises ranked fourth by likelihood and second by impact. The report can be valuable for its emphasis on interconnecting risks ranging from economy to climate. However, the 80-page analysis can bog one down with data and charts weaving together issues.

Second, just over a week ago, the New York Academy of Sciences presented a panel to answer the question, "Where's the water of the future?"

"There is no secret source of water of the future," was the panelists' summary. "Conservation is the best answer."

Meanwhile, two news reports this past week looked at a pair of the globe's largest areas. In "Aspiring Africa," *The Economist* magazine reports that the world's poorest continent is bustling in some areas economically and politically. But water problems loom:

> About a third of Africa's GDP growth comes from commodities. This will not last. Today's prices are near record highs and commodity markets have a habit of collapsing. Furthermore, recent gains in agricultural commodities may be undermined by climate change. Even now, savannahs are drying out, water tables are dropping and rains either failing or becoming more irregular. One in five Africans will be directly affected by 2020. Even as their continent prospers, many of them will continue to depend on agriculture and there is little they can do about the threats to the world's environment.

Roger Armbrust

Further east, *China Daily* on March 7 headlined "Droughts raise water concerns," explaining:

> *Regular droughts in winter, spring and early summer started in 2009 and have continued to affect rural and mountainous areas of Southwest China this year, reshaping the lifestyles of people and causing a major shift in the agricultural industry.*

The report notes in one of the heaviest-hit areas:

> *The lingering drought has hit 15 cities and autonomous prefectures in Yunnan [a province bordering Myanmar, Laos, and Vietnam], affecting 5.58 million people, according to the latest provincial civil affairs department statistics, and of those, 1.2 million face drinking water shortages.*

> *This year's drought has also caused the loss of more than 557,000 hectares of crops, with 70,000 hectares of land facing complete crop failures – an estimated economic loss of up to 2.77 billion yuan ($445.4 million), authorities said.*

Officials both in Africa and China are struggling to provide short-term relief and are yet to find long-term answers.

# Water Supply: State of the World
**Roger Armbrust,** April 22, 2013

We're seeing efforts on the world's continents to grapple with growing populations and providing them with water.

The European Union announced last week that 2.6 million more people in the EU's member states are being served by water supply, and 5.7 million more by wastewater projects.

> The figures are part of an overview of how EU Structural Funds are working in member states. Through its three funds-the European Regional Development Fund (ERDF), the European Social Fund (ESF), and the Cohesion Fund-the EU is investing ‚Ç¨347 billion from 2007-2013 in the 27 member states. This represents 35% of the total EU budget for the same period (‚Ç¨975 billion), according to a European Union release.

Most of the additional population served by water projects, nearly 1.3 million, lives in the following countries: Estonia (around 1,675,488), France (408,300), Portugal (202,700) and Greece (160,800).

You can read the EU's press report, and within it links to the fund studies *here*.

Roger Armbrust

## China

China's water-supply struggles seem to be growing, according to *GreenBiz.com*. These include "Droughts in the north, floods in the south. Toxic industrial runoff, overdrawn ground water and even bloated pigs and dead ducks in major waterways."

But the report by Brooke Barton notes that specific information on the problems is hard to come by:

> *Media censorship and poor government data means limited access to information for many corporate managers we speak to at Ceres who are only beginning to understand the complicated nature of the water risks facing their Chinese supply base.*

But the basic news that is coming out can signal alarm. Barton writes:

> *At least 50 percent of Chinese urban groundwater and 90 percent of urban rivers are considered polluted. About half of all wastewater is released into the environment untreated, affecting ecological and human health alike. And a government assessment released just last week found that half of China's rivers — 28,000 in all — have simply "disappeared" since the country's waterways were last surveyed in the 1990s.*

These issues can have a direct effect on the U.S., Barton explains:

> *We all know that China is the supply chain hub for the American economy. Nearly everything we use — mobile phones, TVs, handbags and even U.S. Olympic team clothing — is made in China, where export jobs support 200 million workers.*

Link to Barton's article and its resources **here**.

## India, Australia Share Water Management

The Australian government and the Indian Institute of Technology have signed a memorandum of understanding to share the Aussies' hydrological modeling platform Source.

Australia's *The Sydney Morning Herald* reported last week:

> *Australia developed the Source software over 15 years, at a cost of more than $300 million, as a modelling tool to improve the management of Australia's major river system, the Murray-Darling Basin.*
>
> *In Delhi, eWater chief executive Gary Jones said there were similarities in India's river basins to the Murray-Darling experience, including competing demands for water from different sectors, conflict between states over water rights, high rainfall variability, and the effects of climate change.*

The news report explained that "many of India's most famous rivers, such as the Ganges and Yamuna, are toxically polluted, and major cities often run dry of drinking water."

Meanwhile, in Mumbai, India, water from the BMC supply chain has grown markedly dirtier, *The Times of India* reported last week.

> *By the civic body's own admission, of the tens of thousands of water samples it tested in 2012-2013, 19% were found unsafe for consumption. This was far worse than in 2011-2012, when the tally of samples found undrinkable was 16%.*
>
> *All year round, the corporation's engineers and health officers randomly collect water samples to study the quality of supply. In 2012-2013, officials gathered 60,726 samples from the 24 municipal wards. Nearly 11,700 of*

*these tested contaminated. And of these dirty samples, 1,474 were found to have the deadly E.coli bacteria.*

**Africa**
Tanzania's newspaper *The Citizen* recently reported that WaterAid, an international non-governmental organization, has challenged the United Nations to set a new global target to achieve its Millennium Development Goal No 7, a universal access to water, sanitation and hygiene by 15 more years, because the UN probably won't meet its 2015 target.

*Medical journal The Lancet conducted a 2012 study which revealed that about 400,000 children under five die every year in sub-Saharan Africa due to diarrhea primarily caused by unsafe water and poor sanitation, The Citizen said. The newspaper's reporter Athuman Mtulya added:*

*WaterAid Pan-Africa programme manager Nelson Gomonda said: "A total of 330 million Africans today live without access to clean water, so the road to travel is long, but we can for the first time see the end in sight. With more than 1,000 African children under five dying every day of diseases due to lack of water and sanitation, Africans will not accept failure. We have to reach this target."*

In 2008, African governments signed the eThekwini Declaration, committing them to spending at least 0.5 per cent of their GDP on sanitation and hygiene. But WaterAid issued a report in February showing the governments were not meeting that commitment.

See *The Citizen* story **here**.

Meanwhile, in Ethiopia, UNICEF and the nation's Ministries of Education; Health; and Water, Mines and Energy, have issued a set of guidelines to improve access and quality of water, sanitation and hygiene (WASH) services in the country's primary schools and health facilities.

Ethiopia's DireTube Media Group reported:

> *Current data from a National WASH Inventory conducted in 2012, revealed that the water supply for primary schools stands at 31 per cent, while sanitation coverage is 33 per cent in an estimated 27,000 primary schools across Ethiopia. In the country's 3, 200 health facilities, a mere 32 per cent have safe water.*

In northwestern Nigeria, the state of Zamfara's Governor Abdulaziz Yari announced his administration has so far spent N7 billion to improve water supply throughout the state in the last two years.

He said the state government had already paid contractors about N4 billion to handle water projects across the state. He was awaiting project completions, and then would pay up the outstanding balance, according to *Premium Times*.

**United States**
The U.S. Supreme Court is scheduled Tuesday to hear a battle between Texas and Oklahoma over water rights. Today's newsok.com reports:

> *The case before the high court was brought by the Tarrant Regional Water District, a Texas agency that provides water to more than 6 million residents of North Texas and says it desperately needs more water to supply the growing population.*
>
> *The agency claims Texas is entitled to water that can only be obtained in Oklahoma, and it argues that the compact implicitly allows for the water to be taken from Oklahoma.*
>
> *Oklahoma and the other two states that are part of the Red River Compact – Arkansas and Louisiana – say the compact doesn't entitle Texas to take water within Oklahoma's boundaries.*

Roger Armbrust

Meanwhile, in Arkansas, Central Arkansas Water's Board of Commissioners is asking ExxonMobil for a plan to move an oil pipeline away from an area that drains into the main source of drinking water for Little Rock and surrounding communities.

*Chem.Info* reports:

> *The request came nearly two weeks after ExxonMobil's Pegasus pipeline ruptured and spilled thousands of barrels of oil in Mayflower, a small city about 25 miles northwest of Little Rock.*
>
> *ExxonMobil has said the March 29 spill didn't affect Mayflower's drinking water supply, which comes from a lake about 65 miles away and is managed by a different supplier.*
>
> *But that hasn't ended concerns about drinking water in the region, as the pipeline runs through part of the Lake Maumelle Watershed, the area that drains into the main drinking water supply for hundreds of thousands of people.*
>
> *Central Arkansas Water's board is also asking ExxonMobil to come up with short-term solutions to reduce the risk of an oil spill in the watershed.*

# The Rising Specter of Privatizing Our Water
**Roger Armbrust,** June 18, 2013

Last September, following the maudlin national political conventions, *Peculiar Progressive*wrote about the five vital issues the political parties didn't want to face. You can read about those five vital realities *here*. Issue number one is water.

The bottom line: The earth's fresh water is decreasing. The world's aquifers are being diminished faster than nature can refill them.

The specter: While this is occurring, an effort is also rising to privatize the world's water. Nestlé is at the forefront of this effort.

Nestlé, the Swiss multinational nutritional, snack food, and health-related consumer goodscompany, is the world's largest food company via revenues. Its bottle water division, Nestlé Waters, produces and distributes 64 brands including Aquarel, Arrowhead Water, Contrex, Deer Park Spring Water, Ice Mountain, Nestlé Pure Life, Ozarka, Perrier, Poland Spring, and San Pellegrino.

In its most recent effort at capturing public water for private profit, Nestlé Waters North America is looking to finalize an exclusive 45-year contract with the water company for

Roger Armbrust

Fryeburg, Maine (pop. 3,449), which sits on the Saco River. Under the contract, Nestle will pay $240,000 a year to annually draw a minimum of 75 million gallons in water for private bottling and distribution.

Last week, Maine Gov. Paul LePage received a petition with 136,000 signatures protesting the contract. The effort is to update a 16-year-old pact with Nestlé's Poland Spring water. Opponents are concerned about the length of the extension with no public input on the process. A spokesman for Poland Spring said any opponents have a process for filing complaints. You can read about the Fryeburg situation *here*.

A 2010 story in *The Colorado Independent* provides a more specific description of the Nestlé process with the company's plan to drain millions of gallons of fresh water from the Arkansas River in Colorado:

> If things go according to plan, in about a month someone at Nestle Waters North America will turn a valve and water will begin running out of a pipeline near Buena Vista and will splash into an empty 8,000-gallon tanker truck. It will take roughly an hour for the truck to fill, and then another truck will take its place. The water will run 24 hours a day, filling approximately 25 trucks each day, every day.

> The trucks will drive 120 miles to a Nestle bottling plant in Denver where the water will be used to fill hundreds and thousands and millions of little plastic Arrowhead Springs water bottles, which will then be trucked to convenience markets, grocery stores, movie theaters, and sports palaces around the West. Each month, Nestle will fill roughly 40.4 million 16.9 ounce bottles with the water from the area's Nathrop spring. By the end of a year, 65 million gallons of Arkansas Valley water will have been driven to Denver, bottled, driven somewhere else, and sold.

There was opposition in Colorado, too. As reporter Scot Kersgaard tells it:

> *Not everyone is happy about this. Buena Vista and Salida have birthed a protest movement that has been more noisy than effective. By some estimates, 80 percent of the roughly 17,000 people in Chaffee County are opposed to this diversion of water. Still, when it came time to issue permits, the three-member Board of County Commissioners was unanimous in approving Nestle's plans.*
>
> *In the end, it was probably a combination of fear and Old-West style property rights values that carried the day for Nestle.*

You can read that full story *here*.

These are just two instances involving the world's largest producer of bottled water at turning public water into private profit. Just as disturbing as a multi-national corporation and local politicians going against local residents' concerns: the attitude of Nestlé leadership toward privatizing water. In recent years, a video interview with Nestlé's chairman Peter Brabeck-Letmathe has emerged. In it, he says water supply is "not a human right," and water should be "valued" through privatization. In other words, don't drink it unless you can pay for it.

Yes, even public water utilities charge for water consumption, but the rates are subject to public hearing and political pressures. That seems less of a possibility with privatization, no matter the political rhetoric that surrounds it.

You can see the video interview with Brabeck-Letmathe *here*.

The problem is that areas suffering from a lack of water often can't afford to pay for it. And human nature shows that, where there's a lack of a resource, greed creeps in to gouge the con-

Roger Armbrust

sumer. Such a case occurred recently in Zimbabwe, where residents have to purchase water from illegal water traders. According to the Inter Press Service News Agency, "These new illegal businesses are the result of the dire need for water, as rationing in towns and cities continues because of shortages of water treatment chemicals in this southern African nation."

We also see the plight elsewhere in the world. Richard Whittell, co-author of the book *Resisting Reform: Water Profits and Democracy*, reports about England on opendemocracy.net. Last week he reported about the company Severn Trent, which supplies water across the Midlands and parts of Wales. Investment consortium LongRiver Partners is attempting to take over the company. Summarizing Whittell's article, opendemocracy.net notes:

> Severn Trent is the latest water company to be targeted for takeover by a motley group of investment funds. An analysis of their past deals reveals huge profits, meagre tax bills and a seemingly casual approach to ethical concerns. Once again public assets are turned into wealth for the few.

These new, illegal businesses are the result of the dire need for water, as rationing in towns and cities continues because of shortages of water treatment chemicals in this southern African nation. – See more at: http://www.ipsnews.net/2013/06/making-a-business-out-of-water-rationing/#sthash.ccbSLI3e.dpuf

*Reuters* reported last week that Singapore's private water companies are looking to profit greatly from China's plan to spend over $850 billion in response to the country's "scarce and polluted water supplies." And the Singapore firms are increasing as they see global water supply needs:

> Since 2006, the number of companies in Singapore's water sector has doubled to about 100 and S$470 million ($371.2 million) has been committed to fund water

*research, government data shows. Over the same period, Singapore-based water companies secured more than 100 international projects worth close to S$9 billion.*

As global aquifers diminish and population grows, the craving for water, and the private sector's efforts to control supply will grow. That's the nature of corporatism. It will be up to the world's citizens to get organized, get educated, and get active so they can protect their local interests in their water supplies, through regulation, legislation, and the courts.

# The World's Water: More Precious than Gold and Oil
**Roger Armbrust,** October 21, 2013

Recent studies and reports on the nation's and world's water supplies are citing specific problems with growing scarcity, and hoping to solve those problems. But the primary solution seems to be conservation as worldwide demand increases while supply does not. Also, getting an accurate handle on water costs is holding back multiple projects to increase supply.

"In more and more places around the world, water demands are bumping up against the limits of Earth's finite water supply," Sandra Postel explains in her *National Geographic* article "More Water Stress than Meets the Eye." "Each year seems to bring another analysis of 'water stress' to help us get a fix on how dangerous our water situation is becoming, whether in a particular country or in the world as a whole."

Postel, director of the Global Water Policy Project, and a Freshwater Fellow of the National Geographic Society, specifically cites a report from the Cooperative Institute for Research in Environmental Sciences at the University of Colorado in Boulder. The team there "examined 2,103 watersheds across the United States and found that in 193 of them – nearly 1 in 10 – water use has surpassed the natural water supply."

Postel says the study found major problems in the western U.S.:

# The Vital Realities for 2020 and Beyond

> *To meet the demands of their farms and cities, these regions typically rely on some combination of multi-year water storage, water imports from other basins, and groundwater pumping.*
>
> *Not surprisingly, most of the stressed watersheds lie in the western part of the country, where irrigated agriculture typically accounts for more than 80 percent of total water withdrawals.*

The research team conducted stress tests on major water use sectors, including agriculture, thermoelectric power plant cooling, and municipal and industrial use.

Three major factors show the water situation will worsen, Postel says:

> *One is that the large volume of water needed to cool nuclear and coal-fired power plants creates pockets of water stress all across the country, including in the fairly well-watered East and Midwest. Thermoelectric power generation demands more water than any other economic sector -some 201 billion gallons a day, or 49 percent of total US water withdrawals.*

The second point focuses on crowded southern California:

> *...most of southern California is classified as water stressed even when looking only at municipal and industrial water use. Farms and power plants worsen the stress...but urban water demands alone exceed the natural supply. Southern California makes up most of the difference by importing water from the northern part of the state, an increasingly contentious solution, as well as from the overtapped Colorado River.*
>
> *A third crucial take-away is that we're not paying enough attention to groundwater, a message we've con-*

Roger Armbrust

> *veyed many times...Even though groundwater makes up a growing share of water use nationally and globally, we don't measure and monitor it carefully enough to come close to getting an accurate picture of its role in our water accounts.*

**Water's Rising Cost**

The Earth Institute's *State of the Planet* blog last week had author Lakis Polycarpou simply asking "End of Cheap Water?"

He opens by citing a Columbia University study of America's municipal water data, and concludes, "Across the country, Americans are paying more for water than they did a decade ago, even as water utilities fall into debt and water infrastructure deteriorates." That 45-page Columbia *study is here*.

Polycarpou also offers a *USA Today* analysis from a year ago which makes clear from its headline and data that "Water Costs Gush Higher." The article surveys 100 municipalities, and finds that "residential water bills in at least one in four places have doubled in the past 12 years."

The article notes:

> The trend toward higher bills is being driven by:
> — The cost of paying off the debt on bonds municipalities issue to fund expensive repairs or upgrades on aging water systems.
> — Increases in the cost of electricity, chemicals and fuel used to supply and treat water.
> — Compliance with federal government clean-water mandates.
> — Rising pension and health care costs for water agency workers.
> — Increased security safeguards for water systems since the 9/11 terror attacks.

## Verifying Cost May Lead to Funding

"Water is the most common substance found on earth, yet some observers predict that it will become as precious and contentious as oil is today," explains an IBM article on its website's *A Smarter Planet* section. "With only 1 percent of the world's supply available for drinking, and roughly 11 percent of the global population lacking access to potable water, it's easy to see why."

But the article notes that, for the globe to send the valuable commodity through new and repaired systems, the financial taps must flow with funding. The article goes on to quote Rajasekar Krishnamurthy, a research manager at IBM's Almaden Research lab:

> *There is a backlog of water development projects, estimated to be about $1 trillion...The true cost of water production, the true efficiency, is not well known. Water is often subsidized in different ways, so it's difficult, almost impossible, to monitor its true cost.*

To help solve this problem, IBM has developed the Water Cost Index. This research comes from the Accelerated Discovery Lab at IBM Research in San Jose, CA. You can learn more about the *Water Cost Index here*.

## Elsewhere around the World

You can take a further look at China's disappearing rivers in this article from *The Economist*.

UK-based pipeline technology company Syrinix says it has been invited to join a European consortium–SmartWater4Europe–to design the drinking water supply of the future. More about that here.

Last week, *The New York Times* reported completion of a water tunnel to serve all of Manhattan:

Roger Armbrust

> *In one of the most significant milestones for the city's water supply in nearly a century, the tunnel – authorized in 1954, begun in 1970 and considered the largest capital construction project ever undertaken in the five boroughs – will for the first time be equipped to provide water for all of Manhattan. Since 1917, the borough has relied on Tunnel No. 1, which was never inspected or significantly repaired after its opening.*

On India's coast, Cyclone Phailin "has wrought havoc in the neighbouring districts but has not had any impact here [in Visakhapatnam], the port city called The Jewel of the East Coast. This report from *The Hindu* newspaper. So the city's water supply should be satisfactory.

Meanwhile, *The Huffington Post* asks why Canada's Prime Minister is selling the nation's fresh water supply to French companies.

And, lastly, *Reuters* on Friday offered a vague report that the FBI "is investigating possible threats to the water supply systems in Wichita, Kansas, and several other Midwestern cities that are as yet unsubstantiated." More here.

# UN and US Water Concerns Increase
**Roger Armbrust,** March 18, 2014

In 2012, completely frustrated with the two leading presidential candidates ignoring responsibility in their campaign speeches, *Peculiar Progressive* pointed out the five vital realities facing America, and the world. The top priority is water. You'll find that column here.

This month, we're seeing concern about water conditions come from both the United Nations due to energy consumption, and in the U.S. from problems both with drought and pollution.

The UN will present its full United Nations World Water Development Report 2014 (WWDR) March 21 in Tokyo for World Water Day. Earlier this month, the UN released a capsuled view of the report, noting the interdependence of water and energy.

The capsule stated in part:

> *Currently, 15 percent of global water withdrawal is used for energy production. This percentage is expected to increase by another 20 percent between now and 2035 as population growth, urbanization and changing consumption patterns, especially in China and India, drives up the demand for energy.*

Roger Armbrust

> *Several world regions are already facing water shortages and the Report foresees that increasing energy demands will weigh heavily on remaining resources, especially in arid areas. The Report urges improved coordination between the water and energy sectors and greater private sector involvement in these areas. It also makes the case for a revision of water pricing policies, arguing that water is generally considered as a "gift of nature" and that its price rarely reflects real costs.*

It will be important to see the UN's attitude stated more specifically regarding "greater private sector involvement" and pricing policy that "reflects real costs." Will the UN face the reality of corporate efforts to take control of water supply? Will the UN encourage it? Will the international body encourage providing water for all, no matter the level of income, or push for water only for those who can afford higher prices? *Peculiar Progressive* looked at the issue of water privatization last June. That column is here.

Earlier this month, *The Motley Fool* (despite its cheek-tongue name a respected investment analysis site) stressed the problems in corporate takeover of water in its article "Coca-Cola and Nestle are Sucking Us Dry Without Our Even Knowing." The article points out:

> *The companies' conflicts with communities in Latin America, Asia, and Africa are too numerous and sordid to be invented from whole cloth. Moreover, the simple fact is that sucking groundwater out of one place, bottling it, and shipping it for sale in another place that typically already has perfectly safe public water ranks high on the list of stupid things to do with scarce water.*

> *So yes, Coca-Cola and Nestle are indeed sucking us dry. So are our modern agricultural practices and unconventional oil and gas extraction, to an even greater extent. A blended privatization scheme may*

indeed be part of the solution, but if it's done right, it will only make life harder for Coke and Nestle.

The Motley article actually opened with concern about the current California drought:

> The droughts currently ravaging California, which will likely send food prices soaring down the road, have highlighted the importance of available freshwater supplies. As 17 communities in California are within 60 days of running out of drinking water, the ability of companies like **Coca-Cola** (NYSE: KO ) and **Nestle** (NASDAQOTH: NSRGY ) to effectively privatize water supplies feels awfully disconcerting. While the rains that just began to fall out west may bring some measure of relief, the fact remains that the world is coming up hard against a water crisis.

Which brings us to national concerns about water here in the U.S. The most precious concern appears to be the dry situation in California, primarily due to the state's high population and its vital place in providing food supply, the number two priority in our earlier column on Five Vital Realities.

The California situation led the *Los Angeles Times* earlier this month to focus on a study revealing Americans' lack of concern about water supply. The study also revealed how we're involved in a national drought:

> The study's conclusions were based on an Internet survey of 1,020 people, and comes amid a national drought that extends from the Pacific Coast to portions of the Mississippi Valley, with the most severe conditions in California.
>
> "Most Americans assume that water supply is both reliable and plentiful," Attari wrote. "However, research

*has shown that with climate change water supply will become more variable due to salinization of ground water and increased variability in precipitation."*

The seriousness of the California issue has also been covered by both *Forbes* and CBS's Sacramento affiliate, seen in these two articles: "Drought Stokes California's Class War,"and "Strong Earthquake Could Pose Serious Threat to Delta Water Supply."

Meanwhile, at the nation's eastern end, the results of pollution continue to sting, seen in articles such as "Duke Energy's $1 Billion Cleanup: Who would pay?" and "The Future of Water Supply in Florida."

As scientists and conservationists look for possible ways to solve the water supply problem, more of those eyes are looking at storage of storm water. The country just celebrated National Groundwater Awareness Week from March 10-16. One article highlighted the U.S. National Academies of Science's 2012 report *Alternatives for Managing the Nation's Complex Contaminated Groundwater Sites*. The article also provided statistics regarding groundwater.

A week earlier, Minnesota Public Radio asked the question "Can We Fill Up Our Underground Water Supply with Stormwater?" Answers are provided here.

So, what do you think? Is it time for you to get organized, get educated, and get active in assuring adequate water supply for your community? Go for it!

# Water as a Weapon of Bloody and Financial War
**Roger Armbrust,** July 2, 2014

Continuing reports are showing us a growing, deadly trend in human-rights abuse. From Ukraine, to Syria and Iraq, to Egypt, to even Detroit, the denial of our most precious resource—water—can prove either an immediate deadly tool or a time bomb set to ignite conflict.

In late June, *Reuters* reported that eastern Ukraine conflicts were threatening water supplies to four million citizens, according to monitors for the Organization for Security and Cooperation in Europe (OSCE):

> *The OSCE's Special Monitoring Mission in eastern Ukraine quoted local officials as saying a water pumping station and a section of pipeline near the town of Semyonovka, close to the bitterly contested city of Slaviansk, had been damaged in fighting between government forces and separatists.*

> *"This pumping station and pipeline constitute the main water supply for Donetsk city's population of 1 million, and a further 3 million inhabitants of the region," it said in a statement following talks with Donetsk mayor Alexander Lukyanchenko.*

Roger Armbrust

> *The OSCE mission quoted the mayor on its Facebook page as saying that the water supply to Donetsk had not been affected yet, but that this was set to change "in a very short while".*

In early June, STRATRISKS, a website dedicated to "Observing the Grand Geopolitical Game of Risk," observed that the Turkish government had cut off the Euphrates River's flow, endangering both Syria and Iraq:

> *Al-Akhbar found out that the water level in Lake Assad has dropped by about six meters, leaving millions of Syrians without drinking water.*

> *Two weeks ago, the Turkish government once again intervened in the Syrian crisis. This time was different from anything it had attempted before and the repercussions of which may bring unprecedented catastrophes onto both Iraq and Syria.*

By June 24, Chatham House: The Royal Institute of International Affairs, announced that Syria was facing an imminent food and water crisis:

> *Syria's essential services are on the brink of collapse under the burden of continuous assault on critical water infrastructure. The stranglehold of extremist group Islamic State of Iraq and al-Sham (ISIS), neglect by the regime, and an eighth summer of drought may combine to create a water and food crisis which would escalate fatalities and migration rates in the country's ongoing three-year conflict...*

> *... The deliberate targeting of water supply networks and related structures is now a daily occurrence in the conflict.*

In Egypt, with a military coup in the last few months and potential revolution still simmering, in the background lies lingering

## The Vital Realities for 2020 and Beyond

hostility between Cairo and Ethiopia over a Nile dam. *Inter Press Service* reported in March:

> *Relations between Egypt and Ethiopia have soured since Ethiopia began construction on the 4.2 billion dollar Grand Renaissance Dam in 2011.*
>
> *Egypt fears the new dam, slated to begin operation in 2017, will reduce the downstream flow of the Nile, which 85 million Egyptians rely on for almost all of their water needs. Officials in the Ministry of Irrigation claim Egypt will lose 20 to 30 percent of its share of Nile water and nearly a third of the electricity generated by its Aswan High Dam.*
>
> *Ethiopia insists the Grand Renaissance Dam and its 74 billion cubic meter reservoir at the headwaters of the Blue Nile will have no adverse effect on Egypt's water share. It hopes the 6,000 megawatt hydroelectric project will lead to energy self-sufficiency and catapult the country out of grinding poverty.*

Meanwhile, at home in the U.S., a growing battle is taking shape over bankrupt Detroit's cutting off water to thousands of its citizens. The situation has grown dire enough for activist organizations to appeal to the United Nations. *Democracy Now* reports:

> *The Detroit Water and Sewerage Department says half of its 323,000 accounts are delinquent and has begun turning off the taps of those who do not pay bills that total above $150 or that are 60 days late. Since March, up to 3,000 account holders have had their water cut off every week. The Detroit water authority carries an estimated $5 billion in debt and has been the subject of privatization talks.*
>
> *In a submission to the United Nations special rapporteur on the human right to safe drinking water and*

*sanitation, activists say Detroit is trying to push through a private takeover of its water system at the expense of basic rights.*

This effort to privatize water through government bankruptcy appeared earlier this year in Greece. However, in late May, one of Greece's top courts blocked that planned privatization. Still, privatization efforts appear to be a growing concern to world citizens who consider water to be a human right. As far back as 2012, globalresearch.ca reported that Wall Street's mega-banks and "elitist billionaires" were ravaging public waters in efforts at privatization:

> *Familiar mega-banks and investing powerhouses such as Goldman Sachs, JP Morgan Chase, Citigroup, UBS, Deutsche Bank, Credit Suisse, Macquarie Bank, Barclays Bank, the Blackstone Group, Allianz, and HSBC Bank, among others, are consolidating their control over water. Wealthy tycoons such as T. Boone Pickens, former President George H.W. Bush and his family, Hong Kong's Li Ka-shing, Philippines' Manuel V. Pangilinan and other Filipino billionaires, and others are also buying thousands of acres of land with aquifers, lakes, water rights, water utilities, and shares in water engineering and technology companies all over the world...*
>
> *...In a JP Morgan equity research document, it states clearly that "Wall Street appears well aware of the investment opportunities in water supply infrastructure, wastewater treatment, and demand management technologies." Indeed, Wall Street is preparing to cash in on the global water grab in the coming decades. For example, Goldman Sachs has amassed more than $10 billion since 2006 for infrastructure investments, which include water.*

Also as early as 2012, *Peculiar Progressive* ranked water as the top vital reality that America's presidential candidates were avoiding discussing. You can read about the top five vital realities here.

Add to this continuing droughts in major U.S. states like California and Texas, as well as water problems for agriculture in China, expect water to affect food supply and food prices. Also, with a recent report citing most American water utilities wallowing in the red, look for efforts to move in and privatize the public systems.

Bottom line: If you believe water is a human right, not a resource to profit private persons or corporations (which the Supreme Court also considers "persons")—and if you want to protect this vital resource for you, your children, and future generations—seriously consider getting organized (you can't do it alone), getting educated, and getting active in protecting your water resources.

# The World's Chief Global Risk? Water Supply
**Roger Armbrust,** February 2, 2015

When the World Economic Forum (WEF), an annual gathering of Earth's money movers, met Jan. 21-24 in Davos, Switzerland, they were confronted with WEF's *Global Risks 2015 Report*. Risks of immediate impact were led, of course, by international conflicts. But the major risk considered to provide the most long-term global impact? Dwindling water supply.

**Drought in California**
Within the 69-page report came this summary:

> *Global water requirements are projected to be pushed beyond sustainable water supplies by 40% by 2030. Agriculture already accounts for on average 70% of total water consumption and, according to the World Bank, food production will need to increase by 50% by 2030 as the population grows and dietary habits change. The International Energy Agency further projects water consumption to meet the needs of energy generation and production to increase by 85% by 2035.*

*Peculiar Progressive*, disgusted in 2012 by presidential candidates avoiding vital issues to the U.S. and world, published a column citing the five vital realities. The first of those is water. That column is here.

# The Vital Realities for 2020 and Beyond

Meanwhile, of immediate concern are water issues ranging from drought in Brazil, the U.S. and water scarcity in China and Africa.

**Drought Lingers in Brazil**
In Brazil, grueling drought is bringing suffering to millions, with dwindling water supplies also endangering provision of electricity. *HydroWorld.com* reported last week:

> Brazil is experiencing a debilitating drought as the nation endures the driest period since South America's most populous country began keeping records in the 1930s. As a result of the arid conditions, reservoir levels and lake water flow to hydroelectric facilities that supply power to Brazil's most densely populated city of Sao Paulo are nearing zero capacity.
>
> According to the federal government, hydroelectric power facilities in the country's southeastern region that supply power to close to 20 million people in the metropolitan region of Sao Paulo (MRSP) are being deactivated. A list of the deactivated facilities is not immediately available, but Brazil normally receives about 70% of its electricity from hydroelectric plants, according to energy officials.

In another report, *bnamericas.com* revealed last week:

> Brazil's São Paulo water utility Sabesp could soon introduce a water rationing plan that involves shutting off supply five days a week.
>
> As the state's Cantareira water supply system – Brazil's biggest – is on the brink of drying up, "the five day per week service shut-off could happen if rainfall does not increase in the reservoir area soon," Sabesp's metropolitan director Paulo Massato Yoshimoto said on national TV.

> There has been a lack of rain in the region for more than a year, according to Yoshimoto, who affirmed that the 2014-15 rainy season looks to be even worse than the already critical 2013-14 season.

**China, Africa Struggle**
A University of Maryland professor and his international team's new paper in the *Proceedings of the National Academy of Sciences* provides a first-time full inventory of water transfers among Chinese provinces. It shows that China's recent years of soaring economic growth are causing the country's water supply to dwindle. The paper notes:

> The geographical mismatch between freshwater demand and available freshwater resources is one of the largest threats to sustainable water supply in China and throughout the world.

In Nigeria, water scarcity is a bigger killer than terrorist group Boko Haram, according to *Bloomberg*:

> While the [recent] terror campaign claimed more than 4,000 lives, the shortage of potable water and poor sanitation led to about 73,000 deaths, according to WaterAid, a London-based nonprofit.

> The water deficit isn't limited to isolated areas in the country's vast north. In Lagos, about 15 million of the coastal metropolis' 21 million have limited access to piped water.

> Africa's accelerating urbanization is colliding with governments' failure to provide the most basic services. Next year alone, Lagos will add more than the population of Boston, worsening its infrastructure shortfall.

In South Africa, according to the Mail & Guardian, the country's "thirst has just begun":

> For many South Africans, the water crisis is already here. For others, research and projections show, it is only a matter of time – and perhaps not a great deal of time.
>
> Thanks to load-shedding, and a shortage of water when electricity is restricted, the thirsty future could arrive in major urban centres as soon as this summer.

## In the U.S., Drought Plagues the West

Drought also continues to gnaw at major U.S. states like California, Colorado and Texas, affecting both citizens and food production.

In California, officials look to dam the situation, according to nbclosangeles.com:

> State water officials say they may dam parts of the Sacramento-San Joaquin Delta in an emergency measure to protect freshwater used by millions of Californians.
>
> The Department of Water Resources said Monday that if the drought persists they may build temporary rocky barriers blocking three channels on the Delta. They say the dams would decrease the amount of water released from upstream reservoirs to keep saltwater from creeping inland from the San Francisco Bay, contaminating the Delta.
>
> The Delta provides 25 million people with drinking water and irrigates millions of acres of farmland.

Meanwhile, Colorado has grown miserly about sharing fresh water with other states, says foxnews.com:

> To understand what's at stake here, a brief overview of the critical nature of the Colorado River and those who depend on it is in order:

Roger Armbrust

> *The river provides water to 40 million people in the states of Arizona, Wyoming, New Mexico, Utah, Nevada, California and Colorado. These seven states also make up one of the driest regions in the nation, dependent on a water flow that is miniscule in comparison to rivers in other parts of the United States.*
>
> *Making matters worse, recent droughts throughout the region have reduced the Colorado's already limited flow and left massive reservoirs like Lake Mead, which sits in Nevada and just over the Arizona border, at record lows.*

In Texas, even recent rains haven't provided sufficient relief for the state's long drought, reports dailytexanoline.com:

> *Despite steady rainfalls over the past six months, University researchers have found that Texas is still far from replenishing its groundwater supply, which is depleted because of a drought that began in 2011.*
>
> *Data gathered from satellites showed that, out of the 76 million acre-feet of water lost during the peak of the drought in 2011, only about 10 percent has been recovered as of November of last year. An acre-foot of water, which equates to about 326,700 gallons of water, covers an acre of land at a depth of one foot.*

Bottom line: Wherever in the world you reside, you'd be wise to get organized, educated, and active in caring for your local and state water supplies, as best you can.

# Water: Reports Point to Worldwide Problems
**Roger Armbrust,** March 30, 2015

*Peculiar Progressive* has consistently reported on the global water supply issue, hoping these repeated reports (including global struggles here, water as war weapon here, and privatizing water here) would help make readers aware of the urgent need to work for water sustainability worldwide.

Now recent reports from Duke University, the United Nations, the World Bank, and the International Committee of the Red Cross specify growing problems with water supply, and possibilities for solving them.

**Better Technology...or Else...**
"Population Could Outpace Water by Mid-Century" states the release headline to the Duke study, adding "Technological advances will be needed in coming decades to avoid water shortages." The report shows both hope and concern, stating:

> Population growth could cause global demand for water to outpace supply by mid-century if current levels of consumption continue. But it wouldn't be the first time this has happened...
>
> Using a delayed-feedback mathematical model that analyzes historic data to help project future trends,

Roger Armbrust

> the researchers identified a regularly recurring pattern of global water use in recent centuries. Periods of increased demand for water — often coinciding with population growth or other major demographic and social changes — were followed by periods of rapid innovation of new water technologies that helped end or ease any shortages.
>
> Based on this recurring pattern, the model predicts a similar period of innovation could occur in coming decades.

However, Anthony Parolari, the study's leader, added a warning:

> But if population growth trends continue, per-capita water use will have to decline even more sharply for there to be enough water to meet demand," he said. The world's population is projected to surge to 9.6 billion by 2050, up from an estimated 7 billion today.
>
> For every new person who is born, how much more water can we supply? The model suggests we may reach a tipping point where efficiency measures are no longer sufficient and water scarcity either impacts population growth or pushes us to find new water supplies...

He pointed to water recycling, and finding new and better ways to remove salt from seawater as two of the more likely technological advances that could help alleviate or avoid future water shortages.

**UN Hopes for Possibilities**
The United Nations 2015 report is entitled "Water for a Sustainable World," and the 139-page study offers solutions for each continent of the globe. But it also provides some huge future global numbers, including both positive and ominous:

> Global water demand is largely influenced by population growth, urbanization, food and energy security policies,

## The Vital Realities for 2020 and Beyond

*and macro-economic processes such as trade globalization, changing diets and increasing consumption. By 2050, global water demand is projected to increase by 55%, mainly due to growing demands from manufacturing, thermal electricity generation and domestic use...*

*...Investments in water and sanitation services result in substantial economic gains; in developing regions the return on investment has been estimated at us$5 to us$28 per dollar. An estimated us$53 billion a year over a five-year period would be needed to achieve universal coverage – a small sum given this represented less than 0.1% of the 2010 global GDP...*

*...The world's slum population, which is expected to reach nearly 900 million by 2020, is also more vulnerable to the impacts of extreme weather events. It is however possible to improve performance of urban water supply systems while continuing to expand the system and addressing the needs of the poor...*

*...By 2050, agriculture will need to produce 60% more food globally, and 100% more in developing countries...*

*...Global water demand for the manufacturing industry is expected to increase by 400% from 2000 to 2050, leading all other sectors, with the bulk of this increase occurring in emerging economies and developing countries.*

**Arab-World Water Crisis**

The World Bank's website offers a brief report headlined "By the numbers: Facts about water crisis in the Arab World". It points out that 6% of the world population lives in the Middle East and North Africa, but that area offers less than 2% of the world's renewable water supply.

Yet the report notes that parts of the region consume more water per capita than anywhere else in the world:

> *To meet water demand, many countries in the Middle East rely on desalination plants. Over 75% of worldwide desalinated water is in the Middle East and North Africa, 70% of which is in the GCC countries (Saudi Arabia, Kuwait, Qatar, Bahrain and the United Arab Emirates) and 6% in Libya and Algeria.*
>
> *In many MENA countries, 85% of water is consumed by the agriculture sector. More water-efficient agricultural practices will save water so it could be used to meet other demands. Good water-resource management depends on good agricultural irrigation policies.*

And, as if war isn't enough to rip Syria apart this year, the report notes:

> *Climate change is expected to bring an expected 20% reduction in rainfall and higher rates of evaporation that will make water scarcer. In Syria for example, a predicted rise in temperature, lack of rainfall and unpredictable weather could result in desertification of 60 % of its land area.*

**Middle Eastern Wars and Water**
On March 25, the Red Cross issued a report stressing that Middle Eastern wars — including in Syria, Iraq, Lebanon, Israel, and the Occupied Palestinian Territory — have pushed "water shortages to the breaking point".

Even without war and current droughts, the growing urban areas and food production demands might max water resources. The report notes:

> *Now with some 7.6 million people displaced within Syria and some 3.8 million seeking safety in neighbouring countries — along with another 2.5 million displaced due to fighting in Iraq — the situation is even more critical.*

## The Vital Realities for 2020 and Beyond

But the Red Cross says it and Islamic fellow organization Red Crescent (affiliated since 1919 as The International Federation of Red Cross and Red Crescent Societies, or IFRC) have been working hard to find solutions, including:

- 9.5 million people received water through emergency repairs or rehabilitation of supply systems.
- 600,000 people received water delivered by tanker trucks or in bottles.
- 1.1 million people benefited from improvements to water-storage or distribution facilities.

**UNICEF Reviews Kids and Water**

Meanwhile, the United Nations Children's Fund (UNICEF) offers good news and bad news:

On the good side, Ethiopia has supplied water to at least 48 million people. UNICEF explains how:

> *The key to Ethiopia's success during these years has been a combination of strong government leadership, persistent donor investment and the development of strong periodic policy instruments. In the year 2000, Ethiopia developed a Water Sector Strategy and Water Sector Development Programme, which paved the way for the progress. Government committed funds to the water supply sector and encouraged donors to invest in lower cost technologies to boost coverage levels. A total of US$ 2 billion has been invested by the Government, development partners, NGOs and the private sector in water supply since 1990.*

On the sadder side, the Ukraine conflict has left 700,000 people in the heavily damaged Donetsk and Luhansk oblasts without access to safe drinking water. UNICEF reveals:

> *In order to respond to the urgent need, UNICEF Ukraine, in collaboration with partners, has provided bottled*

*water to more than 118,000 people in eastern Ukraine. Moreover, UNICEF with the support from the EU Humanitarian Aid and Civil Protection Department (ECHO) has provided three water purification units to Krasnohorivka town (Donetsk oblast), which will secure a continuous supply of safe drinking water to 20,000 people.*

Also, yes, we realize the U.S. has its own Western drought problems, with a parched California fearing for its farm production, as well as struggles stretching over to Texas. We'll continue to keep an eye on this and the world in coming months.

# Your Wallet and Life Crave Water and Air
**Roger Armbrust,** May 16, 2016

Forget about central banks and interest rates. Forget about gas prices. Forget about keeping up with the Joneses. Focus now on what folks like the World Bank and Bank of America Merrill Lynch are focusing on: Water. Focus on what the World Health Organizationis focusing on: Global air pollution. Talk of those two humanly vital issues when you talk of the "sharing economy".

On May 3, the World Bank issued a report titled "High and Dry: Climate Change, Water and the Economy". The study explains that climate change will lead to water scarcity which will "cost some regions up to six percent of their GDP, spur migration, and spark conflict."

The study's executive summary reasons:

> *Water-related climate risks cascade through food, energy, urban, and environmental systems. Growing populations, rising incomes, and expanding cities will converge upon a world where the demand for water rises exponentially, while supply becomes more erratic and uncertain. If current water management policies persist, and climate models prove correct, water scarcity will proliferate to regions where it currently does not exist, and will greatly worsen in regions where water is already scarce.*

Roger Armbrust

The report specifically cites Central Africa, East Asia and the Middle East as the first to experience the economic and societal effects of water scarcity. But we're also seeing news reports from areas around the globe of droughts' heavy effects on economies ranging from India to South America. And we've seen natural drought in the American West, and economic drought in Detroit.

In a May 11 report, Business Insider quoted Bank of America Merrill Lynch's US Trust strategist Joe Quinlan. He cited concerns over hazards to the global economy ranging from China's slowdown, and growing emerging-market debt, to a possible European Union break-up. But he went further to say:

> *They all represent known unknowns — or externalities already acknowledged and discounted by the capital markets. That's the good news. The bad news: None of the hazards just mentioned are as remotely as threatening to the global economy as water-related climate change risks, a dynamic little understood by investors.*

Oh, and lest we forget: The issue of lead in water has grown from not only Flint, MI, but to a national concern.

**Solutions?**
So...are there solutions to the water-scarcity problem?
[pullquote align="right" cite="" link="" color="" class="" size=""]Tell us what you're going to do.[/pullquote]The World Bank suggests policies and investments leading "countries to more water secure and climate-resilient economies. This includes better planning for water resource allocation, adoption of incentives to increase water efficiency, and investments in infrastructure for more secure water supplies and availability."

Peculiar Progressive has doubts about such positive, cooperative generalities becoming reality. We've written often of problems with global water supply, including "Water as a Weapon of Bloody and Financial War". We don't see that going away anytime soon as the U.S. continues its global foreign policy of endless war, including building up its nuclear arsenal — which can instantly devastate water supply, air, and all human external and internal infrastructure.

We also see rising conflicts as corporations and governments continue drives to privatize water supply, with the profit motive cutting off this life-nourishing resource to masses of the dwindling middle class and growing poor.

**And Speaking of Air...**
The World Health Organization reported on May 12 that its new data — now covering 3,000 cities in 103 countries — showed that:

- More than 80 percent of people living in urban areas that monitor air pollution are exposed to air quality levels that exceed the World Health Organization (WHO) limits. While all regions of the world are affected, populations in low-income cities are the most impacted.
- According to the latest urban air quality database, 98 percent of cities in low- and middle-income countries with more than 100,000 inhabitants do not meet WHO air quality guidelines. However, in high-income countries, that percentage decreases to 56 percent...
- As urban air quality declines, the risk of stroke, heart disease, lung cancer, and chronic and acute respiratory diseases, including asthma, increases for the people who live in them.
- A study from the US National Institutes of Health noted in March that, in America, air pollution appears to be causing both premature births and deaths, costing billions of dollars.

Do you believe air pollution and water scarcity will abate? Do you believe that getting organized, educated and active in these two areas will help your community and therefore the world? Let us know what you think. And what you're going to do.

# In 2017, Water Had Better Become Your Top Concern
**Roger Armbrust,** December 26, 2016

If your Merry Christmas is truly going to become a Happy New Year, you the public must force policymakers in 2017 to make the world's water supply the top priority, including in the United States.

Gloomy global water projections, as well as stories of growing problems in specific areas, point to the urgent need for this. These reports have not lessened through 2016. They've become more numerous.

These include a *National Geographic* report of dwindling groundwater threatening global food shock; a World Bank study on climate change's negative effect on water and the global economy; and a panel of experts – including from NASA – who foresee climate change altering Asia's great river systems that feed 1.5 billion people.

In the United States alone, struggles expand. A new *Reuters* investigation has found thousands of U.S. locations with lead levels even higher than Flint's. The *Associated Press* predicts growing tensions in California over how much water will go to agriculture, fish, or humans as a new federal law tries to counter the six-year drought. New Jersey is caught in a drought with a "missing water plan". And last week in California, the city of Clovis won a $22 million court judgment against Shell Oil over toxic drinking water.

Also, America-involved endless wars see water supplies under continued threat in battle-torn areas. For example, toxic waste is leeching into Yemen's capital city's water supply as constant U.S.-supported bombing pummels infrastructure; and Syria's capital Damascus cut its water supply after rebels reportedly polluted it with diesel fuel.

Meanwhile, China continues to struggle with major pollution problems while increasing efforts to solve them. Last week, UK's *The Guardian* newspaper reported how Shanghai's water supply was pelted with 100 tons of garbage.

**The Globe, Solutions...and the Trump Problem**
There are glints of efforts at solutions.

Forest Trends Association, an organization of forest-industry leaders, donors, and environmental groups, reported from Washington, D.C. on Dec. 16:

> *It's been a banner year for green infrastructure, from the roll-out of the Paris climate deal to Peru's groundbreaking new water security strategy to California's recent legislation recognizing nature as a critical part of its water infrastructure.*
>
> *In 2015, governments, water utilities, companies, and communities spent nearly $25 billion on payments for green infrastructure for water. More than 400 programs in 62 countries invested in the natural ability of forests, wetlands, grasslands, and other ecosystems to ensure clean, reliable water supplies for cities and communities, and to combat threats from rapid urban expansion and agricultural pollution.*

Roger Armbrust

On Dec. 18, the *Financial Express* in India reported that 115 Indian cities have launched water supply and sewerage projects under the Atal Mission for Rejuvenation and Urban Transformation (AMRUT):

> *The AMRUT scheme was launched by PM Narendra Modi last year with the focus mainly on the urban renewal projects and to establish infrastructure so as to ensure adequate robust sewerage networks and water supply for urban India thereby fostering transformation.*

Meanwhile, last Tuesday, President Obama placed "a permanent ban on offshore drilling in broad parts of the Arctic and Atlantic coasts", according to the Los Angeles Times:

> *The ban relies on the Outer Continental Shelf Lands Act of 1953, which says the president "may, from time to time, withdraw" federal waters from oil and gas development that are not already leased. It was announced as part of a joint action with Canada, where Prime Minister Justin Trudeau also made long-term, though not permanent, commitments to protect the Arctic from drilling.*

Such a move by Obama might help secure ocean waters for both fishing and expanded efforts of desalination to supply fresh water to mainlands. But there's a problem:

Donald Trump.
The president-elect has made clear his opposition to global efforts of quelling climate change, especially through recent actions of filling his proposed cabinet with execs who are pro-oil, pro-Wall Street, and pro-privatization of public assets.

Can't you see the Money-Dealmaker immediately overturning Obama's permanent offshore drilling ban to please the head of Exxon, his pick for Secretary of State? And opposing any U.S. efforts to help other countries in environmental matters...unless they work out a secret-or-not financial deal for his connections?

## The Vital Realities for 2020 and Beyond

So don't look for the Billionaire President or Millionaire Congress (Republicans and Democrats) to readily or consistently aid the nation's and world's water-supply problems. You're going to have to get organized (you can't do it alone), get educated to issues, and get active if you're going to assure a vital water supply for you, your children, and your grandchildren.

**Nuclear Destruction**

# A Return to a Cold...or Hot... War for You and Your Children
**Roger Armbrust,** May 12, 2012

Ivo Daalder, the U.S. Permanent Representative to the North Atlantic Treaty Organization (NATO), last week seemed to be in a state of denial or ignorance when discussing a planned U.S.-led ballistic missile defense system's effect on Russia. His position should be of particular concern to Americans, because implementing such a system grinds us directly into another cold war, if not a hot one. And it also directly affects America's massive and growing deficit, which will plague our children and generations beyond.

In speaking at a gathering of the Council on Foreign Relations in Washington last Monday, Daalder said that Moscow was wary of the proposed missile defense system, and even wanted legal assurances the system wouldn't threaten Russia.

Daalder said that the missile system's placement "doesn't concern Russia" because its sights will be on the Middle East, which must mean Iran and Syria. Although Daalder didn't mention those two countries specifically, the U.S. Defense Department in a May 3 briefing in Moscow did:

"Shorter-range threats within key regions are growing rapidly: Iran, Syria, and North Korea possess 1000s of short-and medium-range missiles, potentially threatening to U.S. forces, allies, and partners," the PowerPoint briefing said in its opening point "Ballistic Missile Threat Continues to Advance." Yet the briefing also said, while the U.S. will provide missile defense to protect itself and its European partners, the defense system isn't aimed at Russia.

Here's the problem with that rationale: for a long time, Russia has aligned itself with Iran. At one point, while visiting Iran along with other Middle-East countries' reps-to discuss their mutual relationship regarding natural gas supplies and distribution-Russian President Vladimir Putin and the other nations agreed that an attack on any one of their natural-gas alliance members, including Iran, would be an attack on all of them.

More recently, in January 2012, Dmitry Rogozin, Russia's deputy prime minister and former envoy to NATO, said, "*Iran is our close neighbor, just south of the Caucasus. Should anything happen to Iran, should Iran get drawn into any political or military hardships, this will be a direct threat to our national security.*"

So, are Daalder, who represents the Obama administration and our country, and the Defense Department really not aware of these threatening goings-on? Are they in denial about Russia's position? Or do they think America's citizens who heard his question-answer session last Monday aren't smart enough to catch the administration's untruth, or can't connect the dots between Russia and Iran's relationship?

Daalder also told the Washington crowd that NATO is made up of 28 countries and is a Democratic organization in which each nation has a voice and vote in determining NATO policy and actions.

To anyone who understands money and power, that stance is hard to swallow. NATO receives funding from each of the nations, but four of those countries-the United States, United Kingdom, Germany and France-provide 60% of the funds. The

## The Vital Realities for 2020 and Beyond

U.S. contributes nearly 22%. Do you really think those major funders don't decide the directions NATO takes?

We'll get a clearer view of that later this month, when NATO holds its 25th summit in Chicago May 20-21. The agenda will include Afghanistan's future. Also, the media is speculating that France's new socialist president Francois Hollande may want to pull his country out of NATO. That would mean a loss of 12% of NATO's funding. If that happens, who do you suspect NATO would eye to make up that deficit, and increase ours?

Ivo Daalder Q&A: http://www.c-spanvideo.org/program/Stepsfo

Funding NATO: http://www.nato.int/cps/en/natolive/topics_67655.htm

U.S. Ballistic Missile Defense briefing: http://photos.state.gov/libraries/russia/231771/PDFs/U_S_%20Ballistic%20Missile%20Defense%20Briefing%20ENG.pdf

Russia-Iran alliance: http://www.washingtonsblog.com/2012/01/russia-should-anything-happen-to-iran-this-will-be-a-direct-threat-to-our-national-security.html

NATO Summit in Chicago: http://www.nato.int/cps/en/SID-18E5B832-418B2ED0/natolive/news_87077.htm

France and NATO: http://www.iol.co.za/news/world/hollande-victory-rattles-nato-1.1290346

Ivo Daalder: http://en.wikipedia.org/wiki/Ivo_Daalder

# U.S. Activates Trillion-Dollar Nuke Buildup
**Roger Armbrust,** October 13, 2014

The multinational corporations feeding the military-industrial complex, which President Eisenhower warned of, must be creaming in their coffee. The Obama White House has activated refurbishing a nuclear arsenal that will cost taxpayers $1 trillion. Let's call it the insane Flash-to-Ash design for humanity.

The plan first came to light last January in a report from the James Martin Center for Nonproliferation Studies. In a publication called "The Trillion Dollar Nuclear Triad: US Strategic Modernization over the Next Thirty Years" the center reported:

> ...the United States will likely spend over $1 trillion during the next three decades to maintain its current nuclear arsenal and purchase their replacement systems. The necessary level of procurement spending, as a percentage of the defense budget, will peak at levels comparable to the Reagan-era build-up of nuclear forces.

Among the lethal pile-up, the report cites these figures from the government's own budget projections:

- **$100 billion** for 100 long-range strategic manned nuclear bombers. An additional $30-40 billion will be needed to provide the nuclear weapons and cruise

missiles to be deployed on these airplanes. This includes some $45 billion in previously unacknowledged funds required to build the new airplane.
- **$20-120 billion** for a new generation of land based ICBMs. The highest end projection includes a few tens of billions of dollars to make new ICBMs mobile or implement other exotic basing schemes—a plan considered and rejected in the 1980s because of its extreme cost, but under consideration again according to Air Force solicitations.
- Some **$350 billion** in funding for the National Nuclear Security Administration for maintaining current and building more modern nuclear weapons. This averages over $11 billion per year, despite Congress's refusal to provide more than $8 billion in any of the most recent budgets.

Fast-forward from the January report to last month and *The New York Times'* lengthy article headlined "U.S. Ramping Up Major Renewal in Nuclear Arms". It states that Obama plans over the next decade to spend $355 billion on the buildup:

> *The money is flowing into a sprawling complex for making warheads that includes eight major plants and laboratories employing more than 40,000 people.*

One of those developments is in Kansas City, benignly called The National Security Campus. The other plants and labs are located in, west to southeast, California, Nevada, New Mexico, Texas, Tennessee and South Carolina.

## The Nobel Peace President

All this is coming from a president who won the Nobel Prize for Peace in 2009, cited by the Nobel committee for his "extraordinary efforts to strengthen international diplomacy and cooperation between peoples" and his promoting nonproliferation of nuclear arms.

That was then. This is now. Notes the September *Times* article:

Roger Armbrust

> 'The most fundamental game changer is Putin's invasion of Ukraine,' said Gary Samore, Mr. Obama's top nuclear adviser in his first term and now a scholar at Harvard. 'That has made any measure to reduce the stockpile unilaterally politically impossible.'

Of course, Samore fails to mention that the United States backed the right-wing-billionaire-led rebellion against the corrupt pro-Russian, democratically elected government in the Ukraine. And how this has given the U.S. and NATO an opportunity to challenge Moscow, and get a power foothold in a country bordering Russia. And how the Russians aren't going to stand for that.

Paul Craig Roberts, a Reagan assistant treasury secretary and co-creator of Reaganomics, in a recent column condemned the last three White Houses—Democrat and Republican–basically summarizing what he headlined "Washington is Destroying the World":

> ...over the past 21 years three two-term US presidents have taught Moscow that the word of the US government is worthless.

> Today Russia is surrounded by US and NATO military bases, with more to come in Ukraine (part of Russia for centuries), Georgia (part of Russia for centuries and the birthplace of Joseph Stalin), Montenegro, Macedonia, Bosnia-Herzegovina, and perhaps also Azerbaijan...

> ...Washington always picks the puppet who serves as Secretary General of NATO. The latest is a former Norwegian politician and prime minister, Jens Stoltenberg. On Washington's orders, the puppet quickly antagonized Moscow with the statement that NATO has a powerful army that has a global policing role and can be deployed wherever Washington wishes. This claim is a total contradiction of NATO's purpose and charter.

All this warmonger maneuvering while the nuclear arms are being made ready. The U.S. State Department, in an Oct. 1 fact

## The Vital Realities for 2020 and Beyond

sheet (yes, this month), listed the current lethal scorecard in what the U.S. and Russian Cold Warriors of the '70s and '80s termed the Mutual Assured Destruction (MAD) policy:

| Category of Data | United States of America | Russian Federation |
|---|---|---|
| Deployed ICBMs, Deployed SLBMs, and Deployed Heavy Bombers | 794 | 528 |
| Warheads on Deployed ICBMs, on Deployed SLBMs, and Nuclear Warheads Counted for Deployed Heavy Bombers | 1642 | 1643 |
| Deployed and Non-deployed Launchers of ICBMs, Deployed and Non-deployed Launchers of SLBMs, and Deployed and Non-deployed Heavy Bombers | 912 | 911 |

**Follow the Money**
Could nukes make them the last presidents?

*Peculiar Progressive*, through a number of columns, has consistently argued that, when a nation gets into deep financial trouble, its policymakers look for a foreign enemy to jerk the citizenry's minds away from their economic problems and stir nationalism. In the case of the U.S., recreating enemies ranging from Russia to the Middle East has also primed funding for endless war. And, in this new case, perhaps the only thing that can stop endless war: a nuclear holocaust.

Meanwhile, the U.S. still suffers economically from...yes, we'll keep repeating them...a student loan debt of over $1 trillion, a credit card debt of $1 trillion, a national debt (owed by the public) of $12.8 trillion, and infrastructure needs of $2.3 trillion. All this while we've also written about two major international reports warning of a global economic meltdown worse than 2008.

Which leads to a basic question: Can the U.S. afford a trillion-dollar nuclear build-up?

Roger Armbrust

The September *Times* article quotes an authority who says no:

> In the end, however, budget realities may do more than nuclear philosophies to curb the atomic upgrades. "There isn't enough money," said Jeffrey Lewis, of the Monterey Institute of International Studies, an expert on the modernization effort. "You're going to get a train wreck."

The article also quotes from the federal Government Accountability Office, indicating the nuclear upgrades have been planned since Obama's first term, "over five years," meaning in 2009 when he was accepting the Nobel Peace Prize:

> Across the nation, 21 major upgrades have been approved and 36 more proposed, according to the Government Accountability Office. In nearly two dozen reports over five years, the congressional investigators have described the modernization push as poorly managed and financially unaccountable.

> They recently warned — in typically understated language — that the managers of the atomic complex had repeatedly omitted and underestimated billions of dollars in costs, leaving the plan with 'less funding than will be needed.'

So, are you ready yet? Will you get organized, educated and active in taking control of your government, starting with the November midterm elections? Or are you resigned to you and your family experiencing endless war, or the end of it and civilization with the Flash-to-Ash design?

# China, the U.S. and Looming War
**Roger Armbrust,** June 8, 2015

> *...with its actions in the South China Sea, China is out of step with both international norms that underscore the Asia-Pacific's security architecture, and the regional consensus in favor of a non-coercive approach to this and other long-standing disputes.*
>
> *China's actions are bringing countries in the region together in new ways. And they're increasing demand for American engagement in the Asia-Pacific, and we're going to meet it. We will remain the principal security power in the Asia-Pacific for decades to come.*

That was a May 27 salvo that U.S. Defense Secretary Ashton Carter fired at China, an aggressive assurance that the U.S. is continuing its "Asian Pivot" policy, an effort to contain China's growing global economic influence.

The Obama Administration's efforts to solidify the "Asian Pivot" — through increased military "flyovers" and naval patrols in the area, and attempting to fast-track the Trans-Pacific Partnership (TPP) in Congress — has just moved Beijing to public pronouncements of aggressive response. In fact, viewing the attitudes of both sides, it's possible the growing feud could eventually lead to nuclear confrontation because both sides are showing increasing efforts at nuclear arming.

Roger Armbrust

For the first time, China has issued a military policy paper —"China's Military Strategy" — clarifying what actions it plans to take to strengthen itself globally. Through a decade of releasing these military policy statements, China's offered only tepid reviews of numbers and statistics regarding the Chinese military. But last month, China changed that approach, obviously to show the U.S. it's tired of America's global military aggression to assure its "exceptionalism" and to control global markets and natural resources, primarily for energy.

In the new century, the U.S. has continued to try controlling global markets militarily — and to aid its weapons sales by fomenting conflict, particularly in the Middle East and through the North Atlantic Treaty Organization (NATO). China, meanwhile, has touted a foreign policy of noninterference in other nations' internal affairs, and in stressing economic cooperation through trade and infrastructure-construction agreements globally.

China and its partners in BRICS — Brazil, Russia, India, and South Africa — have also over the last couple of years moved to challenge the dollar as the world's ruling reserve currency. The economic threat from BRICS, *Peculiar Progressive* believes, is at the center of both the Asian Pivot and TPP (against China), and supporting the revolution in Ukraine and expansion of NATO (against Russia).

When a nation is suffering economically, it looks for an enemy and potential conflict to try to deflect attention from domestic problems and unite the public. The U.S. has tried that with Russia, both fomenting the Ukraine situation and pushing the European Union to join Washington in implementing sanctions on Russia.

Now, Washington's neocons also see a need to challenge China. But China isn't Iraq or Afghanistan or even Russia. And China obviously decided to make that clear with its recent aggressive military white paper.

## China's Military Strategy Paper

Released on May 26, Beijing's military strategy paper emphasizes maintaining the peace and cooperation with other countries, and maintaining a military based on defense and not aggression. It specifically mentions strong cooperation with Russia, as well as continued cooperative efforts with the U.S. and the Asian countries.

But it also notes it will "oppose hegemonism" which obviously means the U.S., because China's President Xi Jinping has consistently alluded to America hegemony in speeches during his world travels. The paper's strategy also repeats often that China's military is preparing for combat, and for "winning", whether the threat is by land, air, sea, or nuclear.

The paper sites major "strategic tasks" for the Chinese military:

*— To deal with a wide range of emergencies and military threats, and effectively safeguard the sovereignty and security of China's territorial land, air and sea;*
*— To resolutely safeguard the unification of the motherland;*
*— To safeguard China's security and interests in new domains;*
*— To safeguard the security of China's overseas interests;*
*— To maintain strategic deterrence and carry out nuclear counterattack;*
*— To participate in regional and international security cooperation and maintain regional and world peace;*
*— To strengthen efforts in operations against infiltration, separatism and terrorism so as to maintain China's political security and social stability; and*
*— To perform such tasks as emergency rescue and disaster relief, rights and interests protection, guard duties, and support for national economic and social development.*

Roger Armbrust

There's a lot of weight in these few words. For example, China has signed major trade agreements with Russia, India, and nations in Africa and South America. And President Xi has introduced his vision for a new Silk Road Economic Belt and 21$^{st}$ Century Maritime Silk Road, establishing modern land and sea trade routes linking Asia, eastern Europe and Africa. The two projects have become simply known as "One Road, One Belt".

So, when China's military paper stresses the "strategic tasks" of both safeguarding China's security and interests in *new domains*, as well as the security of China's *overseas interests*, to *Peculiar Progressive* this means Beijing is prepared to protect its global investments, even militarily if necessary.

Also keep in mind that China and Russia have recently cooperated in military operations, that China has closed major natural gas and oil deals with Russia, and offered to help Moscow if it hits an economic bottom due to sanctions. The point: in a war, China's enemy could quickly become Russia's enemy.

Their foreign policies have shown that the U.S. would rather fight a war than negotiate, and China would rather negotiate than fight a war. But these recent hostile words and efforts show a marked change. And we'll close by looking at China's view of nuclear force, because if confrontation gets that far, negotiation will join everything else in the incinerating mushroom clouds.

Keep in mind that China knows the U.S. has begun a plan of a 10-year, $1 trillion refurbishing of its nuclear arsenal. We wrote about that in our column "U.S. Activates Trillion-Dollar Nuke Buildup" last October.

Consider that as you read the next paragraph which further explains what Beijing means by its strategic task "to maintain strategic deterrence and carry out nuclear counterattack":

## The Vital Realities for 2020 and Beyond

*The nuclear force is a strategic cornerstone for safeguarding national sovereignty and security. China has always pursued the policy of no first use of nuclear weapons and adhered to a self-defensive nuclear strategy that is defensive in nature. China will unconditionally not use or threaten to use nuclear weapons against non-nuclear-weapon states or in nuclear-weapon-free zones, and will never enter into a nuclear arms race with any other country. China has always kept its nuclear capabilities at the minimum level required for maintaining its national security. China will optimize its nuclear force structure, improve strategic early warning, command and control, missile penetration, rapid reaction, and survivability and protection, and deter other countries from using or threatening to use nuclear weapons against China.*

Keep this in mind, too, if these two major nations increase hostilities through cyberwar, which might somehow set off nuclear war.

Don't you think the two sides might be better off, instead of their current jabbing at each other — which George Washington warned of, cited in my recent column — to sit down and have honest negotiations to quell this growing conflict? This can't wait until Xi visits President Obama at their scheduled September gathering. This should start now, before some "Concord shot" starts military war for real.

# NukeBuild:
# This Will Not End Well
**Roger Armbrust,** June 22, 2015

While the corporate media's flashing you constant images of 2016 presidential candidates and the tragic Charleston massacre, don't let it cloud your focus on the rising conflict that won't end well: the U.S. challenging both China and Russia – all three nations possessing and increasing nuclear arms. Let's call the growing tensions NukeBuild.

*Peculiar Progressive* wrote recently of the growing belligerence between Washington and Beijing: "China, the U.S. and Looming War". We stressed how the U.S. is planning a 30-year, $1 trillion rebuilding of its nuclear arsenal. How China knows this. And how this, President Obama's effort to solidify his "Asian Pivot" with the Trans-Pacific Partnership, and the Pentagon's war words about controlling the South China Sea and Pacific have all led China to publicly voice its own global military action plan.

Meanwhile, last week Russian President Vladimir Putin announced a smaller modernizing of Moscow's nuclear arms. Not a lot. Just enough to incinerate and/or poison the planet:

> Mr Putin said that "more than 40 new intercontinental ballistic missiles (ICBMs) able to overcome even the most technically advanced anti-missile defence systems" would be added to Russia's nuclear arsenal this year...

*...The president also announced that the military was beginning testing a new system of long-range early warning radar "to monitor in the western direction".*

*After Mr Putin's address, Russia's deputy defence minister Anatoly Antonov told Russia Today his country was being "pushed into an arms race" by NATO.*

NATO (North Atlantic Treaty Organization) is heavily funded and influenced by Washington, which supported the fascist overthrow and replacement of a democratically elected government in Ukraine – a voter-selected regime supporting Moscow, and also corrupt.

That regime change and the move by the eastern Ukraine region of Crimea to secede and be annexed by Russia has led NATO's effort to move troops closer to Russia's borders. NATO's foreign ministers in April 2014 announced they would "suspend all practical civilian and military cooperation between NATO and Russia."

This chess-playing with Ukraine lives also led Washington to push the European Union to agree on U.S.-EU economic sanctions against Russia. The EU just extended those sanctions through the end of 2015.

All this has led Moscow to begin expanding its military and nuclear strength.

**China, U.S. Meet This Week**
China and the U.S. on Monday, June 22 began its seventh annual Strategic and Economic Dialogue in Washington, three days of banter about serious issues which will come to a head in September when China's President Xi Jinping travels to the U.S. capitol to meet with President Obama.

The two sides feel they can expand some issues of mutual agreement. But the reality is this: China continues to grow as an equal economic power with the U.S., and Washington is trying to find ways to prevent that. Meanwhile China and Russia are growing closer while both are experiencing deep disagreements and distrust with the U.S. and its military threats. Both sides have been involved in cyber warfare.

According to Channel NewsAsia:

> *The two sides will try to ease tensions by stressing areas of cooperation, including climate change, shared concerns about Iran and North Korea's nuclear programmes, the fight against Islamist militancy, and support for global development.*
>
> *'We have agreed with the Chinese that we are going to try to expand those areas where our interests overlap and expand cooperation in those areas,' the [unnamed] US official said. But the aim was not to 'paper over' contentious issues, or to 'agree to disagree,' but to narrow differences to avoid miscalculations.*

It's those "miscalculations" which concern *Peculiar Progressive*, seeing the belligerent dialogue and military "shoving" by the three powers as the dangerous buildup grows toward war, and even nuclear war. And we're not alone.

**Roberts Sees 'Armageddon'**
Paul Craig Roberts was an Assistant Secretary of the Treasury under Ronald Reagan, and was part of the brain trust in forming Reaganomics. He realizes the Washington neocons' shoutings are efforts at activating Reagan's hawkish actions toward Russia — only without Reagan's willingness to negotiate. And he basically said so in a speech to the Conference on the European/Russian Crisis, in Delphi, Greece this past weekend. The talk's title: "Washington is Impotent to Prevent Armageddon".

Roberts, tracing the American attitude of exceptionalism and efforts to build empire, opens his talk with this:

## The Vital Realities for 2020 and Beyond

> *The United States has pursued empire since early in its history, but it was the Soviet collapse in 1991 that enabled Washington to see the entire world as its oyster.*
>
> *The collapse of the Soviet Union resulted in the rise of the neoconservatives to power and influence in the US government. The neoconservatives have interpreted the Soviet collapse as History's choice of "American democratic capitalism" as the New World Order.*

He moves on to discuss the Wolfowitz Doctrine and its chief priority of hegemony. The two chief enemies of the doctrine are Russia and China he says, adding:

> **We come to the bottom line.** *Washington's position is not negotiable. Washington has no interest in compromising with Russia or China. Washington has no interest in any facts. Washington's deal is this: 'You can be part of our world order as our vassals, but not otherwise.'*
>
> *European governments and, of course, the lapdog UK government, are complicit in this implicit declaration of war against Russia and China. If it comes to war, Europeans will pay the ultimate price for the treason of their leaders, such as Merkel, Cameron, and Hollande, as Europe will cease to exist.*
>
> **War with Russia and China is beyond Washington's capability. However, if the demonized "enemy" does not succumb to the pressure and accept Washington's leadership, war can be inevitable.**

He also notes, "**The agenda of American hegemony serves the interests of Wall Street and the mega-banks.**"

You can read Roberts' entire speech here. Perhaps it will help urge you to get organized, get educated, and get active in changing the destructive dynamic we're all being drawn into.

# Ban Nuclear Weapons, Despite Washington

**Roger Armbrust,** October 31, 2016

Last Thursday, the United Nations' member states took a positive step toward perhaps saving the world. It voted for the first time to begin talks on a nuclear-weapons-ban treaty— a first step to quell the New Cold War that's getting hotter. Yes, discussing a ban for the first time since the UN's forming 71 years ago. Making history.

We should say, 123 member states made positive history, voting to begin talks in March 2017. Another 38 countries – including major nuclear-weapons powers such as the United States, Russia, Israel, France and the United Kingdom – voted no, continuing their making negative history.

We've been expressing concern about the New Cold War and increasing tensions for a while, including our column "Nuke-build: This Will Not End Well", which includes information on the U.S. $1 trillion, 30-year rebuilding of its nuclear-weapons arsenal, going on now. It has caused both Russia and China to ramp up their nuclear weapons. Great for the nuclear-weapons industry. Great for the Millionaire Congress that supports it. Not great for us.

Why is the US opposing a nuclear-weapons-ban treaty? The Huffington Post published a column on Thursday by Joe Cirincione, author of the book *Nuclear Nightmares: Securing the*

*World Before It's Too Late*. He quoted the Obama administration's rep:

> *The Obama Administration was in fierce opposition. It lobbied all nations, particularly its allies, to vote no. 'How can a state that relies on nuclear weapons for its security possibly join a negotiation meant to stigmatize and eliminate them?' argued Ambassador Robert Wood, the US special representative to the UN Conference on Disarmament in Geneva, 'The ban treaty runs the risk of undermining regional security.'*
>
> *The US opposition is a profound mistake. Ambassador Wood is a career foreign service officer and a good man who has worked hard for our country. But this position is indefensible.*
>
> *Every president since Harry Truman has sought the elimination of nuclear weapons.*

That, of course, includes President Obama, who early in his administration won a later-undeserved Nobel Peace Prize for efforts with Russia to reduce nuclear warheads. Obama even recently preached against nuclear war on a visit to Hiroshima. But politicians, of course, are known for talking out both sides of their mouths. And speaking against nuclear war is not nearly as meaningful as actively pushing us toward nuclear war.

And the United States seems set on doing that through three recent simultaneous activities: (1) the US-led NATO aggression toward Russia's borders; (2) Obama's "Asian Pivot" in an effort to militarily control the Pacific and surround Eurasia; and (3) efforts to place THAAD missiles in South Korea, which both Russia and China have called a threat to their security.

Meanwhile, as Washington leads us back into the cycle of the old Cold War's Mutual-Assured Destruction (MAD) policies, a large majority of other nations in the U.N. are trying to pull us away from self-destruction.

Roger Armbrust

**How You Can Take Action**

Ironically or not, the day before the UN vote, an international legislative group released a potentially vital booklet offering an action plan to ban nuclear weapons: "Time to Move the Nuclear Weapons Money: A Handbook for Civil Society and Legislators." Potentially vital because the group consists of nations' legislators, those who fund defense policies. They call themselves Parliamentarians for Nuclear Non-Proliferation and Disarmament (PNND), and add to their title the action line, "Engaging legislators worldwide in steps towards nuclear disarmament."

PNND launched the handbook at the 135th Assembly of the Inter-Parliamentary Union, (IPU) an organization of 170 member parliaments from around the world. The group is debating the issue of military spending versus Sustainable Development Goals (SDGs), policies approved last year at the major climate conference in Paris. The PNND website quoted IPU's president:

> 'Over $100 billion is spent annually on nuclear weapons — funds that are sorely needed to meet the SDGs,' says Saber Chowdhury, IPU President. 'Parliamentarians have a key role to play in setting budgets, developing policy and providing oversight on government investments. This handbook provides a guide for effective parliamentary action to invest in peace and sustainability rather than on maintaining the threat of nuclear war.'

A bit of a different view, eh, than US Ambassador Wood?

One section you might find particularly valuable in the handbook: "How to Engage with Legislators." *Peculiar Progressive* has insisted for years that, if you want to create change, you can't do it alone. You'll need to get organized, get educated and get active. This handbook should help you do that, if you want to remove the nuclear-weapons threat for you and your children.

# Endless War and World War

# Op-Ed: Obama, Congress and Our Afghan Reality
**Roger Armbrust,** June 29, 2010
***Special to The Clyde Fitch Report***

The Washington Post reported Tuesday that "Congress will debate its divisions over U.S. policy on Afghanistan." Let's not let political rhetoric fog our view of historic reality.

President Barack Obama and Congress' efforts to secure the invasion of Afghanistan represent a continuum going back to Jimmy Carter. Our present president realizes, just as his predecessors did, that the object of maneuvering in Afghanistan is not to destroy the Taliban — which obviously no nation's been able to do since we first gave them weapons in the early 1980s — but to continue efforts to neutralize Russia while also forcing the Taliban eventually to reach an agreement. On what? Allowing multibillion-dollar Trans-Afghanistan pipelines for natural gas and oil, stretching from Turkmenistan to Pakistan, India and beyond. Why? Controlling energy is the key to superpower. American presidents and lawmakers know this, although they don't seem to want to talk about it.

Carter's national security advisor, Zbigniew Brzezinski, revealed in a 1998 interview that Carter in 1979 had provided the catalyst for the Soviet Union's invasion of Afghanistan. The president signed a secret directive on July 3 of that year which aided enemies of Kabul's pro-Soviet regime. Brzezinski said the move was calculated to induce the Soviets into the "Afghan trap," thus "giving to the USSR its Vietnam war."

U.S. arming of Islamic fundamentalists in Afghanistan pushed the Taliban into a power foothold. Brzezinski's 1998 view of that:

> **"What is most important to the history of the world? The Taliban or the collapse of the Soviet empire? Some stirred-up Moslems or the liberation of Central Europe and the end of the cold war?"**

In his 1997 book *The Grand Chessboard: American Primacy and Its Geostrategic Imperatives*, Brzezinski presents his premise that the U.S. must concentrate on Eurasia to remain the lone global superpower and "to make certain that no state or combination of states gains the capacity to expel the United States from Eurasia." To do that, it helps to control energy sources and supplies.

Brzezinski went on to become a consultant for Amoco, which later became a player in the push for Trans-Afghan pipelines. Henry Kissinger, Nixon's former secretary of state, got involved, too, through consulting for California-based Unocal, which led negotiations with the Taliban in a major Trans-Afghan effort. Dick Cheney's Halliburton also joined the mix, as did Chevron when Condoleezza Rice sat on its board. Enron chief Ken Lay, a George W. Bush crony, also worked for an Afghan pipeline to feed a gigantic Enron-built Indian power plant. All this in the 1990s after the Soviet Union's fall, allowing the strong Western attempt to take control of gas and oil in the Caspian region.

Bill Clinton stalemated oil companies' efforts at the Trans-Afghan lines in the late '90s, classifying the Taliban as an enemy. In April 1999, excluding U.S. interests, Afghanistan (under the Taliban), Pakistan and Turkmenistan reactivated the Trans-Afghan effort. In July, Clinton froze the Taliban's U.S. assets and prohibited trade with Afghanistan, economically frustrating the pipeline effort.

Meanwhile, Clinton had put millions of U.S. tax dollars and thousands of administrative man hours in developing the Baku-Tblisi-Ceyhan (BTC) pipeline, moving the Caspian Sea's oil and gas through Azerbaijan, Georgia and Turkey to the Mediterranean — a way to get energy to Europe and circumvent Russia.

Then, Clinton's out of the White House, and oilman George W. Bush is in, bringing Cheney and Rice, along with other oil connections, with him. And the Trans-Afghan pipelines again become a quiet priority.

One Bush cohort, Paul Wolfowitz, joins them with a position paper describing how the U.S. could seize the Persian Gulf's oil wells: "some catastrophic and catalyzing event — like a new Pearl Harbor" (see page 51). Bush and Cheney obviously respond to that. Bush later canonizes Wolfowitz president of the World Bank, where he begins rerouting hundreds of millions of dollars, designed originally for fighting poverty, to Pakistan and other nations supporting the U.S. in its invasions of Afghanistan and Iraq.

After Sept. 11, 2001, news reports began appearing, revealing how the Bush Administration had attempted to negotiate with the Taliban about the Trans-Afghan pipelines, as well as trying to get the Afghan rulers to turn Osama bin Laden over to the U.S. The BBC reported that U.S. representatives had informed a former Pakistani foreign secretary in mid-July 2001 that Bush — tired of negotiating — was preparing to attack Afghanistan as early as October. A U.S. State Department report noted that U.S. reps met with the Taliban, for the last time, five weeks before Sept. 11.

After invading Afghanistan, Bush placed Hamid Karzai as head of the interim government. He now reigns after a disputed election. Karzai is a former consultant to Unocal. Under him, in December 2002, Afghanistan, Turkmenistan and Pakistan again signed an agreement to build the Trans-Afghanistan natural gas pipeline. Meanwhile, the war has kept the Trans-Afghan pipelines from developing.

But news reports surfaced last week that Karzai had recently met with Taliban leader and al-Qaida affiliate Sirajuddin Haqqani in an effort to build a "separate peace" with the Taliban. The New York Times reported that Karzai was discussing with Haqqani (who has a $5 million U.S. price on his head) a "power sharing" arrangement.

Meanwhile, as President Obama and Congress scurry to replace U.S. military leadership in Afghanistan, the Trans-Afghan pipelines just might remain quietly in their plans. And not so quietly in the mind of Brzezinski (called by Obama "one of our most outstanding thinkers"). Brzezinski was reported saying after the 2008 Russia-Georgia war how "the construction of a pipeline from Central Asia via Afghanistan to the south…will maximally expand world society's access to the Central Asian energy market." The news report, by Asia Times correspondent Pepe Escobar, placed the price on the 1,600 km gas pipeline at more than $7.6 billion. And where there's a natural gas pipeline in place through Afghanistan, would an oil pipeline not be far behind?

# Libya, the Invasion Continuum, and Us

**Roger Armbrust,** March 27, 2011
*Special to the Clyde Fitch Report*

Some members of Congress, led by Democratic Rep. Dennis Kucinich of Ohio, have been challenging President Obama's aerial invasion of Libya, calling it "unconstitutional" and even "impeachable."

You remember Kucinich? He's the Congressman who had the guts to file bills in the House of Representatives calling for impeachment of both George W. Bush and Dick Cheney for implementing the U.S. military invasion of Iraq. It seems he doesn't care which party an empire-minded president belongs to.

It's interesting that this year more members of Congress seem prone to bring criticism of the chief executive for a military invasion. It's only taken over a decade for the fear-the-president mood to begin changing on Capitol Hill — which is interesting because the U.S. Constitution hasn't changed for quite a while. The inaction of a cowardly Congress during the Bush administration led this journalist, in 2007, to write about our lawmakers' lack of resolve and avoidance of defending our nation's basic document. Unfortunately, since history is basically repeating itself, it's time to expand on this vital issue.

Here's the reality: Within the borders of the U.S., neither

political rhetoric — including President Obama making our actions in Libya "very clear" — nor United Nations documents, nor Congressional resolutions, take precedence over the U.S. Constitution in designating who has the power to make and end war.

The Constitution states clearly and simply in Article 1, Section 8:

***The Congress shall have power...to declare war, grant letters of marque and reprisal, and make rules concerning captures on land and water.***

That's the only paragraph that speaks specifically to war.

The article also provides Congress with powers "to raise and support armies...to provide and maintain a navy; to make rules for the government and regulation of the land and naval forces," and to "provide for calling forth the militia," which we would call the National Guard. The Constitution's Article 2, Section 2 states, "The President shall be commander in chief of the Army and Navy of the United States, and of the militia of the several states, when called into the actual service of the United States." The "calling" is left up to Congress, not the president.

That's it. Nowhere in the executive powers article does it say the president has the right to declare or wage war at his own will and in his own way.

The president, as commander in chief, should execute not his own will, but the will of Congress, and therefore more closely the will of the American people.

Presidents, including our present one, have usurped that will and power, usually from a weak-kneed Congress.

One such Congress, following Vietnam, felt a political need to "clarify" the roles of the two branches regarding war-making powers. The result was the War Powers Resolution of 1973.

Roger Armbrust

The resolution stresses that the president can only send forces into hostile action in one of three ways: (1) Congress's declaration of war; (2) "specific statutory authorization," meaning Congress must pass a law allowing the hostile action; or (3) "a national emergency created by attack upon the United States, its territories or possessions, or its armed forces."

The Congress, in 1973, showed its weakness in later paragraphs, where the resolution does give in, wordily allowing the president to initiate hostile action if he quickly reports back to Congress, justifying the action's legality. Obama could say he's following this law, if he does quickly report.

The problem is, *Congress does not have the Constitutional right to abdicate its power to declare and wage war to the executive branch. That would take a Constitutional amendment.* But this 1973 resolution basically does that.

This 1973 Congressional resolution was also the primary document cited by President Bush's deputy counsel, John C. Yoo, in his Sept. 25, 2001 memorandum opinion on the president's having "broad constitutional power to use military force." But Yoo's word isn't law. It's only a biased opinion within the then-Bush administration.

Congress also cited the 1973 document in its 2002 resolution allowing the president to send American forces into Iraq. But that 2002 resolution is simply Congress ignoring the Constitution.

Kucinich says he'll introduce a budgetary amendment to defund any military attack on Libya. A courageous Congress might have taken such action on both Afghanistan and Iraq, saving American and Middle East citizens' lives and greatly lowering our national debt.

But if Kucinich is going to push any such legislation through, he'll need the support of voters nationwide who can convince their own representatives to gather some courage. If you agree with him, it's time to get organized, get educated and get active. Kucinich and others need to scrap that 1973 Congressional resolution. The courts should also gather the guts to rule on the resolution's constitutionality. Members of Congress, on two occasions, have filed suit against a president in federal courts to challenge the resolution's constitutionality — once in 1999-2000 and again in 2005. Both times lower federal courts avoided the issue, ruling that members of Congress "lacked standing to sue the President." The U.S. Supreme Court let those judgments stand, and refused to hear the appeals.

Meanwhile, Congress and the courts continue to "piddle, twiddle, and resolve," presidents continue to invade, and we continue to lose lives, dive deeper into debt and further dissolve our nation's standing worldwide.

# Memorial Day: Recalling and Caring for Our Constant Brave
**Roger Armbrust,** May 28, 2012

How shall we recall and care for these, our constant brave: the individuals who have volunteered, trained, and sacrificed so much in the name of America and its military?

First, let's remember the solemn oath they have taken when inducted into the armed services. Here's the Army enlistment oath:

> I, _____, do solemnly swear (or affirm) that I will support and defend the Constitution of the United States against all enemies, foreign and domestic; that I will bear true faith and allegiance to the same; and that I will obey the orders of the President of the United States and the orders of the officers appointed over me, according to regulations and the Uniform Code of Military Justice. So help me God.

Millions of courageous men and women have taken this oath. When they did, they should have received the right to demand an oath in return from us, the American people: to support and protect them from elected officials who have allowed the flagrant expansion of a military-industrial complex which Dwight D. Eisenhower warned us about.

## The Vital Realities for 2020 and Beyond

Eisenhower saw the dangers of money and power turning America's military missions into greedy, aggressive, endless war for the sake of the profit of a few, rather than the protection of many. On leaving the presidency in 1961, this greatest of World War II's heroes, a Republican, said publicly:

> *A vital element in keeping the peace is our military establishment. Our arms must be mighty, ready for instant action, so that no potential aggressor may be tempted to risk his own destruction…*
>
> *This conjunction of an immense military establishment and a large arms industry is new in the American experience. The total influence – economic, political, even spiritual – is felt in every city, every statehouse, every office of the federal government. We recognize the imperative need for this development. Yet we must not fail to comprehend its grave implications. Our toil, resources and livelihood are all involved; so is the very structure of our society. In the councils of government, **we must guard against the acquisition of unwarranted influence, whether sought or unsought, by the military-industrial complex**. The potential for the disastrous rise of misplaced power exists and will persist.*
>
> *We must never let the weight of this combination endanger our liberties or democratic processes. We should take nothing for granted. Only an alert and knowledgeable citizenry can compel the proper meshing of the huge industrial and military machinery of defense with our peaceful methods and goals so that security and liberty may prosper together.*

Are we "an alert and knowledgeable citizenry?"

Would an alert and knowledgeable citizenry allow a homeless

population of over 600,000 to exist in the U.S., with one-third of them consisting of our military veterans?

Would we allow 18 U.S. veterans, men and women, to *daily* commit suicide, primarily due to psychiatric drugs? (ABC News)

Would we allow our dedicated warriors to be sent into an aggressive invasion based on a lie, and which our political leaders knew would turn into a quagmire?

Listen to Dick Cheney's explaining in 1984 why George H. W. Bush refused to invade Iraq's capitol of Baghdad, which would put our military irrationally in harm's way:

> *It's a quagmire if you go that far and try to take over Iraq.*
>
> *The other thing was casualties. Everyone was impressed with the fact we were able to do our job with as few casualties as we had. But for the 146 Americans killed in action, and for their families — it wasn't a cheap war. And the question for the president, in terms of whether or not we went on to Baghdad, took additional casualties in an effort to get Saddam Hussein, was how many additional dead Americans is Saddam worth?*
>
> *Our judgment was, not very many, and I think we got it right.*

Cheney didn't get it right the second time on Iraq, when the U.S. invaded, resulting in the death of over 4,400 U.S. forces (as of Feb. 13) and nearly 32,000 wounded. Add to that over 16,600 Iraqi military and police, 26,000 Iraqi "insurgents" and over 66,000 civilian deaths.

All this, because George W. Bush lied to his electorate and the world about Weapons of Mass Destruction existing in Iraq. And Colin Powell carried that lie to the United Nations.

## The Vital Realities for 2020 and Beyond

Powell's former chief of staff, U.S. Army Col. (ret.) Lawrence B. Wilkerson-who helped prepare Powell for his U.N. speech-said Powell wasn't aware of the falsehoods in his presentation, but it was a "hoax." Wilkerson told PBS in 2006:

> I participated in a hoax on the American people, the international community and the United Nations Security Council. How do you think that makes me feel? Thirty-one years in the United States Army and I more or less end my career with that kind of a blot on my record? That's not a very comforting thing...

> ...we turned to the National Intelligence estimate as part of the recommendation of George Tenent and my agreement with. But even that turned out to be, in its substantive parts–that is stockpiles of chemicals, biologicals and production capability that was hot and so forth, and an active nuclear program. The three most essential parts of that presentation turned out to be absolutely false.

The Afghanistan invasion-prompted by 9/11, which appeared to be set up by the Bush administration (see Peculiar Progressive column "The Afghanistan Plan: A Pipeline, an Invasion, a Pipeline, and an "Exodus")-followed by America's Iraqi aggression both cost the U.S. over one trillion dollars. According to the Congressional Research Service report from March 29, 2011:

> ...based on DOD, State Department/USAID, and Department of Veterans Administration budget submissions, the cumulative total appropriated from the 9/11 for those war operations, diplomatic operations, and medical care for Iraq and Afghan war veterans is $1.283 trillion including:
> $806 billion for Iraq;
> $444 billion for Afghanistan;
> $29 billion for enhanced security; and
> $6 billion unallocated

Roger Armbrust

While the decade-long quagmires have bled our brave military and our taxpayers, Cheney's folks seem to have profited from the invasions. Before becoming vice-president, he was serving as CEO of Halliburton. That corporation and its subsidiaries, while Cheney was vice president, pulled in billions from work in Iraq and Afghanistan. While it's difficult to get a total figure, sources list Halliburton subsidiary Kellogg, Brown and Root (KBR) getting $16 billion in contracts from 2004-06 alone. *Politifact* cites KBR government work for Iraq reconstruction from 2001-10 of $31 billion. Cheney was vice president from 2001-2008. Halliburton broke ties with KBR in 2007.

Halliburton, of course, wasn't the only corporate profiteer benefiting from the efforts of our American brave. In the sources listed at this column's end, you can find links to the top 20 and top 100 defense contractors.

Eisenhower pointed out in his farewell address that the military-industrial complex was something new in the '50s. America's founding fathers opposed a standing army, and the U.S. basically didn't have one until World War II when the Nazi onslaught required it. America's brave met that onslaught and defeated it.

In the Nuremberg trials of the Nazi leaders, the Army's prosecutors including Benjamin Ferencz, told the court that the defendants' chief crime was "aggressive war" which led to all other offenses they committed. Sixty years later, in the summer of 2006, Ferencz claimed that George W. Bush should be charged with the same crime:

> The United Nations charter has a provision which was agreed to by the United States, formulated by the United States, in fact, after World War II. It says that from now on, no nation can use armed force without the permission of the U.N. Security Council. They can use force in connection with self-defense, but a country can't use force in anticipation of self-defense. Regarding

> *Iraq, the last Security Council resolution essentially said, 'Look, send the weapons inspectors out to Iraq, have them come back and tell us what they've found — then we'll figure out what we're going to do.' The U.S. was impatient, and decided to invade Iraq — which was all pre-arranged of course. So, the United States went to war, in violation of the charter.*

But, of course, Congress refused to impeach Bush or Cheney, and reluctantly and rarely has prosecuted contractors. Only our brave warriors and their families are expected to suffer patriotically, with death, physical wounds, and psychological trauma. As are the civilian victims in Iraq and Afghanistan.

And the truth is, our military brave will suffer patriotically. They have dedicated and trained themselves to do so. Some do it without questioning. A few have challenged our government on its endless, aggressive war, and paid the consequences under military law.

This conniving by the military-industrial complex isn't new. Our experience with the Vietnam quagmire surely should have taught us. Our young soldiers and sailors and airmen and women may not be old enough to remember it. But members of Congress are certainly aware of its history, as is the American taxpayer.

Now the White House is making war taunts toward Pakistan, Syria, and heavily toward Iran. Powell's Col. Wilkerson, in the documentary "The Israel Lobby," predicted that, if the U.S. attacks Iran, the American military will see a major exodus of veteran officers who oppose aggressive war.

How can we stop the military-industrial complex from embroiling us in future fiascos like Vietnam, Afghanistan and Iraq? We need to remove any president and Congress that continues the profiteering practice, and replace them. And we need to get Congress and the White House to truly regulate and break

Roger Armbrust

up the mammoth conglomerates that have taken control of government.

It will require the American voters to get organized, get educated and get active. It will take work to become the "alert and knowledgeable citizenry" Eisenhower encouraged us to become. As citizens, at a minimum, we owe our brave military forces and veterans that much.

The Army enlistment oath:
http://www.history.army.mil/html/faq/oaths.html

Eisenhower's full farewell address:
Eisenhower Farewell Address (Full)

Details of the military-industrial complex:
http://en.wikipedia.org/wiki/Military-industrial_complex

Homeless American veterans:
http://voices.yahoo.com/our-lost-soldiers-wandering-americas-10480585.html?cat=70

The New York Times articles on homeless:
http://topics.nytimes.com/top/reference/timestopics/subjects/h/homeless_persons/index.html

Veterans' suicides:
http://www.cchrint.org/2011/06/04/18-u-s-veterans-commit-suicide-daily-largely-due-to-psychiatric-drugs/

Military women's suicides:
http://today.msnbc.msn.com/id/47556147/ns/today-today_health/#.T8EvF1Kdh8E

Cheney on Iraq in '94:
Invading Baghdad would create quagmire
http://www.infowars.com/articles/iraq/cheney_video_1994_warning_of_iraq_invasion_quagmire.htm

# The Vital Realities for 2020 and Beyond

Col. Lawrence Wilkerson interview about "hoax":
http://www.pbs.org/now/politics/wilkerson.html

Total cost of Iraq and Afghanistan invasions:
http://www.fas.org/sgp/crs/natsec/RL33110.pdf
http://costofwar.com/en/

Halliburton:
http://www.corpwatch.org/article.php?list=type&type=15
http://www.halliburtonwatch.org/
http://www.politifact.com/truth-o-meter/statements/2010/jun/09/arianna-huffington/halliburton-kbr-and-iraq-war-contracting-history-s/

Top defense contractors:
http://defensesystems.com/articles/2010/05/27/top-20-defense-contractors.aspx
http://en.wikipedia.org/wiki/List_of_United_States_defense_contractors

Nazi prosecutor Benjamin Ferencz on Iraq:
http://www.alternet.org/world/38604/could_bush_be_prosecuted_for_war_crimes/

# Ferencz Condemns Drone Attacks: "A Crime Against Humanity"
**Roger Armbrust,** June 21, 2012

**"Innocent people are being blown up... somebody has to write about these things."**

Nicole Kidman speaks these words in the film "Hemingway and Gellhorn." She plays Martha Gellhorn, perhaps the world's greatest war correspondent, reacting to the Russians attacking Finland in World War II.

The words hold true today with America's obsessive drone attacks in its worldwide aggressive war on "terror."

In news article after news article, reports site American drones killing "suspected terrorists" and often innocent people. In rare cases, the U.S. has actually reported the demise of a leading insurgent. Meanwhile, authorities on international law have responded to the drone attacks, including the latest CIA drone maneuvers in Pakistan and Yemen, with everything from condemnation to wary questioning of their legality.

"The illegal use of armed force knowing that it will inevitably kill large numbers of civilians is a crime against humanity, and those responsible should be held accountable by national and international courts," Benjamin B. Ferenzc told *Peculiar Progressive* by email on June 16, when asked for a statement about America's drone attacks. "The use of any weapon that will unavoidably kill a disproportionate number of non-combatants is an inhumane act that should be condemned and punishable as a crime against humanity under customary international law."

Ferencz was an Army prosecutor in the Nuremberg trials of Nazi leaders following World War II. He told the court that the defendants' chief crime was "aggressive war" which led to all other offences they committed. Sixty years later, in the summer of 2006, he claimed that George W. Bush should be charged with the same crime for ordering the illegal invasion of Iraq. Now Ferencz is condemning his country's drone assaults. Since drone strikes began under George W. Bush as early as 2001, Ferencz's complaint of crimes would include both Bush and Barack Obama.

Ferencz isn't alone in his criticisms. Congressman Dennis Kucinich (D-Ohio) and twenty-five fellow Members of Congress on June 13 wrote to President Obama demanding the White House's legal justification for "signature" drone strikes, which could significantly increase the risk of killing innocent civilians or those who have no relationship to a potential attack on the U.S.

In their letter, the Congress members specifically sought "the process by which 'signature' strikes are authorized and executed (drone strikes where the identity of the person killed is unknown); mechanisms used by the CIA and JSOC to ensure that such killings are legal; the nature of the follow-up that is conducted when civilians are killed or injured; and the mechanisms that ensure civilian casualty numbers are collected, tracked and analyzed."

The lawmakers went on to say:

> *We are concerned that the use of such 'signature' strikes could raise the risk of killing innocent civilians or*

> *individuals who may have no relationship to attacks on the United States. Our drone campaigns already have virtually no transparency, accountability or oversight. We are further concerned about the legal grounds for such strikes under the 2001 Authorization for the Use of Military Force.*
>
> *The implications of the use of drones for our national security are profound. They are faceless ambassadors that cause civilian deaths, and are frequently the only direct contact with Americans that the targeted communities have. They can generate powerful and enduring anti-American sentiment.*

Peculiar Progressive had checked on June 19 with Kucinich's office to see if Obama had responded to the letter, but had not heard back as of noon.

In a June 1 news story, the *Times of India* states that "a July 2009 Brookings Institution report shows that 10 civilians die for every one suspected militant from US drone strikes." Also, the report cites another study by the New American Foundation which "concluded that out of 114 drone attacks in Pakistan, at least 32 per cent of those killed by the strikes were civilians."

The Bureau of Investigative Journalism shows drone strikes going back to 2001 in Yemen. Its latest figures as of June 18 for Pakistan, Yemen, and Somalia show:

**CIA Drone Strikes in Pakistan 2004 – 2012**
Total US strikes: **332**
Obama strikes: **280**
Total reported killed: **2,486-3,188**
Civilians reported killed: **482-832**
Children reported killed: **175**
Total reported injured: **1,192-1,308**

**US Covert Action in Yemen 2001- 2012**
Total confirmed US operations (all): **44-54**
Total confirmed US drone strikes: **33-43**
Possible additional US operations: **95-108**
Possible additional US drone strikes: **52-62**
Total reported killed (all): **317-884**
Total civilians killed (all): **58-138**
Children killed (all): **24**

**US Covert Action in Somalia 2007 – 2012**
Total US strikes: **10-21**
Total US drone strikes: **3-9**
Total reported killed: **58-169**
Civilians reported killed: **11-57**
Children reported killed: **1-3**

By June 18, Navi Pillay, United Nations High Commissioner for Human Rights, brought her concern about American drone attacks in Pakistan to the UN Human Rights Council. According to an advance copy (June 17) of her speech, she stated:

> *During my visit [to Pakistan the previous week], I also expressed serious concern over the continuing use of armed drones for targeted attacks, in particular because it is unclear that all persons targeted are combatants or directly participating in hostilities. The Secretary-General has expressed concern about the lack of transparency on the circumstances in which drones are used, noting that these attacks raise questions about compliance with distinction and proportionality. I remind States of their international obligation to take all necessary precautions to ensure that attacks comply with international law. I urge them to conduct investigations that are transparent, credible and independent, and provide victims with effective remedies.*

Pillay's statement, while seeming reasonable, is actually a step back for the UN. In October 2009 a UN human rights investigator warned that the U.S. drone attacks might breach international law. Philip Alston told the UN General Assembly:

> *Of the many concerns that I raised, one has grown dramatically in importance since June [2009]. It concerns the use of unmanned drones or predators to carry out targeted executions. While there may be circumstances in which the use of such techniques is consistent with applicable international law, this can only be determined in light of information about the legal basis on which particular individuals have been targeted, the measures taken to ensure conformity with the international humanitarian law principles of discrimination, proportionality, necessity and precaution, and the steps taken retrospectively to assess compliance in practice. I consider that, unless the US Government moves to answer these questions, it will increasingly be perceived as carrying out indiscriminate killings in violation of international law.*

The major question: Considering the gravity of conditions listed in both the Congress members' June letter and Alston's 2009 UN report, what's taken the federal legislators and UN so long to push the drone issue, and with weaker language compared to historic Nazi-prosecutor Ferencz?

The drone strikes agenda surely lies in Obama's hands, according to *The New York Times*. In a May 29 article entitled "Secret 'Kill List' Proves a Test of Obama's Principles and Will," reporters Jo Becker and Scott Shane note, "Mr. Obama has placed himself at the helm of a top secret 'nominations' process to designate terrorists for kill or capture, of which the capture part has become largely theoretical. He had vowed to align the fight against Al Qaeda with American values; the [kill] chart, introducing people whose deaths he might soon be asked to order, underscored just what a moral and legal conundrum this could be."

## The Vital Realities for 2020 and Beyond

And in an appalling opposition to America's innocent-until-proven-guilty justice system, the Obama drone policy, according to the *Times* article, calls any adult a combatant, only judged innocent after death:

> *It is also because Mr. Obama embraced a disputed method for counting civilian casualties that did little to box him in. It in effect counts all military-age males in a strike zone as combatants, according to several administration officials, unless there is explicit intelligence posthumously proving them innocent.*

Asked about the *Times* article the same day in a press briefing, White House press secretary Jay Carney explained:

> *I think your [the Times] description of the policy is not quite exact. I would refer you to John Brennan's speech not long along on these matters, in which he was very explicit and transparent about methods that are used in our counterterrorism operations and the care that is taken to avoid civilian casualties. We have at our disposal tools that make avoidance of civilian casualties much easier, and tools that make precision targeting possible in ways that have never existed in the past.*
>
> *And I think that this administration's commitment, this President's commitment to, A, go after those who would do harm to the United States and do harm to our allies is clear. This President's first and primary — this President's first priority is the protection of the United States, protection of the citizens of this country, and he takes that responsibility enormously seriously. And that is why he has pursued the fight against al Qaeda in the very direct way that he has.*

Carney was referring to John O. Brennan, Obama's chief counter-terrorism adviser. In a May 1 speech at the Woodrow Wilson Center, Brennan said:

> *Targeted strikes conform to the principle of distinction, the idea that only military objectives may be intentionally targeted and that civilians are protected from being intentionally targeted. With the unprecedented ability of remotely piloted aircraft to precisely target a military objective, while minimizing collateral damage, one could argue that never before has there been a weapon that allows us to distinguish more effectively between an al-Qaida terrorist and innocent civilians.*

The statistics offered by the Brookings Institution, The New American Foundation, and the Bureau of Investigative Journalism would seem to disagree with Brennan's assessment.

In columns to come for the *Clyde Fitch Report*, we'll have *Peculiar Progressive* take a look at Obama's responding, or not, to Congress and the UN, along with other issues dealing with drone attacks overseas and drone surveillance throughout America's air space.

# Drone Control: Secret Killings Take Center Stage

**Roger Armbrust,** February 10, 2013

Since our relaunch last summer, *CFR* has covered the U.S. drone surveillance/killing issue, with particular concern about the CIA's seeming indifferent assaults on innocent global citizens.

In June, we pointed out how international law authorities both condemned drone attacks and questioned their legality. This included Benjamin B. Ferenzc, an Army prosecutor in the Nuremberg trials of Nazi leaders following World War II, who called drone attacks "a crime against humanity."

In July, we reported how some in Congress were questioning drone use in the U.S. following a June crash of a Navy drone in Maryland.

In August, former U.S. Associate Attorney General Webb Hubbell, in his *CFR* column "Hubbell's Telescope," listed surveillance drones and targeted killings as two of five alarming policing trends in America.

In September, *CFR*'s staff reported on an NYU/Stanford legal report which criticized U.S. drone killings, citing deaths of innocents and questioning legality of the attacks.

In November, *Peculiar Progressive* wrote of Congressman

Dennis Kucinich's scheduled Washington briefing to criticize the drone program.

Throughout these months, even with *The New York Times* publicizing President Obama's "kill list" for the drones program, Congress as a whole has remained hands-off on criticizing the drones killing policy, has continued to quietly fund it, and has even mutely approved the FAA's allowing licensing of drone use throughout the United States. Obama has continued to refuse transparency on the deadly drone program, citing security reasons.

**Sudden Visibility**
Then, just in recent days, the drone issue has visibly surged in the United Nations, in Washington, and even in the progressive city of Seattle.

In late January, the UN launched a legal inquiry into drone killings of innocent civilians in Pakistan, Yemen, Somalia, Afghanistan and the Palestinian territories. We still await an outcome of that investigation. Meanwhile, this past week a UN body monitoring children's rights reported that hundreds of children have died in the last four years from U.S. military attacks, including air strikes, in Afghanistan.

Also this past week in Washington, the Senate Intelligence Committee held its hearing on Obama's choice for the new CIA director, John Brennan, mastermind of the White House's drone program who also ran George W. Bush's national counter-terrorism center.

Brennan had responded to a pre-hearing questionnaire, and stuck to his views there during his panel interview. Chris McGreal, a reporter for London's *The Guardian* newspaper, relayed information on that questionnaire:

*In written answers* to questions prepared by the Senate

intelligence committee, Brennan defended drone strikes as a more humane form of warfare. He said that "extraordinary care" is taken to ensure they conform to the "law of war principles" – a phrase human rights groups say is notable in that it does not claim to *actually adhere to international law.*

*Brennan said drones are better than bombs and artillery. "They dramatically reduce the danger to US personnel and to innocent civilians, especially considered against massive ordnance that can cause injury and death far beyond the intended target," he said.*

*Brennan acknowledged that there have been "instances when, regrettably and despite our best efforts, civilians have been killed."*

*But he added: "It is exceedingly rare, and much rarer than many allege".*

Brennan isn't specific about civilians being killed because it allows him to use general statements, like the last two, which appear to be untrue.

*CFR* has cited figures from the Bureau of Investigative Journalism regarding civilian deaths, and the NYU/Stanford legal study includes psychological trauma of civilians suffering drone attacks. McGreal's *Guardian* article also includes statistics from various sources citing increased attacks and civilian deaths under Obama's administration. You can see those here.

Just as disturbing as the deaths and psychological harm on innocent victims: the administration's attitude that it can be judge, jury and executioner through its drone program. Brennan portrayed that cold-blooded attitude in his remarks. This from *The Washington Times*, quoting Brennan during the hearing:

*The actions that we take on the counterterrorism front, again,* are to take actions against individuals where we believe that the intelligence base is so strong and the nature of the threat is so grave and serious, as well as imminent, that we have no recourse except to take this action that may involve a lethal strike.

He is, in fact saying, the White House has a right to take any life without having to consult with Congress, the judiciary, or consideration of international law. *The New York Times* has reported that the White House itself has said, regarding individuals killed by drone attacks, it "counts all military-age males in a strike zone as combatants, according to several administration officials, unless there is explicit intelligence posthumously proving them innocent." But what good is it for you if you're found to be innocent after you're dead?

**Droneless in Seattle**
While Congress has approved use of surveillance drones within America's borders, and agencies are lining up to seek FAA licenses for drones, the mayor of Seattle this past week has balked, according to the *Associated Press*:

*Seattle's mayor on Thursday ordered the police department to abandon its plan to use drones after residents and privacy advocates protested.*

*Mayor Mike McGinn said the department will not use two small drones it obtained through a federal grant. The unmanned aerial vehicles will be returned to the vendor, he said.*

Could this be a turning of the tide? Polls have shown that a majority of Americans favor using drones to survey and kill people in other countries, evidently buying the administration's argument that it saves American lives.

Maybe that attitude will continue to change as drones become increasingly visible at home, which they will. Authorities predict the sky will fill with 30,000 drones worldwide by 2020, 15,000 of those in the U.S.

# "Mali? Why?" We'll Whisper
**Roger Armbrust,** February 24, 2013

"The war against terror," Gore Vidal chided, "is like the war against dandruff." And the endless dandruff now seems to have spread to the landlocked West African country of Mali. The question for the financially struggling United States and its equally cash-strapped European allies is this: Will Mali become our next Viet-ghanistan?

France has sent troops into the independent state (pop. 13.8 million)-once a French colony-to battle radical Islamist fighters who have taken over Mali's vast northern desert area. The French have returnedto bolster weak defense efforts by the Mali military-which has operated a suppressive dictatorship in the south since a March 2012 coup-while the radical Islamists control with oppression in the north.

Actually the Europeans' problem-including France's-with West African rebellion began, not with radical Islamists, but with the Tuareg: a nomadic people who for centuries have lived in the expansive Sahara Desert, including areas of Mali, Niger, Algeria and Libya. The Tuareg has considered the area one living space. But the Europeans forcefully divided it up, making the Tuareg citizens of several nations. They haven't liked that, and have rebelled consistently since the 1960s. In 2007, Tuareg rebels fought unsuccessfully to gain control of Niger's lucrative uranium deposits.

Roger Armbrust

In Mali, Tuareg leaders have said they won't oppose the radical Islamists unless they turn and reach some kind of cooperation with the invading French and U.S.

**Natural Resources**
Which leads us to this question: Why should Paris care to get involved in a former now-independent colony's current conflict? Well, France has been greedy since the 16th century to grab its share of West African natural resources, ranging from food products to gold to slaves. Mali remains the third largest producer of gold in the African continent, a product of growing desire internationally, but of little good to the Mali economy itself because foreign companies control the gold interests and operate the mines and distribution.

The world's central banks are looking now to protect their gold, primarily because they've continued to print paper money that's becoming less and less valuable, and sooner or later will have to require a stable bullion source to brace themselves in the growing currency war. As an example, the German court recently demanded the Bundesbank account for its gold supply, and the bank in turn called on the U.S. to return the German gold it's been holding. Just part of a gold maneuvering international process that could get really sloppy, and even lead to national conflicts.

So gold seems to be growing more valuable in the global eye, and Mali has an exploitative supply of it.

But other natural resources remain in play, too.

France began its Mali military intervention in January of this year with air strikes and then land troops. Militants retaliated by seizing hostages and an *internationally* operated gas field in Mali's neighbor Algeria.

We just spoke of the 2007 Tuareg effort to control Niger's uranium. Niger's another Mali neighbor, which always seems to draw U.S. interest if our troops are in the area, and we seem to be everywhere these days.

So, you see, while Mali and its neighboring states are allegedly independent, their natural resources are controlled by multinational corporations. Rebels, including but not limited to radical Islamists, are very aware of their own history of enslavement, and who's currently running the natural-resource pipeline.

**United States Involvement**
If you're not a history buff, we'll just remind you of three points about the U.S. invasion of South Vietnam in the 1960s: (1) France preceded us there. (2) Both Presidents Kennedy and Johnson warned we had to be there because of the alleged "domino effect": if Vietnam falls, all of Southeast Asia could fall. (3) It was a war we could never win.

Now, think about those points regarding U.S. invasion policy in Afghanistan, Iraq, Pakistan, and Iran.

Okay, now let's look briefly at the U.S. and its policy in Mali and West Africa:

As much as 10 years before the March 2012 military coup and radical rebellion in Mali, the U.S. state and defense departments had run counter-terrorism operations in Mali. *The Washington Post* details them here.

Long story short, the U.S. feared radical Islamist fighters would exodus **Afghanistan** and settle in northern Mali. And guess who would drive them out of Aghanistan?

So, we began sending special forces in to train Mali military-as we had in Vietnam and Afghanistan, etc.-in the early 2000s. We also spent about $45 million from 2004-08 for defense projects and other aid. Then pumped it up to $461 million in good will for "good governance, economic freedom, and investing in their citizens" as a part of the U.S. Millennium Challenge from 2006 to 2012.

Roger Armbrust

Meanwhile, the World Bank reports that 9 out of 10 people in Mali live in dire poverty, with 72% of the population having less than a dollar a day to live on.

*The Washington Post's* Walter Pincus in his Jan. 16 column asks what went wrong with the U.S. counter-terrorism effort, and suggests Congress should look into it. A practical question and suggestion.

And the war drumbeat goes on. In June of last year, the Army Times announced that a brigade of 3,000 soldiers "and likely more" would deploy to Africa this year "in a pilot program that assigns brigades on a rotational basis to regions around the globe." The article added:

> *...U.S. Army Africa will continue to strengthen ties with regional militaries and governments by teaching military tactics, medicine and logistics, as well as combating famine, disease and terrorism in secure environments. The Army currently allows conventional soldiers to enter only 46 of the 54 African states due to security risks.*

Just three months ago, in early December, the *Associated Press* http://www.armytimes.com/news/2012/12/ap-us-military-says-intervention-in-mali-now-would-fail-120312/reported:

*The top U.S. military commander in Africa warned Monday against any premature military action in Mali, even as he said that al-Qaida linked extremists have strengthened their hold on the northern part of the country.*

> *Army Gen. Carter Ham said that any military intervention done now would likely fail and would set the precarious situation there back "even farther than they are today."*

But Ham also expressed concern about cooperative efforts among radical groups:

## The Vital Realities for 2020 and Beyond

*Ham's comments provided greater public detail on the worrisome coordination between al-Qaida in the Islamic Maghreb, which bases its operations in Mali, and the radical Islamist sect Boko Haram, which is based in Nigeria. The growing linkage between the terror groups, Ham said, poses the greatest threat to the region.*

*The Washington Post* reported on Feb. 22 that President Obama had announced that "about 100 U.S. troops have been deployed to the West African country of Niger, where defense officials said they are setting up a drone base to spy on al-Qaeda fighters in the Sahara."

*Reuters* last Monday revealed:

*The United States is likely to eventually resume direct support for Mali's military, but only after full restoration of democracy through elections, the head of a visiting U.S. Congress delegation said on Monday.*

*Senator Christopher Coons, chairman of the Senate Foreign Relations subcommittee on Africa, was leading the first American congressional visit to the West African nation since France sent a military force there last month to halt an offensive by al Qaeda-allied insurgents.*

Will Mali become our next Viet-ghanistan?

# Syria: Symbol of Our Government's Endless-War Addiction
**Roger Armbrust,** August 26, 2013

Back in June, *Peculiar Progressive* outlined for you four major factors showing "1984" is alive and ill in America. One of those is the combined addiction of nationalism and endless war. At that time, we said:

> Today, the United States sees the decaying effects of a decade of invasions of Iraq and Afghanistan, drone invasions into Pakistan, and looking to spread its military aggression possibly into Iran, Syria, Africa, and beyond.

This week, that endless-war addiction now is aiming its drone-slanted eyes toward Syria. This weekend, UK newspaper *The Independent* ran the headline "Syria: air attacks loom as Britain and US pledge to use force within two weeks." *Reuters* published a head reading, "Russia warns US not to repeat in Syria past mistakes in region," meaning Iraq and Afghanistan. And this afternoon (Monday) *The Washington Post* just ran a "news alert" headline shouting, "Kerry says Obama will hold Syria accountable for use of chemical weapons."

So here we go again. What didn't work in Korea, and didn't work in Vietnam, and didn't work in Iraq and Afghanistan, and didn't work in Libya, appears about to repeat itself in Syria.

Why does the US keep sticking its flaring military nostrils in the Middle East, Asia and also create other combat hotspots? Here are just two major reasons to contemplate:

**Military-Industrial Complex**
For the multinational corporations that control Washington, endless war is their meal ticket. As just one example, Dick Cheney's Halliburton and its subsidiaries, while Cheney was vice president, pulled in **billions** from work in Iraq and Afghanistan. While it's difficult to get a total figure, sources list Halliburton subsidiary Kellogg, Brown and Root (KBR) getting $16 billion in contracts from 2004-06 alone. *Politifact* cites KBR government work for Iraq reconstruction from 2001-10 of $31 billion. Cheney was vice president from 2001-2008. Halliburton broke ties with KBR in 2007.

But Halliburton is just one of a battalion of corporations living off America's military. To review a couple of lists and see where your tax money's going, check the links *here* and *here*.

**An Eroding Economy**
Political power mongers (we dare not call them leaders) historically have understood that, when the economy sucks, they need to find a national enemy to turn your attention away from your money miseries. So they'll invade Iraq (by lying about weapons of mass destruction) or preach that Iran's use of atomic energy will devastate the world.

Meanwhile, Washington doesn't want you to think about this:

The US Federal Reserve continues to hold interest rates artificially low, killing consumers' chances to make money on savings, while the big bucks go to the big banks and Wall Street, who are selling billions in bonds back to the Fed. Meanwhile, the banks once again are bundling mortgages with other financial risks, which led to the financial meltdowns and depressions of the 1930s and post-2008. That process can only lead to another meltdown, probably worse than 2008. Washington knows it, and needs an enemy to preach about so the US doesn't turn into another Egypt. Considering where Congress has languished in the polls' slimy bottom over the last couple of years, a "manufactured" foreign enemy may not wash when the economy dissolves.

Stats show the top 20 percent of incomes in the US own 90 percent of the wealth, the middle class has been shrinking, and executive incomes have been rising, but not employees' incomes. And most of the jobs being created since the 2008 meltdown have been low-end and part-time work.

Now, ask yourself this:

Do you think Congress, nearly half of whom are millionaires, and the president, who's also a millionaire, really want to change that? Oh, they'll pabulum-feed the major media with their efforts at minor fines for banks and corporations, and putting low-level execs behind bars. But anything more than that? Don't bet on it.

Not when the big bucks keep going to their big-bellied cronies in the big corporations as this country continues to wage endless war.

That is...unless you decide to get organized, get educated, get active, and take back your Congress, your White House and your country. We showed you how to do that *here*.

# Obama the Invader: Tightening His Own Noose

**Roger Armbrust,** September 8, 2013

"The 'New American Century' proclaimed by the neoconservatives came to an abrupt end on September 6 at the G20 meeting in Russia," Paul Craig Roberts said this weekend. "The leaders of most of the world's peoples told [President Barack] Obama that they do not believe him and that it is a violation of international law if the US government attacks Syria without UN authorization."

Identifying President Obama with the neoconservatives is an impactful statement from Roberts. An American economist, he served as Assistant Treasury Secretary in the Reagan Administration and was noted as a co-founder of Reaganomics. Neoconservatives-who primarily push for religious opposition of evil via military power, with calculated focus on the Middle East and Islam-held influential positions in both the Nixon and Reagan administrations.

Still, Roberts, a columnist for Creators Syndicate, clarified his view in his weekend writing:

> [Russian President Vladimir] Putin told the assembled world leaders that the [Syrian] chemical weapons attack was "a provocation on behalf of the armed insurgents in hope of the help from the outside, from the countries

> which supported them from day one." In other words, Israel, Saudi Arabia, and Washington-the axis of evil.
>
> China, India, South Africa, Brazil, Indonesia, and Argentina joined Putin in affirming that a leader who commits military aggression without the approval of the UN Security Council puts himself "outside of law."
>
> In other words, if you defy the world, Obama, you are a war criminal.

Realizing opposition against his plan was rising, Obama last week-even while at the G20-was also taking his plan to Congress. After all, Congress has given the last two presidents basically everything they've wanted for hawking, ranging from invasions of other countries to creating a surveillance state in America. But Congress, who appeared to be leaning Obama's way early, evidently began hearing from their more-than-skeptical constituents. As a result, opposition to the president began to grow, particularly in the House of Representatives.

Seeing support waning in Washington, Obama has decided to present his endless-war continuum on television, planning to make an address Tuesday. He'll be talking to an American people experiencing a $1 trillion credit-card debt, a $1 trillion college-loan debt, a $17 trillion national debt, infrastructure repair requirements of $2 trillion, a still staggering unemployment rate and most job creation going to low-scale and part-time jobs. In other words, he'll be addressing a less-than-happy public. But, odds are, he won't address those negative economic points.

The president will be banking (good word for him and who he really supports) that the audience will buy his argument that the Assad regime, and not the Syrian insurgents, have used chemical weapons-even though that's not the way the United Nations and the G20 countries have observed it.

## The Vital Realities for 2020 and Beyond

He'll also be banking that the American public has no sense of history, particularly regarding the U.S. government's extensive assaults with chemical weapons. *Peculiar Progressive* offered a column on that last week. You can read that here.

It appears that Obama finally may have carried his efforts at abusive power abroad and at home too far. We've traced those efforts over the past couple of years in columns covering his endless-war invasions ranging from drone strikes in Pakistan to military maneuvers in Mali, to the current Syrian crisis; and in his tyranny at home ranging from massive surveillance to, when he was campaigning, avoiding the five vital issues facing America.

He's hoping that on Tuesday, he'll be talking to an uninformed public, and he'll probably be right. But he'll also be addressing an exhausted American public, and he may not be able to overcome that.

# The Coming Conflict over Santa's Home
**Roger Armbrust,** December 25, 2013

St. Nick, the missus, their elves and eight tiny reindeer are about to be joined by major nations' military forces, in what could lead to conflict over possession of the North Pole's oil, gas, and fresh-water reserves.

Scientists consider the Arctic-one of the last vast wilderness areas-vital to biodiversity and extremely sensitive to global warming. The northern global sector, a wide ice-covered ocean surrounded by treeless permafrost, has seen recent years of warmer temperatures and melting sea ice.

But the jolly old elf's homeland is also deep in natural resources, including oil, gas, and fresh water, along with fish and, in the subarctic, forestlands-all considered economic boons to the major nations. A number of those countries claim property rights to sections of the area. Those sovereignties include Canada, Russia, the United States (Alaska), Denmark (Greenland), Norway, Sweden, Finland, and Iceland. They are limited to a 200-nautical-mile economic zone around their border coasts which lie within the Arctic region.

Under the United Nations Convention on the Law of the Sea, a country has ten years to claim an extended continental shelf beyond those 200 nautical miles. Russia, Canada, Norway, and

Denmark all have started projects to claim extended territories. All are signees to the U.N. convention on sea law.

Canada has made the most recent and controversial move, last week marking a claim, and it appears to be extensive. According to the article "Did Canada Just Claim the North Pole?" in *The Diplomat*, a Tokyo-based, online magazine covering politics, society and culture in the Asia-Pacific region:

> *Canada may have positioned itself to eventually claim sovereignty over the North Pole. Canadian Foreign Minister John Baird made a statement last week that revealed that a scientific and geographical survey regarding its claim to Arctic territories will be submitted to the UN Commission on the Limits of the Continental Shelf and may contain data robust enough to lay claim to the North Pole. The submission is necessitated by Canada's participation in the UN Convention on the Law of Sea (UNCLOS). The move represents a bold political push by Stephen Harper's conservative government to extend Canada's rights in the Arctic.*
>
> *The Canadian decision to assertively pursue a claim to the North Pole has a clear foundation in its national interest: the Arctic seabed is expected to contain over one-quarter of the world's undiscovered energy resources, according to The Globe and Mail. The U.S. Geological Survey provides more specific numbers: the Arctic may contain 13 percent of the world's undiscovered oil reserves, 30 percent of undiscovered gas deposits, and 20 percent of the undiscovered natural gas liquids.*

According to UK's *The Guardian* newspaper, the Canadian move has led Russia to increase its military presence in the Arctic. Territorial claims before the U.N. could drag on for years, with other countries' approval required. But that's not stopping active military buildup, according to the paper:

Roger Armbrust

> *In the meantime Canada and Russia have been stepping up their military footprint in the oil- and gas-rich region. [Russian President Vladimir] Putin has said Russia will restore Arctic bases that fell into disrepair after the collapse of the Soviet Union, including one on the New Siberian Islands. On Tuesday he said this base and others were crucial to protecting Russia's "security and national interests".*

How the U.S. will respond to Canada's and Russia's actions isn't clear yet. But two things are clear:

First, the U.S. has not even signed the U.N. convention on sea law, even though it helped form it. Republican senators have opposed the convention and held back the Senate's ability to attain a two-thirds majority vote favoring the treaty.

Second, America's vast military seems to need conflict to survive, having a record of constant invasion of foreign lands ranging from the Middle East to Africa, either through direct fighting or as "advisers" or supporters of reigning governments. Congress doesn't ever seem to declare war or call them wars anymore. It just keeps funding presidents' decisions to militarily enter other nations' borders for "regional conflicts," with U.N. approval or no.

And the U.S. is preparing militarily for a move in the Arctic, according to a *Reuters* Nov. 22 article:

> *U.S. Defense Secretary Chuck Hagel announced on Friday the Pentagon's first Arctic strategy to guide changes in military planning as rapidly thawing ice reshapes global commerce and energy exploration, possibly raising tensions along the way.*

So stay tuned. And if your kids want to write Santa a thank-you letter after hauling in their loot this Christmas, suggest to them they warn St. Nick to stay alert for invading foreigners.

## The Vital Realities for 2020 and Beyond

Meanwhile, you may want to contact your senators and find out if they're going to approve the U.N. sea-law convention, and if they want to send Americans to fight in the Arctic.
Merry Christmas.

# Confronting (Encouraging?) War in 2014
**Roger Armbrust,** January 6, 2014

*Foreign Policy* magazine has published an article predicting the top 10 most likely places 2014 wars will begin, or continue, and shake global stability.

The new entries: Bangladesh, Central African Republic, Honduras, Libya, and North Caucasus. The continuing hotbeds: Central Asia, Iraq, the Sahel, Sudan, and Syria/Lebanon.

The Dec. 30 article, "Next Year's Wars," is authored by Louise Arbour, president and CEO of the International Crisis Group (ICG), an "anti-conflict" non-profit crowded with U.S. and NATO politicians and diplomats. Arbour is a former UN High Commissioner for Human Rights, a former justice of the Supreme Court of Canada and the Court of Appeal for Ontario and a former chief prosecutor of the International Criminal Tribunals for the former Yugoslavia and Rwanda.

Arbour also finds Syria and Central Africa the worst of the lethally worrisome:

> ...it is Syria and the recent muscular interventions in Central Africa that best illustrate alarming deficiencies in our collective ability to manage conflict.

# The Vital Realities for 2020 and Beyond

> *In Syria, the speed and decisiveness with which the international community acted to eliminate Bashar al-Assad's chemical weapons can't help but underscore its failure to act with equal determination to end the fighting; even concerted humanitarian action remains elusive...*
>
> *...In the Central African Republic, meanwhile, the international community was apparently taken by surprise by the collapse into violence. There is no excuse for this: Decades of misrule, under-development, and economic mismanagement had left behind a phantom state long before this year's coup unleashed turmoil and now escalating confessional violence. France's robust support for the African Union (AU) in a full-fledged humanitarian intervention was commendable. But without concerted, sustained commitment to rebuilding the Central African Republic (CAR), it is unlikely to make much difference in the long run.*

But Arbour is too experienced to believe that a top ten list is the limit of the growing global unrest, or that broiling tensions in other countries couldn't easily impose on the leading war zones:

She adds to her concerns Pakistan, Turkey, Afghanistan, Somalia, the Democratic Republic of the Congo, and South Sudan.

Hearing Arbour, and considering realities, one could question whether the West, and Russia, really want to "manage conflict." Arbour doesn't say this, *Peculiar Progressive* says this: Where there's regional conflict, the U.S. and Russia seem to dutifully follow. In the U.S., it's our way of keeping the military-industrial complex (which President Eisenhower warned us about) growing. This involves our government operating as military advisers in foreign conflicts, or taking part in conflicts through NATO (the North Atlantic Treaty Organization), or simply invading nations, or selling arms to countries to aid their war efforts.

Roger Armbrust

U.S. and Russian arms sales continue to grow in controlling the global arms market. The Congressional Research Service in August 2012, reviewing arms sales since 2004, reported:

> *Developing nations continue to be the primary focus of foreign arms sales activity by weapons suppliers. During the years 2004-2011, the value of arms transfer agreements with developing nations comprised 68.6% of all such agreements worldwide. More recently, arms transfer agreements with developing nations constituted 79.2% of all such agreements globally from 2008-2011, and 83.9% of these agreements in 2011.*
>
> *The value of all arms transfer agreements with developing nations in 2011 was over $71.5 billion. This was a substantial increase from $32.7 billion in 2010. In 2011, the value of all arms deliveries to developing nations was $28 billion, the highest total in these deliveries values since 2004.*

From 2008-11, America and the largest of the former Soviet countries ranked first and second in arms sales:

> *From 2008 to 2011, the United States made nearly $113 billion in such agreements, 54.5% of all these agreements (expressed in current dollars). Russia made $31.1 billion, 15% of these agreements. During this same period, collectively, the United States and Russia made 69.5% of all arms transfer agreements with developing nations, $207.3 billion in current dollars) during this four-year period.*

You can read the entire Congressional Research report here.

But, while the U.S. and Russia lead the arms suppliers' pack, other NATO nations are also involved. Germany, France, the United Kingdom, Italy, all reap annual sales in the hundreds of millions to a billion dollars. Do you really think those countries want to see regional conflicts end any time soon?

Farther down in Arbour's long article, she speaks of how the African country Mali is "far from stable today." *Peculiar Progressive* covered the Mali situation at length in a column last year, predicting that it could possibly become America's next "Viet-ghanistan."

Arbour didn't mention the possibility of conflict over oil, minerals, and water in the Arctic. But we reviewed the growing potential in our Christmas Day column, which is here.

How can you affect these continuing efforts in endless war, and U.S. involvement in them? You'll need to order your U.S. senators and Congressmembers to quit funding military invasions into foreign lands, and Congress's supporting multinational corporations—and the Defense Department—benefiting from arms sales. You'll have to get organized, get educated, and get active with others to do this. Can you do that? Sure you can. A worthy project to benefit you and your children in 2014. Bring it!!

# How Do World Wars Ignite?
**Roger Armbrust,** March 3, 2014

World Wars, history shows us, don't just begin. They ignite. Combusted by sudden sparks resulting from constant decades of friction. And they tend to occur when nations' economies suck, and politicians need to find an enemy. Like now.

The West vs Russia, grappling which now we're seeing about to explode in the Ukraine, is older than most of us. But its most significant jousting, leading to the current crisis, seems to have begun with manipulation by the U.S. and the North Atlantic Treaty Organization (NATO...the U.S.-led European military force) and the dissolution of the Union of Soviet Socialist Republics (USSR), commonly called the Soviet Union.

The USSR dissolved in 1991, following both economic struggles and President Mikhail Gorbachev's successful efforts at Perestroika, or liberalizing the society, including press freedoms. Russia, by far the largest and most populated state, represented the Soviet Union's motherload, with the smaller states geographically connected to it.

NATO, created following World War II with a membership mainly from Europe and North America, immediately went to work, hoping to assure the Soviet breakup stayed that way. NATO began approaching the former Soviet states, offering to form Partnerships for Peace(PfP), working relationships to create trust. By 1994, 10 of the 15 Soviet states had become

# The Vital Realities for 2020 and Beyond

PfP members. They included the Ukraine, who joined in February, and Russia, who came aboard in June.

So Russia, while losing the USSR's designation as a superpower, still has maintained a role as a major world power. It's a member of the United Nations' Security Council which can affect international relations, and Russia's treaties, political and economic connections also rank it among global leaders. In fact, it followed the Soviet breakup by building back its economy, led by energy production.

**Oil and Gas**
And here's a major element in why the current crisis in the Ukraine–and the West's growing criticism of Russia's voting to possibly send troops into that turbulent country—could spark a major conflict in Europe, if not beyond:

Russia is a key oil and gas supplier to most of the European countries. The media, including the *Wall Street Journal*, have referred to it as an energy superpower, and with reason. *Wikipedia* well summarizes Russia's strong energy position:

> The country has the world's largest natural gas reserves, the 8th largest oil reserves, and the second largest coal reserves. Russia is the world's leading natural gas exporter and second largest natural gas producer, while also the largest oil exporterand the largest oil producer. On 1 January 2011, Russia said it had begun scheduled oil shipments to China, with the plan to increase the rate up to 300,000 barrels per day in 2011.
>
> Russia is the 3rd largest electricity producer in the world and the 5th largest renewable energy producer, the latter because of the well-developed hydroelectricity production in the country.

This is perhaps the chief disturbing factor in the current political jousting over Ukraine, which by today, Monday, appeared to be a growing political conflict, and unpredictable.

Both Russia and the West are accusing each other of disrupting Ukrainian stability.

Russia claims that Western interference in internal Ukrainian affairs led to the overthrow of President Viktor Yanukovych, who was removed from power by the parliament on Feb. 21.

President Obama, ignoring that charge, has given a tough response, according to CNN:

> *Obama said any violation of Ukraine's sovereignty and territorial integrity would be "deeply destabilizing, and he warned "the United States will stand with the international community in affirming that there will be costs for any military intervention in Ukraine."*

Also this week, NATO and German Chancellor Angela Merkel echoed Obama, saying any Russian use of force in Ukraine would go against international law.

Russia doesn't seem to be buying that. A Russian council member, interviewed today, said that Russia is following its constitution and respecting Ukraine's constitution. He also basically said he doesn't believe the European Union is in any economic shape to push Russia. He also called it strictly political, according to RT America television:

> *"All this hysteria in the European Union are nothing more than a PR bubble created in the lead-up to European Parliamentary elections on May 25," Andrey Klimov, a deputy head of the Federation Council's committee for international relations, told Russian mass circulation daily Izvestia.*

He has a point. EU countries are all still struggling from the

## The Vital Realities for 2020 and Beyond

2008 global economic meltdown. And what if the EU did decide to declare even economic sanctions on Russia, or worse, send forces into Ukraine, or even Russia?

What do you think would be Russia's logical move? Yep. Cut off that precious oil and gas it's supplying EU countries.

Also, the U.S. doesn't seem to have much room for complaint. Since both U.S. diplomat Victoria Nuland and Sen. John McCain had visibly shown support for the rightest rebels who ousted the democratically elected Ukrainian president, Russia has that card to call marked. And with the U.S. invasions of Afghanistan and Iraq, and support for overthrow of Syria's leader (a Russian ally), Russia won't give credence to Obama's complaints. Nor NATO's. Remember NATO's invasion of Libya?

Also, give Russia a strong ally with China. Reuters reported today:

> *Russian Foreign Minister Sergei Lavrov discussed Ukraine with his Chinese counterpart on Monday and their views coincided on the situation there, the ministry said.*
>
> *In a statement, Russia's foreign ministry said the two veto-wielding U.N. Security Council members would stay in close contact on the issue.*

Recall earlier in this column, we noted that in 2011 Russia began shipping 300,000 barrels of oil to China each day. You bet they'll stay in touch on the Ukraine issue. And don't expect the U.S. to receive any slack from either country if it keeps pushing them on Ukraine. Obama's bravado may sound good to nationalists here in America. But it's difficult to see our nation in a military position to start another foreign war, particularly one so close to Russia and China.

Nor are we in an economic position, with the government so

deep in debt. While the Federal Reserve has continued printing money for the banks, and keeping interest rates artificially low, snubbing American savers, both China and Russia have been producing and purchasing gold, a solid insurance in the growing currency wars.

China is also a major holder of American debt. And has been gradually positioning itself to move the yuan as the major international currency replacing the dollar. A major conflict with Russia, and therefore China, rather than discouraging the yuan's progress, might insure it.

Too, both Russia and China are members of BRICS, acronym for those two countries aligning with Brazil, India and South Africa, the five major emerging national economies. All, no doubt, will have something to say to the U.S. and EU should they see Ukraine's growing turbulence begin to spill across borders. And it's getting close.

In the last couple of days, Ukraine military have begun to defect from the new national government in Kiev in favor of regional governments. And growing protests in two regions are refusing to recognize two billionaire oligarchs, who supported the government overthrow, and have been appointed regional governors.

So we're seeing the turmoil in Ukraine mirror the global scene from Athens to Detroit to London, with oligarchs and austerity sucking monies out of national economies leading to larger debts and dissolving middle classes, and even deaths. It's a growing unrest politicians have attempted to deflect by finding an enemy to impress a country with nationalism. But as the public more and more begins to see through the dictatorial process, we'll only see more revolt like that now rising in the Ukraine regions. And that turmoil, rather than leading to world peace, could lead to its opposite.

# Wannabe Gov Opposes Nat'l Guard Invading Foreign Nations
**Roger Armbrust,** April 11, 2014

Through the United States' decade-long invasions of Afghanistan and Iraq, a heavy burden of military involvement abroad has been placed on each state's National Guard. Curtis Coleman, a conservative Republican candidate for governor in Arkansas, openly opposes sending his state's troops into such undeclared wars.

*Peculiar Progressive* has been opposing these military invasions, and has wondered if any state's governor would ever show courage enough to buck the federal government in its forcing a state's citizens to continually risk and lose their lives, limbs and psyches.

Internet research has shown only one—a Green Party candidate for governor in 2009, Rich Whitney of Illinois—who publicly opposed sending National Guard troops overseas. Perhaps others have braved such stances, but they're certainly rare and surely not heavily publicized by a profit-minded corporate media that supports endless war.

These days, the states' governors have united behind their National Guards, but it's because of funding-cut threats coming from Washington. As far as reluctance to offer their citizens in sacrifice in undeclared wars, no state executive seems to have opposed that.

Enter Coleman, a successful businessman and conservative Arkansas Republican. That's right: Arkansas, home of Bill Clinton, who as president—although he signed legislation that turned the nation's media over to a handful of moguls and bared the world economy to the wolves of Wall Street—did avoid invading foreign lands and miring us down in any new Vietnam.

We haven't been so lucky under George W. Bush or Barack Obama. And they've freely exploited the country's National Guards in their futile efforts—with Congress's consent— to militarily control the Middle East and its oil and gas all under the guise of an elusive war on "terror."

Obama and Congress, who also allowed NATO's invasion of Libya to overthrow Muammar Gaddafi, have made overtones at also invading Iran, Syria, and certain countries in Africa. And now are supporting a rightist new government in Ukraine in a challenge to Russia, and may send troops to support NATO's Ukraine efforts. Who knows when or if Washington might approve military action in those areas without declaring war, and include our National Guards in the effort.

Coleman says, if elected Arkansas's governor, he'll challenge any effort by the president, whoever it is, to send the Arkansas National Guard into foreign lands and into an undeclared war. He bases his stance on a document both our recent presidents and Congress seem to ignore: the United States Constitution.

On his website, candidate Coleman provides his stance on policies, one of which is titled "Caring for Arkansas' Military Service Members and Veterans." Since he's a Republican, you'd expect him to support caring for military veterans, and to seek tax exemptions for employers who hire them. And he does.

But the first sentence of his care for military members is the surprising uppercut that led to this column:

> *I will be a governor who, to the extent of my constitutional and legal authority, will resist the federalization of our Arkansas National Guard by repeated deployments to military engagements in which Congress has not issued a declaration of war according to the Constitution.*

So, what does the U.S. Constitution say about declaration of war. We've looked at this question in earlier columns, and it's pretty simple.

**The Constitution and War Powers**
Here's the reality: Within the borders of the U.S., neither political rhetoric — including President Obama making our actions in Libya and toward Ukraine "very clear" — nor United Nations documents, nor Congressional resolutions, nor the bible or any other religious publication take precedence over the U.S. Constitution in designating who has the power to make and end war.

The Constitution states clearly and simply in Article 1, Section 8:

> ***The Congress shall have power…to declare war, grant letters of marque and reprisal, and make rules concerning captures on land and water.***

That's the only paragraph that speaks specifically to war.

The article also provides Congress with powers "to raise and support armies…to provide and maintain a navy; to make rules for the government and regulation of the land and naval forces," and to "provide for calling forth the militia," which we would call the National Guard. The Constitution's Article 2, Section 2 states, "The President shall be commander in chief of the Army and Navy of the United States, and of the militia of the several states, when called into the actual service of the United States." The "calling" is left up to Congress, not the president.

That's it. Nowhere in the executive powers article does it say the president has the right to declare or wage war at his own will and in his own way.

The president, as commander in chief, should execute not his own will, but the will of Congress, and therefore more closely the will of the American people.

Presidents, including our present one, have usurped that will and power, usually from a weak-kneed Congress.

One such Congress, following Vietnam, felt a political need to "clarify" the roles of the two branches regarding war-making powers. The result was the War Powers Resolution of 1973.

The resolution stresses that the president can only send forces into hostile action in one of three ways: (1) Congress's declaration of war; (2) "specific statutory authorization," meaning Congress must pass a law allowing the hostile action; or (3) "a national emergency created by attack upon the United States, its territories or possessions, or its armed forces."

The Congress, in 1973, showed its weakness in later paragraphs, where the resolution does give in, wordily allowing the president to initiate hostile action if he quickly reports back to Congress, justifying the action's legality.

The problem is, *Congress does not have the Constitutional right to abdicate its power to declare and wage war to the executive branch. That would take a Constitutional amendment.* But this 1973 resolution basically does that.

This 1973 Congressional resolution was also the primary document cited by President Bush's deputy counsel, John C. Yoo, in his Sept. 25, 2001 memorandum opinion on the president's having "broad constitutional power to use military force." But Yoo's word isn't law. It's only a biased opinion within the then-Bush administration.

Congress also cited the 1973 document in its 2002 resolution allowing the president to send American forces into Iraq. But that 2002 resolution is simply Congress ignoring the Constitution.

**Coleman's Revolution**
Gubernatorial candidate Coleman, in effect, is challenging this entire process. He's saying the governor, as the state's chief executive, has the state constitutional right to oppose "federalization of our Arkansas National Guard" in undeclared wars.

Coleman has another ace to play in his case. It was World War II's greatest war hero, Dwight D. Eisenhower, who warned us about the growing military-industrial complex. He did it in his farewell address as our nation's president. He also was a Republican, which Coleman can call on for any within his party who oppose his stance.

Some of Coleman's other positions are troublesome to any voters outside conservative Republicans and those on the religious right. For example, he opposes gay marriage for religious reasons. He says:

*God instituted and defined marriage as between a man and a woman before He instituted government. Government has no authority to re-define an institution that pre-dated it.*

That's a concern for more than a stance on marriage. He's basically saying that religious law supersedes constitutional law, in essence the political philosophy of radical Islamists who believe that Sharia law supersedes a country's constitution—a pet peeve of conservative Republicans. It's one of the contradictions conservatives have yet to admit and deal with. And that's a problem for Coleman if he—on the one hand is defending the Constitution, and on the other hand is trying to supersede it.

But his stance regarding the National Guard and undeclared war is a courageous one. It could be exciting to see if Coleman's effort picks up any steam. Neither his Republican opponent nor either Democratic gubernatorial candidate have touched this issue, except seeming to support the military unquestionably.

If Coleman's able to set himself apart from his opponents by pushing this issue, and is able to pull off a win as an underdog, his National Guard stance just might have powerful legs. Politicians go with what they see work. And if other Republican governors, and there are a lot of them, see Coleman's defense of the Guard and the Constitution develop staying power, they just might jump on board. That could lead to a real confrontation of states' rights versus federal-government power—which was at the basis of the forming of our Declaration of Independence and eventually our national Constitution.

# Will World War III Be a "Dollar" Conflict?
**Roger Armbrust,** April 20, 2014

It's appearing more and more that the United States' major concern with Russia is not the Ukraine conflict, but the Great Bear's alliance with China and other countries in the Shanghai Cooperation Organisation (SCO). That group seems poised to replace the dollar with another currency, perhaps the yuan, as the international choice for trade. And to organize a banking system for its members separate from the normal international banking channels.

Such an action would greatly reduce U.S. power over world markets and global influence, which is just what Russia and China would prefer. The Ukraine conflict, then, would be the latest in ongoing struggles among the nations for positions of economic power, and the international political force that comes with it. It is also the most serious step toward a World War III of finance as the U.S. attempts to directly affect political affairs in the Ukraine, and oppose Russia's efforts to do the same. America is united with the European Union in the effort, along with their military wing the North Atlantic Treaty Organization (NATO).

With the outbreak of the Ukraine crisis, *Peculiar Progressive* considered the possibilities of a military world war. We also pointed to the danger of taking on Russia due to its growing connection with China, both through BRICS, and a 2011 agreement for Russia to send 300,000 barrels of oil a day to China.

Roger Armbrust

It recently became clear that the Russia-China energy connection is growing even stronger. Russia's natural gas producer Gazprom literally added more fuel to the mix last week, announcing that it expected a long-sought supply contract with China would "come into force by the end of 2014," according to Reuters.

These Russia-China agreements, in turns out, are growing fruits of the SCO, founded in 2001 in Shanghai by leaders of China, Kazakhstan, Kyrgyzstan, Russia, Tajikistan, and Uzbekistan.

According to Wikipedia:

> *By 2007 the SCO had initiated over twenty large-scale projects related to transportation, energy and telecommunications and held regular meetings of security, military, defence, foreign affairs, economic, cultural, banking and other officials from its member states.*
>
> *The SCO has established relations with the United Nations, where it is an observer in the General Assembly, the European Union, Association of Southeast Asian Nations (ASEAN), the Commonwealth of Independent States and the Organisation of Islamic Cooperation.*

This was activity preceding the world economic meltdown. A year later, the disastrous 2008 financial crisis occurred, affecting countries throughout the globe.

In 2007, observing the financial meltdown beginning, Iranian Vice President Parviz Davudi suggested to the SCO that it form "a new banking system which is independent from international banking systems."

By this time Iran was one of the Observer States to the SCO. Others are Afghanistan, India, Mongolia, and Pakistan. The U.S. applied for observer status in the SCO, but was turned down in 2006.

## The Vital Realities for 2020 and Beyond

Alasdair Macleod, a financial analyst, said in a TV interview last Thursday that at least Russia, China, India, and Iran, and perhaps others involved with SCO, would like to see the dollar replaced as the international currency. The dollar has held that position since the end of World War II. The U.S. is fighting to keep that from happening to the dollar. He said this situation could set the stage for a World War III, not based on military action, but on currencies.

Russia, China, India are also united with Brazil and South Africa in BRICS, an acronym for the association of these emerging national economies. BRICS, too, in its first formal summit in 2009, called for a new global reserve currency. So the U.S. and EU are seeing through these two organizations–SCO and BRICS–these growing nations solidify and expand their unity.

Macleod also wrote on his blog *goldmoney.com* on March 21:

> *Assuming military options are a non-starter, the West's financial condition is too fragile to withstand an alternative financial war with the world's largest energy exporter and eighth largest economy [Russia], let alone a combination of Russia and China working together...*
>
> *...the West is not just confronting Russia, but potentially China and the other SCO members as well. Russia's relationship with the SCO brings with it the possibility of using gold as a weapon against the West, because most governments involved with the SCO have been actively buying gold while western central banks have been providing it. So far the SCO members have been content to accumulate the west's gold on falling prices, being careful not to disrupt the market.*

In a 2010 special to *CFR*, we discussed the U.S. interest in controlling Eurasia. We pointed to President Jimmy Carter's national security advisor, Zbigniew Brzezinski, revealing in a

Roger Armbrust

1998 interview that Carter in 1979 had provided the catalyst for the Soviet Union's invasion of Afghanistan. The president signed a secret directive on July 3 of that year which aided enemies of Kabul's pro-Soviet regime. Brzezinski said the move was calculated to induce the Soviets into the "Afghan trap," thus "giving to the USSR its Vietnam war."

Before that, in his 1997 book *The Grand Chessboard: American Primacy and Its Geostrategic Imperatives*, Brzezinski presented his premise that the U.S. must concentrate on Eurasia to remain the lone global superpower and "to make certain that no state or combination of states gains the capacity to expel the United States from Eurasia."

That, and more, is what Russia and China would like to make occur. And that is what the U.S. and EU would like to avoid, and hope a foothold in the Ukraine will help them avoid. They may have done that this past week. Following a summit meeting on Ukraine involving the U.S., Russia, the Ukraine's new government, and the EU, a statement resulted indicating an agreement. The pact included the Ukraine stepping away from armed confrontation that could lead to civil war, and working to revise its constitution in a transparent way.

But a report Thursday evening from Sky News indicated policymakers remain wary:

*Western leaders have reacted cautiously to an agreement reached with Russia over a plan to ease tensions in Ukraine.*

*US President Barack Obama warned the West stood ready to impose further sanctions on Russia if no progress was made in de-escalating the continuing crisis.*

Understanding that the Ukraine crisis represents a part of a larger conflict over international finance and political influence, expect the struggle to continue.

# A Bush Insider Cites War Crimes Against His President, VP
**Roger Armbrust,** May 30, 2014

This week, George W. Bush's former chief counterterrorism officer accused the once-was president and his administration of committing war crimes. Could it lead to some type of legal action? We'll see.

Richard Clarke–who served a brief stint as Bush's national coordinator for security and counterterrorism—perked up Amy Goodman's ears in a Tuesday television interview on *Democracy Now!* The show's host, Goodman asked Clarke if he thought Bush, former VP Dick Cheney, and former Defense Secretary Donald Rumsfeld should be tried for war crimes via attacking Iraq.

Clarke tried to soften his response, but basically said yes:

> *I think things that they authorized probably fall within the area of war crimes. Whether that would be productive or not, I think, is a discussion we could all have. But we have established procedures now with the International Criminal Court in The Hague, where people who take actions as serving presidents or prime ministers of countries have been indicted and have been tried. So the precedent is there to do that sort of thing. And I think we need to ask ourselves whether or not it would be useful to do that in the case of members of the Bush administration. It's clear that things that the Bush*

> *administration did — in my mind, at least, it's clear that some of the things they did were war crimes.*

*Democracy Now!* hasn't aired the interview yet, only taped it, and released that juicy bit to urge our watching. But that's indeed a ferocious bite when you recall that Iraq resulted in the death of over 4,400 U.S. forces and nearly 32,000 wounded. Add to that over 16,600 Iraqi military and police, 26,000 Iraqi "insurgents" and over 66,000 civilian deaths. Plus a cost of $806 billion.

Also, it's valuable when people with authority, or former authority, raise such accusations. Clarke isn't the first. In May 2012, *Peculiar Progressive* wrote about Benjamin B. Ferencz's take on the U.S. invasion of Iraq. Lawyer Ferencz was an investigator of Nazi war crimes after World War II and the Chief Prosecutor for the United States Army at the Einsatzgruppen Trial, one of the twelve military trials at Nuremberg, Germany. Later, Ferenzc became a vocal advocate of the establishment of an international rule of law and of an International Criminal Court.

The U.S. prosecutors at Nuremberg charged that the Nazis' chief crime was "aggressive war" which led to all other offenses they committed. Sixty years later, in the summer of 2006, Ferenzc claimed that George W. Bush should be charged with the same crime for ordering the illegal invasion of Iraq:

> *The United Nations charter has a provision which was agreed to by the United States, formulated by the United States, in fact, after World War II. It says that from now on, no nation can use armed force without the permission of the U.N. Security Council. They can use force in connection with self-defense, but a country can't use force in anticipation of self-defense. Regarding Iraq, the last Security Council resolution essentially said, 'Look, send the weapons inspectors out to Iraq, have them come back and tell us what they've found — then we'll figure out what we're going to do.' The U.S.*

*was impatient, and decided to invade Iraq — which was all pre-arranged of course. So, the United States went to war, in violation of the charter.*

*Peculiar Progressive* specifically asked Ferencz by email his legal view on killer drone strikes which Bush conducted and President Barack Obama has continued. Ferencz condemned them, saying:

> *The illegal use of armed force knowing that it will inevitably kill large numbers of civilians is a crime against humanity, and those responsible should be held accountable by national and international courts. The use of any weapon that will unavoidably kill a disproportionate number of non-combatants is an inhumane act that should be condemned and punishable as a crime against humanity under customary international law.*

In June 2008, Congressman Dennis Kucinich introduced legislation to impeach Bush over the Iraq invasion, but Democratic House Speaker Nancy Pelosi eventually quelled the effort. As *CNN* reported at the time, "House Speaker Nancy Pelosi has repeatedly said she would not support a resolution calling for Bush's impeachment, saying such a move was unlikely to succeed and would be divisive."

*CNN* also described Kucinich's specific legislation:

> *Most of the congressman's resolution deals with the Iraq war, contending that the president manufactured a false case for the war, violated U.S. and international law to invade Iraq, failed to provide troops with proper equipment and falsified casualty reports for political purposes.*

> *Kucinich also charges that Bush has illegally detained without charge both U.S. citizens and 'foreign captives' and violated numerous U.S. laws through the use of*

*'signing statements' declaring his intention to do so.*

**A Trial and Conviction Far, Far Away**
Bush, Cheney and Rumsfeld actually were convicted in absentia of Iraq war crimes in 2012 in Kuala Lumpur–the federal capital and largest city in Malaysia, which is in Southeast Asia. The trial and its five-panel group of senior judges were initiated by Malaysia's retired Prime Minister Mahathir Mohamad. He had heavily opposed the 2003 American-led invasion.

Also found guilty were the administration's legal advisers, including former Attorney General Alberto Gonzales, David Addington, William Haynes, Jay Bybee and John Yoo. According to *Foreign Policy Journal*:

> *The trial held in Kuala Lumpur heard harrowing witness accounts from victims of torture who suffered at the hands of US soldiers and contractors in Iraq and Afghanistan...At the end of the week-long hearing, the five-panel tribunal unanimously delivered guilty verdicts against Bush, Cheney, Rumsfeld and their key legal advisors who were all convicted as war criminals for torture and cruel, inhumane and degrading treatment.*
>
> *Full transcripts of the charges, witness statements and other relevant material will now be sent to the Chief Prosecutor of the International Criminal Court, as well as the United Nations and the Security Council.*

The International Criminal Court (ICC) is a relatively new body, founded in 2002, created by the Rome Statute, a treaty adopted in 1998 which established four core international crimes: genocide, crimes against humanity, war crimes and the crime of aggression.

Currently, 122 states are parties to the ICC, but the United States and Israel have refused to ratify, recognize or adhere to statutes of the court. Because the U.S. is not a state party to the court, no U.S. official can be tried, unless the alleged crime(s) took place in the territory of a state that has accepted the court's jurisdiction. Iraq is not a state member.

However, in 2006, the ICC's prosecutor reported that he had received 240 communications alleging various war crimes in connection with the invasion of Iraq. Some of those appear to involve the UK, a state party to the ICC, and the country that worked most closely with the U.S. in Iraq. It's possible the prosecutor may find the U.S. complicit in UK alleged war crimes, which would be considered a war crime in itself.

Still–although a former prosecutor of Nazi crimes, a U.S. Congressman, and a court of five judges in Malaysia have found specific charges against Bush and company for war crimes–the ICC prosecutor hasn't. The only charges brought before the court so far have been alleged crimes in Africa.

But perhaps Clarke, having been involved in the Bush administration, through his interview will be a catalyst for a deeper look into Bush's actions. That would be good for humanity, who needs to have major policymakers brought to justice for crimes against it, no matter what their nationalities.

# Is War a Racket? An Honored Marine General Said "Yes!"
**Roger Armbrust,** June 17, 2014

Have you heard of Smedley Butler? Perhaps not lately. He was a U.S. Marine who received the Congressional Medal of Honor TWICE. Also the Corps' highly respected Brevet Medaland the Army and Navy Distinguished Service Medal. He retired as a Major General in 1939.

But before he retired, in 1935, he wrote a book. Was it called *Courage in Battle*? No. Was it called *We Defend the World*? No. Was it called *America, Love It or Leave It*? No. It was called *War is a Racket*.

Based on his career as a military officer, Butler discussed—first in a speech then later in book form—how business profiteered from war. In the book, he summarized his view this way:

> War is a racket. It always has been. It is possibly the oldest, easily the most profitable, surely the most vicious. It is the only one international in scope. It is the only one in which the profits are reckoned in dollars and the losses in lives. A racket is best described, I believe, as something that is not what it seems to the majority of the people. Only a small 'inside' group knows what it is about. It is conducted for the benefit of the very few, at the expense of the very many. Out of war a few people make huge fortunes.

## The Vital Realities for 2020 and Beyond

Butler suggested three actions to quell the war racket. First, take the profit motive out of war:

> *It can be smashed effectively only by taking the profit out of war. The only way to smash this racket is to conscript capital and industry and labour before the nation's manhood can be conscripted. ... Let the officers and the directors and the high-powered executives of our armament factories and our steel companies and our munitions makers and our ship-builders and our airplane builders and the manufacturers of all other things that provide profit in war time as well as the bankers and the speculators, be conscripted — to get $30 a month, the same wage as the lads in the trenches get.*

Second, decide to go to war only by a limited referendum, with the only eligible voters being those who would fight on the front lines.

Third, limit the military to only actions of self-defense, with the Navy staying within 200 miles of the U.S. coastline, the army held within the country's territorial limits.

By 1940, he was dead at age 58, via an illness similar to cancer.

By 1961, Dwight D. Eisenhower, another war hero and a Republican president, was warning America of the military-industrial complex's potential to take over Washington. By 1964, we saw it spreading with our invasion of Vietnam, followed in our new century with the quagmires of Afghanistan and Iraq.

Which brings us to this week, and the Obama administration beginning to ingrain us again in Iraq. This from today's *Associated Press*:

> *Obama met with his national security team Monday evening to discuss options for stopping the militants known as the Islamic State of Iraq and the Levant. Officials said the president has made no final decisions on*

> how aggressively the U.S. might get involved in Iraq, though the White House continued to emphasize that any military engagement remained contingent on the government in Baghdad making political reforms.
>
> Still, there were unmistakable signs of Americans returning to a country from which the U.S. military fully withdrew more than two years ago. Obama notified Congress that up to 275 troops would be sent to Iraq to provide support and security for U.S. personnel and the American Embassy in Baghdad. The soldiers — 170 of which have already arrived in Iraq — were armed for combat, though Obama has insisted he does not intend for U.S. forces to be engaged in direct fighting.
>
> "We are hard-wired into their system," the fledgling democracy that America helped institute, said Ryan Crocker, a former U.S. ambassador to Baghdad. "We can't walk away from it."

This, of course, is an exercise in military frustration and continued corporate profit. Frustration because a foreign nation that's a couple of hundred years old (America) is trying to end a 14-centuries-old religious rivalry. National Public Radio summarized that yesterday in a report, which you can read and listen to here.

Meanwhile, the multinational corporations will benefit by continuing to support America's efforts in nationalism and endless war, and also in rebuilding destroyed areas in the aftermath. And don't forget how both the U.S. and Russia profit from weapons sales.

You can find a listing of corporations profiting from the military here. A good place to begin as you get organized, get educated, and get active in changing your government's racket that Washington doesn't want to change.

# Hurtling Toward World War III
**Roger Armbrust,** August 6, 2014

We're not kidding around. This is serious.

Earlier this year, when United States officials helped push Ukraine billionaires to foment an angry citizenry into a continuing revolution, *Peculiar Progressive* asked the question "How Do World Wars Ignite?" We noted how history shows a spark from continued friction can lead to massive explosion, and applied this to the U.S, European Union, Russia and China. China, you see, has become closely allied with Russia, India, Brazil, and South Africa through BRICS. And Moscow and Beijing are involved in major energy contracts sending oil and planned natural gas from Russia to China.

The international conflict is currently taking place with the U.S.-EU versus Russia on two levels: economic and military.

On the economic level, the U.S. and EU have been piling sanctions on Russia in an effort to fiscally corner Moscow. But today (Wed., Aug. 6), Russian President Vladimir Putin announced one-year sanctions against the West, including on all U.S. agricultural products. It appears he may also ban fruits and vegetables from the EU.

*The Associated Press* reported today that Russian agricultural imports in 2013 totaled $1.3 billion from the U.S. and 11.8 billion euros ($15.8 billion) from the EU.

Roger Armbrust

On the military level, the North Atlantic Treaty Organization has been looking for a way to contain Russia ever since the Soviet Union's breakup in the 1990s. NATO has used the current Ukraine conflict to again eye moving toward Russia's borders.

Putin also responded militarily this week, adding 8,000 more troops to the 12,000 already lined along the Ukraine border with Russia.

Now history watchers, ranging from respected U.S. scholars to seasoned economists of Ronald Reagan's administration, are expressing grave concerns about current political tug-of-wars leading to global war. Again. Unless citizens can force policymakers to stop the insanity. So we continue to urge you to get organized, educated, and active in making your policymakers start taking care of the world instead of destroying it for the greedy benefit of a few.

Foreign relations scholars from Johns Hopkins, New York University, U. of Chicago, and U. of Illinois all spoke out in the last two weeks, critical of the U.S. trying to corner Russia, and concerned about bravado leading to nuclear war.

Dr. Steve H. Hanke of The Johns Hopkins Institute for Applied Economics, Global Health, and the Study of Business Enterprise in late July called Washington officials "war mongers."

Veteran Russian history professor Stephen Cohen of NYU expressed grave concerns that the attitude in Washington to try and corner Putin, who won't be cornered, could lead to nuclear war.

John Mearsheimer, a foreign relations scholar at the University of Chicago, said through his decades of dialogues with Washington officials, he's never before seen a consistent attitude that the U.S. knows what's good for the world, and the rest of the world doesn't. He added that the major nations such as Russia, China and India don't agree with that attitude, and he believes they'll defy it. The interviews with Cohen and Mearsheimer can be seen here.

Two important former members of the Reagan administration have also recently expressed great worries about the growing drumbeats from the West. Paul Craig Roberts — former Assistant Secretary of the Treasury under President Reagan and one of the creators of Reaganomics — on July 28 published a column entitled "War is Coming." He bluntly opened it by saying:

> *The extraordinary propaganda being conducted against Russia by the US and UK governments and Ministries of Propaganda, a.k.a., the "Western media," have the purpose of driving the world to war that no one can win. European governments need to rouse themselves from insouciance, because Europe will be the first to be vaporized due to the US missile bases that Europe hosts to guarantee its "security."*

David Stockman, former director of the OMB under President Reagan, and former US Representative, in an early August interview showed concern over a "perfect storm" forming from what he considers U.S. failures in foreign, economic, and fiscal policy.

Meanwhile, Wall Street's banks and corporate oligarchs continue to rake in cash from the growing chaos. This involves weapons sales, led globally by the U.S. and Russia. Big bucks also reign with the U.S. involvement in endless war through invading foreign countries, destroying their governments, culture and infrastructure, then sending in multinational corporations to make billions rebuilding that infrastructure.

*Peculiar Progressive* gave you a clearer view of the oligarch cash cow in our column "Is War a Racket? An Honored Marine General Says 'Yes!'"

What's pushing this World War button? The economy. When

countries' economies crumble, policymakers look for an enemy outside their borders, and so many nations are in financial trouble, the time for global military conflict is ripe. Policymakers (we dare not call them leaders) look to nationalism to unite their struggling citizens and take the focus off their government officials' foibles.

The news has run lately with Argentina's defaulting on international loans. But USAToday carried an article this week revealing that 11 nations are in danger of fiscal defaults. They are, besides Argentina: Ecuador, Egypt, Pakistan, Venezuela, Belize, Cuba, Cyprus, Greece, Jamaica, and, yep, Ukraine. All of this can foment into, if not involvement in a military war abroad, most likely revolution at home. They've already experienced various levels of unrest, ranging from revolution to public protests.

And we'll repeat our mantra of concern about the U.S. economy's shaky position: Americans' credit card debt is $1 trillion. Add to that an over $1 trillion college-loan debt, a national debt of $12.5 trillion (held by the public), and national infrastructure needs of $2.3 trillion.

**Will Nerds Prevail?**
Of course, the global digital wars have been waging for some time now. The U.S. has been spying on the world—from its own citizens to foreign countries and leaders—through the National Security Agency. China has been working to infiltrate American government networks. And while spying on other countries, the U.S. has also been working with their intelligence agencies to spy yet on other countries.

*Peculiar Progressive* has wondered for the last couple of years if the digital wars may prove the place where power finally ends in the hands of a few that no oligarchs planned for. We envisioned the computer geniuses of the globe, who quietly work at keeping the world running, finally becoming fed up, coming down from out of the hills, and organizing an electronic shutdown of Earth.

We've seen hints of this in recent years from the rebel computer organization Anonymous, who has broken into government computers around the U.S. and globe to publicly reveal files ranging from finances to personal information of officials. Most recently, it tapped into Israel's intelligence agency to disrupt it and other networks, a protest against the Israeli invasion of Gaza.

Also, news came today that a Russian gang hacked over 1 billion passwords. That's one-seventh of the world population. But, of course, these examples could be just the tip of the iceberg, should the digital geniuses break loose.

If the Nerds of Digital Navigation ever do decide to make their move, they could perhaps begin by shutting down the world's major electric grids—a long concern of intelligence agencies. They, of course, would also be looking for ways to hack into government emergency power systems, both intelligence and military.

It would make for an awe-inspiring historic experience, wouldn't it? Seeing the world's military and spy machines dismantled? Complete peace. For at least a while. No doubt, we'd all be better off.

# Six Films Link Warmongers' Warped Mind

**Roger Armbrust,** September 1, 2014

"The Godfather," "Three Days of the Condor" and four documentaries—two on espionage, one on art, and a major, in-depth review of the Cold War—clarify man's inhumanity to man, the insanity of the nuclear arms race, and how it's all based on economics...also known as business. And in 2014 known jointly as Big Business: Big Agri, Big Arms, Big Oil, Big Banks and Big Government. And referred to by the late war hero and Republican President Dwight Eisenhower as the Military-Industrial Complex.

Collectively, the films also substantiate how a human race of such great potential, consistently dumbed down, prepares to kill itself.

These six films aren't connected, nor meant to be. They've been produced in different decades. Yet, when considered on a single canvas, their images and intent unmuddy the coercive mindset and manipulation of warmongers in power. The films, besides "The Godfather" and "Condor," are "American Coup," "Secrets of Her Majesty's Secret Service,'""This is Civilization," and CNN's 24-hour documentary "The Cold War."

**"The Godfather" (1972)**
Two of the most famous lines from "The Godfather" set the

stage for the Warmonger Mindset: "Tell Mike it was just business," and "I'll give him an offer he can't refuse." Both deal with killing. The first, killing you is nothing personal; it's how we stay in power and keep the money flowing in. It's required. No options. The second phrase connotes putting a gun to your head and giving you an option: you follow orders, or your brains coat the wall.

But "The Godfather" takes that Warmonger Mindset from that one-on-one level to the Family level, with a collection of people (gangs) involved. As Michael Corleone prepares to commit a double murder to "defend the family," he watches his father's old friend Clemenza prepare a meal for the guys. Clemenza explains to Michael why war will follow the assassination. It is inevitable:

> Michael: How bad do you think it's gonna be?
> Clemenza: Pretty goddam bad. Probably all the other Families will line up against us. That's all right. These things gotta happen every five years or so, ten years. Helps to get rid of the bad blood. Been ten years since the last one.

Then there's the scene where Michael takes the image to the level of the federal government as he tries to defend his father's Warmonger actions to Kay, who he wants to marry:

> Michael: My father is no different than any powerful man, any man with power, like a president or senator.
> Kay Adams: Do you know how naive you sound, Michael? Presidents and senators don't have men killed.
> Michael: Oh. Who's being naive, Kay?

## "Three Days of the Condor" (1975)

In the closing scene, Higgins, a Central Intelligence Agency (CIA) assistant director, attempts to explain to protagonist Joe Turner why the clandestine agency really exists:

Roger Armbrust

> *Higgins: It's simple economics. Today it's oil, right? In ten or fifteen years, food. Plutonium. Maybe even sooner. Now, what do you think the people are gonna want us to do then?*
> *Joe Turner: Ask them?*
> *Higgins: Not now – then! Ask 'em when they're running out. Ask 'em when there's no heat in their homes and they're cold. Ask 'em when their engines stop. Ask 'em when people who have never known hunger start going hungry. You wanna know something? They won't want us to ask 'em. They'll just want us to get it for 'em!*

No thought of multinational cooperation, communication, planning and distribution. Warmongers don't profit from that.

## "American Coup" (2010)
*Peculiar Progressive* took an in-depth look at this film in a 2012 column: "American Coup: When U.S. versus Iran Really Began." The 53-minute documentary traces the CIA's clandestine overthrow of Iran's democratically elected government in 1953.

That's DEMOCRATICALLY ELECTED government. The U.S. replaced it with the Shah, who would assure the West access to Iranian oil. Hey, Iran. It was nothing personal. It was just business. Every Warmonger understands that.

## "Secrets of Her Majesty's Secret Service" (2014)
Aired on PBS this past Sunday, this intriguing British-made nearly hour-long film is a melding of documentary and public relations to show the history and value of the UK's MI6 intelligence agency.

We cite it here because one brief segment basically shows that, during the Cold War, neither the U.S. nor Russia had a responsible grasp on what they were doing in their Warmongers shoving match.

The Reagan administration had put into play a full-scale mock military preparation—basically a war game, including the president's involvement—to flex a show of strength. Trouble was, Russia suspicioned it to be the real thing, and began revving up its military and missiles...in a hurry. Their chief concern, according to MI6, was seeing that the president was directly involved.

The film explains that it took a call to MI6 from a Russian double agent who saw what really was happening. That allowed the British to immediately communicate to the White House, resulting in Reagan personally stepping away from the military exercise, and making clear to the Russians the U.S. effort was only an internal scrimmage, so to speak. The Russians stood down.

**"This is Civilization" (2007)**
Art critic Matthew Collings in this splendid 2007 four-part documentary traces civilization's evolution from ancient Egypt to modern day through our art.

We speak of it here because Collings devotes one entire program to John Ruskin, the insightful, impactful 19$^{th}$ century British art-and-society critic. Collings explains how Ruskin saw, with the advent of the Industrial Revolution, the beginnings of civilization's devolution: a turning from dependence on God and nature to an addiction with greed, money, and subservience of modern society.

It was then, Ruskin saw, and Collings seems to agree, that we turned from humans who cared for our souls to machines, that don't care about our spirit. Collings titles that episode "Save Our Souls." Not save our money. He believes Ruskin still may have the key on how to do that.

The Industrial Revolution, of course, led to the Technological Revolution, including the ability to immediately nuclear destruct.

**"The Cold War" (1998)**
In January, CNN re-aired this dedicated, exhaustive look at humanity's destructive nature ranging from World War II

through the rest of the 20th century. The network should re-air it often, and also distribute its 24-hour, six-disk DVD package internationally to schools.

Why? We emphasize again: Because this vast reporting effort paints the clearest picture—through both news films and interviews with eye witnesses—of man's senseless inhumanity to man, as well as the sadly laughable insanity of nuclear weapons and the arms race.

One segment, in just a small portion of its hour, shows brief but deeply revealing interviews with a former American GI and a Russian woman. The GI speaks of walking with his squad down a German road near war's end. They see a squad of Russians coming the other way. They've never met Russians before, but know that they're allies. They approach and greet each other.

And the GI recalls how he was surprised to find, "They looked just like us. If you'd have put them in American uniforms, you wouldn't have known the difference."

The Russian woman, in a separate experience, echoes that surprise. She speaks of standing on a riverbank and seeing American soldiers approach her and her companions by boat. As the soldiers came ashore and greeted them, the woman recalls, "They looked just like us."

What does this tell you about government propaganda? About painting pictures of another culture as an enemy to fear...an enemy who's nothing like us and can't be trusted...and must even be eventually destroyed.

In another hour's segment, members of President Kennedy's staff and two Russian military officers are interviewed separately about the rationale of the Mutual Assured Destruction (MAD) philosophy they were operating under. Each interviewee begins to nervously laugh—realizing in these interviews years later how truly insane the nuclear arm wrestling is.

## The Vital Realities for 2020 and Beyond

We'll close by reminding you of our earlier column about the late Marine Brigadier General Smedley Butler. He gave a speech and followed it with a book titled "War is a Racket." Having won two Congressional Medals of Honor and other military decorations, he's hard to argue with.

# Ron Paul: Washington's Peacenik Nemesis
**Roger Armbrust,** November 24, 2014

Ron Paul has never liked war. Perhaps because Dr. Paul's medical residency had been in obstetrics and gynecology, daily experiencing the origin and promise of life, the nurture of mothers during pregnancy and at birth.

Perhaps it was because he understands like Brigadier General Smedley Butler, the multi-decorated Marine hero, that war is a racket, through which many die and a few profit in millions...and now billions...of dollars.

Perhaps it's both. Whatever the reason, Paul's never liked war or the military-industrial complex. And he's never been quiet about it. Even when he ran twice as a Republican presidential candidate, he'd complain about America's constantly invading sovereign nations during the past and new century. Republican audience members would boo him for it. He didn't seem to care. It just increased his resolve, and he'd further explain himself.

No doubt, when Mitt Romney won the Republican nomination and Paul suddenly became silent, the neoconservatives—both in the Republican Party and the Obama administration—breathed a sigh of relief, believing they had finally ridded themselves of this Libertarian(he was that party's presidential nominee in

1988) in Republican clothing. The neocons may have thought they'd never hear from that thorny peacenik again.

They were wrong. Paul simply returned to his native Texas, and has evolved from a single thorn into a thorntree (we dare not say thornBush), just beginning to spread its branches. He has formed The Ron Paul Institute for Peace and Prosperity (RPI), has created an Internet TV station, become an active presence in social media, and has brought into the fold a brain trust who serves as a board of advisors and columnists. In their constant daily messages, they hammer away at the Washington neocons and their ravenous desire for endless war, and its offspring at home, such as massive surveillance in the U.S.

Only today, reports have come of Paul's praising Congress's refusal to approve the USA Freedom Act, because—though it would have imposed certain restrictions on the controversial National Security Agency's (NSA) Orwellian surveillance of Americans–it would have renewed portions of the post-9/11 Patriot Act increasing government limits on freedom. He said in his Sunday column on the foundation's website:

> *The abuses of the Constitution in the PATRIOT Act do not need to be fully recounted here, but Presidents Bush and Obama both claimed authority based on it to gut the Fourth Amendment. The PATRIOT Act ushered in the era of warrantless wiretapping, monitoring of our Internet behavior, watering down of probable cause, and much more. After the revelations by whistleblower Edward Snowden, we know how the NSA viewed constitutional restraints on surveillance of American people during the PATRIOT Act period.*

But Paul's and his foundation's obsessive concentration of late has been on Washington's addiction to endless war. Here are recent examples of columns and video pouring from Paul's group:

1. Today (Monday) the foundation's executive director Daniel McAdams said in a TV interview that U.S. Defense Secretary Chuck Hagel's sudden resignation did not bode well for America. McAdams indicated it only means the White House's neocon base led by Susan Rice, the national security advisor, will continue to try and remove Syrian President Bashar al-Assad from power, further increasing Middle East instability.

2. On Nov. 19, the website ran journalist Robert Parry's piece headlined "Still Letting the Neocons Lead". Parry complained in the piece:

*It may be highly naïve at this point to think that President Obama will ever demonstrate true leadership by repudiating the neocon "group think" regarding a whole variety of issues including today's hotspots, such as Iran, Syria, Iraq, Russia and Ukraine.*

3. On Nov. 10, John W. Whitehead, attorney and founder of The Rutherford Institute, considered a conservative ACLU, had a column called "The Devil's Bargain: The Illusion of a Trouble-Free Existence in the American Police State". He quoted CNBC:

*One out of 100 American adults is behind bars — while a stunning one out of 32 is on probation, parole or in prison. This reliance on mass incarceration has created a thriving prison economy. The states and the federal government spend about $74 billion a year on corrections, and nearly 800,000 people work in the industry.*

4. Former Democratic Congressman Kucinich
   On Nov. 7, the website carried an interview with former Democratic Congressman Dennis Kucinich, an advisory board member of Paul's foundation, titled "The U.S. Must Work to Re-establish Friendly Relations with Russia". Kucinich contended:

> *Because the Democratic Party voted most recently to support giving arms to the so-called Syrian rebels, the Democrats once again voted for war. And the party has consistently voted for war. It has not distinguished itself from the Republican Party at matters of perpetual war which means that there is a vacuum in American politics, there is a vacuum with respect to addressing the need of the people for jobs, the need of the country for rebuilding its infrastructure which is in need of trillions of dollars worth of repairs, and the need for redefining America's role in the world as a means of recognizing that this is not a unipolar world. This is a world of multiple interests and multiple countries, and there is folly for any nation including America to try to sell itself up there as the only nation that matters because indeed we have to be ready to recognize the concerns of all people.*

Some in DC must be wincing from the thorny nicks. We saw a C-SPAN panel recently discussing the NSA and the ever-pervasive propaganda on the war on terror. One of the panelists, who appeared to be a neocon college professor, was blasting Paul for his anti-neocon campaign. That, of course, to Paul and his cohorts is a good sign—getting under the military-industrial complex's armored skin.

But will the Paul-led antiwar effort be enough to stop President Obama's and Congress's military onslaught into the Middle East and the continuance of endless war? RPI's McAdams in a Nov. 7 report concludes the onslaught was continuing. His headline: "Obama Demands Another 1,500 Troops and $5.6 Billion for War Expansion".

The headline alone rings a ghostly bell of Vietnam and America's gradual incursion of military troops into a war we could not win:

**1959 760 troops**

Roger Armbrust

**1960 900**
**1961 3,205**
**1962 11,300**
**1963 16,300**
**1964 23,300**
**1965 184,300**
**1966 385,300**
**1967 485,600**
**1968 536,100**

Then the bloody, slow withdrawal finally ending after the 1972 presidential election.

Oh, and let's not forget the U.S. surprise invasion of Iraq in March 2003. By May 1, President George W. Bush declared "Mission Accomplished". But it took until December 2011 to withdraw our military...who are on the way back for another futile effort that will bring billions of dollars to a chosen few.

Ron Paul and his peacenik cohorts no doubt will keep reminding us of that.

# Paul Craig Roberts: Economic Peace Monger
**Roger Armbrust,** March 2, 2015

Paul Craig Roberts's bottom line seems to be this: Endless war and greed are bad for the economy, and therefore harmful to humanity.

Roberts slipped into the globe's view back in the '80s, when he became an Assistant Secretary of the Treasury under Ronald Reagan, and was part of the brain trust in forming Reaganomics.

Now, 30 years later, he's taken the mantle of gutsy maverick opposing Congress and the White House's fascist obsession with endless war, Wall Street's obsession with endless greed, and both the politicians' and bankers' addiction with feeding the military-industrial complex—and the American corporate media supporting that.

He does this primarily through publishing on his Institute for Political Economy website (paulcraigroberts.org), and in speeches and TV and radio interviews. He's concerned most about an approaching global economic meltdown, and also Washington's (Republicans and Democrats') determination to cause chaos in the Middle East and its fixation on lashing at Russia, which he believes could lead to nuclear war. As a former federal Treasury official, he understands it's all about money and power.

Roger Armbrust

Take a look at some of his recent statements, and see whether or not you agree with him. You can be pretty certain that Washington's pro-war machinery won't. And remember, this guy served under Ronald Reagan:

**"War on Terror" – February 7, 2015**

*Consider the "war on terror." According to a Nobel economist and a Harvard University budget expert, Washington's 14 years of war on terror has cost Americans a minimum of $6 trillion. That's 6,000 billion dollars. This sum, together with the current PayRoll tax revenues is enough to keep Social Security and Medicare in the black for years to come. Without the vast sum wasted on the war on terror, Republicans would not have an excuse to be trying to cut Social Security and Medicare for budget reasons and to privatize the old age pensions and health care of people, thus turning Medicare and Social Security pensions into fee income for Wall Street.*

*Combatting terrorism is the excuse for squandering a minimum of $6,000 billion dollars.*

*What were the terrorist events that serve as a basis for this expenditure?*

*There are five: 9/11, the London transport system bombings, the Spanish train bombing, the Boston Marathon Bombing, and the French Charlie Hebdo rifle attack.*

*In other words, 5 events in 14 years.*

*The loss of life in all these events combined is minuscule compared to the loss of life in the war on terror. Even the deaths of our own soldiers is greater. Washington's wars against terror have caused more deaths of Americans than the alleged terrorist events themselves.*

## The Vital Realities for 2020 and Beyond

**Threat of Nuclear War – February 25, 2015**
*Washington and its neoconservative monsters have destroyed trust with demonization and blame of Russia for violence in Ukraine for which Washington is responsible.*

*Creeping closer?*
*Washington has forced Europe to impose economic sanctions on Russia that are based entirely on lies and false accusations. The Russians know this. They recognize the blatant hostility, the blatant lies, the never-ending crude propaganda, the hypocritical double-standards, the push toward war.*

*Simultaneously China is experiencing hostile encirclement with Washington's "pivot to Asia."*

*By destroying trust, Washington has resurrected the threat of nuclear armageddon. Washington's destruction of trust between nuclear powers is the crime of the century.*

**U.S. International Aggression – February 26, 2015**
*The neoconservative ideology raises the United States to the unique status of being "the exceptional country," and the American people acquire exalted status as "the indispensable people."*

*If a country is "the exceptional country," it means that all other countries are unexceptional. If a people are "indispensable," it means other peoples are dispensable. We have seen this attitude at work in Washington's 14 years of wars of aggression in the Middle East. These wars have left countries destroyed and millions of people dead, maimed, and displaced. Yet Washington continues to speak of its commitment to protect smaller countries from the aggression of larger countries. The explanation for this hypocrisy is that Washington does not regard Washington's aggression as aggression, but as History's purpose.*

*We have also seen this attitude at work in Washington's disdain for Russia's national interests and in Washington's propagandistic response to Russian diplomacy.*

*The neoconservative ideology requires that Washington maintain its Uni-power status, because this status is necessary for Washington's hegemony and History's purpose.*

**Myth of Economic Recovery – February 23, 2015**
*According to the official economic fairy tale, the US economy has been in recovery since June 2009.*

*This fairy tale supports America's image as the safe haven, an image that keeps the dollar up, the stock market up, and interest rates down. It is an image that causes the massive numbers of unemployed Americans to blame themselves and not the mishandled economy.*

*This fairy tale survives despite the fact that there is no economic information whatsoever that supports it.*

*Real median household income has not grown for years and is below the levels of the early 1970s.*

*There has been no growth in real retail sales for six years.*

*How does an economy dependent on consumer demand grow when real consumer incomes and real retail sales do not grow?*

*Not from business investment. Why invest when there is no sales growth? Industrial production, properly deflated, remains well below the pre-recession level.*

*Not from construction. The real value of total construction put in place declined sharply from 2006 through 2011 and has bounced around the 2011 bottom for the past three years.*

*How does an economy grow when the labor force is shrinking? The labor force participation rate has declined since 2007 as has the civilian employment to population ratio.*

*How can there be a recovery when nothing has recovered?*

**Summary**
So...why is *Peculiar Progressive* quoting from this rebellious Reaganomics renegade? Because on these key issues–endless war, nuclear war, and a dissolving economy–we've written columns through recent years. We've seen these problems in much the same light as Roberts. We've called on readers to get organized (you can't do it alone), get educated, and get active in changing these detriments to you and your children's future. So what do you think? And even more important, will you do anything to create change?

# "Apocalypse: WWI" Will Teach Your Children Well
**Roger Armbrust,** March 17, 2015

*Peculiar Progressive* watched for the first time this weekend "Apocalypse: World War I", a five-part documentary series which will make clear to your children the evolution, horror, and futility of world war — which today's corporate news media avoids and Washington's neocons continue to strive for. It's history which young adults need to see. It will help them learn, and help us all to recall, how corporate greed and military aggression can cause generations globally to suffer.

The 2014 series is an original French production, translated into English for the *National Geographic Channel*, and shown this past weekend on *American Heroes Channel*, an irony since the series emphasizes that war's devastation creates tragedy rather than heroes.

The series' five episodes are bluntly titled "Fury", "Fear", "Hell", "Rage", and "Deliverance".

Fury develops with the assassination of Archduke Ferdinand, heir to the Austrian empire, and his wife by a 19-year-old Serbian nationalist. That basically — to keep it simple — leads to Germany and Austria-Hungary attacking Serbia, leading in turn to Russia, France and England getting into the clash.
Fear reaches a global pitch as German troops near Paris,

and Australia and New Zealand enter the conflict, answering England's call. Hell arrives in the fall of 1915 when millions are shocked by a now industrial and chemical war involving new artillery, chlorine and mustard gas.

Rage rises by 1917 as anti-war revolution threatens governments — including overthrow of the Russian czar — and growing military efforts in different nations. And alleged Deliverance arrives with U.S. war entry, Germany's defeat and 1918's austerity-demanding Treaty of Versailles, which actually set the stage for World War II.

What each episode repeats for emphasis: the war racket begins primarily because military leaders and industrialists — not the people — want it. And that the weapons makers and warmongers financially benefit while average families get separated from loved ones and millions lose lives and homes for the war leaders' benefit.

Too, it seems every documentary we've seen on war — this most recent on WWI, another on WWII, and *CNN*'s vast 24-hour documentary "The Cold War" — that military leaders who are losing always want to fight to the last human. For honor, they say.

They came close in WWI. It resulted in 37 million casualties, including 17 million deaths (10 million military and 7 million civilians) and 20 million wounded. If the documentary numbered the millions of refugees, we missed it. But they may have somewhere in the 5 hours.

Due to today's conflicts, one brief segment in the doc quickly caught our attention: Germany funding Vladimir Lenin's return to Russia to foment revolution, and Lenin's agreement to turn Ukraine over to Germany. That was foiled when Germany lost the war. Research shows that in WWI, 3.5 million Ukrainians fought with the Imperial Russian Army, while 250,000 fought for the Austro-Hungarian Army aligned with Germany. That

Roger Armbrust

Russia-Western Europe split still affects Ukraine today, with the U.S. urging it on.

And today, as we've discussed in earlier columns — "Memorial Day: Recalling and Caring for Our Constant Brave"; "Syria: Symbol of Our Government's Endless-War Addiction"; "American Coup: When U.S. Versus Iran Really Began"; and "Hurtling Toward World War III" — industrialists and warmongers continue to push toward endless war.

# Memorial Day: Reflecting on Our Nation's Father and Ike
**Roger Armbrust,** May 24, 2015

Memorial Day was established to remember those in the U.S. military who died in service to their country. This column reflects on two of our greatest war heroes who went on to serve our country as president – George Washington and Dwight D. Eisenhower — on what they said in their farewell addresses to their fellow countrymen, and in what they might think of America's current policies of foreign relations, endless war, massive weapons sales, and global surveillance of citizens. And if this is what our brave warriors should fight, suffer, and die for.

### George Washington
Washington's farewell letter runs over 1,300 words, the first draft written in 1792 with James Madison's assistance. He was planning to step away from the presidency then, but a bitter feud between Alexander Hamilton, his treasury secretary, and Thomas Jefferson, his Secretary of State, prompted Washington to serve another term, hoping to bring peace to his cabinet and help sustain the government and the nation.

He finally published the letter, revised with help from Hamilton, in 1796. Within the extensive missive covering the nation's welfare from the Constitution to unity to education, he discusses the united idea of foreign relations and free trade. And he makes no doubt where he stands.

Roger Armbrust

**Foreign Relations**

Washington stressed the need to avoid permanent opposition or alliances with foreign nations, often summarized as "foreign entanglements". As our nation's father stated in part:

> ...*nothing is more essential than that permanent, inveterate antipathies against particular nations, and passionate attachments for others, should be excluded; and that, in place of them, just and amicable feelings towards all should be cultivated. The nation which indulges towards another a habitual hatred or a habitual fondness is in some degree a slave. It is a slave to its animosity or to its affection, either of which is sufficient to lead it astray from its duty and its interest. Antipathy in one nation against another disposes each more readily to offer insult and injury, to lay hold of slight causes of umbrage, and to be haughty and intractable, when accidental or trifling occasions of dispute occur. Hence, frequent collisions, obstinate, envenomed, and bloody contests. The nation, prompted by ill-will and resentment, sometimes impels to war the government, contrary to the best calculations of policy. The government sometimes participates in the national propensity, and adopts through passion what reason would reject; at other times it makes the animosity of the nation subservient to projects of hostility instigated by pride, ambition, and other sinister and pernicious motives. The peace often, sometimes perhaps the liberty, of nations, has been the victim.*
>
> *So likewise, a passionate attachment of one nation for another produces a variety of evils...*
>
> *Taking care always to keep ourselves by suitable establishments on a respectable defensive posture, we may safely trust to temporary alliances for extraordinary emergencies.*

One can't help but think – when considering "permanent, inveterate antipathies against particular nations" – of Russia and a bit less so China and Iran, and the Washington establishment's ceaselessly demonizing them, as well as other smaller nations not falling into line with Beltway neocons' worldview.

**World Trade**
Washington made it clear he felt American businesses should be encouraged to continue trading with foreign countries, but should keep commerce separate from politics.

> *The great rule of conduct for us in regard to foreign nations is in extending our commercial relations, to have with them as little political connection as possible. So far as we have already formed engagements, let them be fulfilled with perfect good faith...*
>
> *... Harmony, liberal intercourse with all nations, are recommended by policy, humanity, and interest. But even our commercial policy should hold an equal and impartial hand; neither seeking nor granting exclusive favors or preferences; consulting the natural course of things; diffusing and diversifying by gentle means the streams of commerce, but forcing nothing; establishing (with powers so disposed, in order to give trade a stable course, to define the rights of our merchants, and to enable the government to support them)...*

We think immediately of the White House, Congress, and the hundreds of multinational corporations currently involved in the SECRET negotiations – and efforts to fast-track through Congress – the controversial Trans-Pacific Partnership. A number of opponents complain that the agreement would give corporations power over individual nations and their citizens. How do you think the Father of Our Country would feel about that? Do you believe that's the type of governing the American colonists fought and died for?

Roger Armbrust

**Ike's Grave Warning**

While Eisenhower is famous for helping lead the Allies' troops in defeating Adolph Hitler, he may be even more famous for his wise, grave warning during his 1961 farewell address: beware the growing Military-Industrial Complex:

> *A vital element in keeping the peace is our military establishment. Our arms must be mighty, ready for instant action, so that no potential aggressor may be tempted to risk his own destruction...*
>
> *This conjunction of an immense military establishment and a large arms industry is new in the American experience. The total influence – economic, political, even spiritual – is felt in every city, every statehouse, every office of the federal government. We recognize the imperative need for this development. Yet we must not fail to comprehend its grave implications. Our toil, resources and livelihood are all involved; so is the very structure of our society. In the councils of government,* **we must guard against the acquisition of unwarranted influence, whether sought or unsought, by the military-industrial complex**. *The potential for the disastrous rise of misplaced power exists and will persist.*
>
> *We must never let the weight of this combination endanger our liberties or democratic processes. We should take nothing for granted. Only an alert and knowledgeable citizenry can compel the proper meshing of the huge industrial and military machinery of defense with our peaceful methods and goals so that security and liberty may prosper together.*

In writing about Memorial Day in 2012 ("Memorial Day: Recalling and Caring for Our Constant Brave"), I dealt in depth with our nation's problems, due to the growth of the military-industrial complex and the fact that we're NOT "an alert and knowledgeable citizenry".

Were Washington and Eisenhower with us today, do you think America would be involved in its obsessive endless Middle-East wars leading to the loss of millions of lives (including thousands of American lives and over 750,000 American military suffering from TBI and PTSD), efforts to goad Russia into war, the National Security Agency's global surveillance of citizens, and the secret connivance of trade efforts like the Trans-Pacific Partnership? Oh, and let's also remember the thousands of veterans who are homeless.
Well...what do you think?

I think it's time we become aligned with George Washington's "harmony, [and] liberal intercourse with all nations", and Eisenhower's "an alert and knowledgeable citizenry". It's time we get organized, get educated, and get active, and take our country back, turning it away from oligarchy and return to striving for democracy. After all, that's what our brave military fought and died and still suffer for.

# Global Hot Spots: Both Climate and Military Conflict
**Roger Armbrust,** August 31, 2015

Signs abound this week of potential for future global conflict. Here's a brief look at five: (1) China's propagandized celebration of the 70th anniversary of victory over Japan; (2) An international summit on the Arctic; (3) growing revolution, again, in Ukraine; (4) announcement of a European Union emergency meeting on Middle East war refugees; (5) and agonizing dissolution of the global economy.

**China, Japan, and the U.S.**
In June, *Peculiar Progressive* warned of rising tensions with China in our column "China, the U.S. and Looming War", emphasizing America's saber-rattling over China's growing economic strength, and China's active response to it. We also warily examined recent efforts at nuclear-weapon buildup in the U.S., Russia and China in our column "Nukebuild: This Will Not End Well".

Now China, on Sept. 3 ups the ante on its anti-Japan/U.S. jousting with a major holiday and military parade celebrating its World War II victory over Japan. Chinese media have been stressing the approaching holiday, emphasizing Japan's aggression and war crimes. The U.S. military newspaper *Stars and Stripes* has covered the Chinese effort at increasing public ill-will against Tokyo with the recent article "China's leadership fans smoldering antipathy toward Japan".

## The Vital Realities for 2020 and Beyond

The list of who will attend and avoid China's celebration appears to draw deeper global lines of separation. Russia will be there, further solidifying economic and military ties with China. The U.S. will not be there, nor will leaders of the European Union, two of China's major allies in World War II. Chinese media points out its gratitude to the U.S. military's Flying Tigers, the crack air squadron that fought Japan in the air above China's mainland.

Also today (Monday), news outlets began reporting that Washington is considering sanctions against China over alleged hacking of federal government websites. China has denied responsibility for the hacking and has countered with accusations against the U.S. of hacking Chinese sites.

All this points the way to what could be a stressful face-to-face meeting scheduled between President Barack Obama and China President Xi Jinping in late September.

**Arctic Summit**
On Dec. 25, 2013, Peculiar Progressive published the column "The Coming Conflict over Santa's Home". We discussed what could lead to battling over possession of the North Pole's oil, gas, and fresh-water reserves. The Arctic, which has seen 65% of its ice melted, is deep in natural resources, including oil, gas, and fresh water, along with fish and, in the subarctic, forestlands — all considered economic boons to the major nations. A number of those countries claim property rights to sections of the area. Those sovereignties include Canada, Russia, the United States (Alaska), Denmark(Greenland), Norway, Sweden, Finland, and Iceland.

Both Sunday and Monday (today), the U.S. has brought together the highest-emitting-pollutant countries for a closed-door summit on global warming's effect on the polar region.

Closely following will be the Sept. 28-30 2015 Arctic Energy Summit bringing together "several hundred industry officials, scientists, academics, policy makers, energy professionals and community leaders together to collaborate and share leading approaches on Arctic energy issues", according to the summit's website.

In our 2013 column, we already predicted the possibility of military conflict over the region. Eight nations, including six NATO countries, also suggested that with military exercises in the area this summer.

**Ukraine**
We've been writing about Ukraine since early 2014 when United States officials helped push Ukraine billionaires to foment an angry citizenry into a continuing revolution. That resulted in the overthrow of the democratically elected government and rise to power of billionaire Petro Poroshenko as president.

Now the neo-fascist parties who pushed him into power are rebelling against his government. Their protests in front of parliament in Kiev led to violence, a death, and injuries.

Ukraine is basically a failed state, unable to pay bills, seeing increased hardships on citizens, and growing unrest. The U.S. has used Ukraine as an excuse to challenge Russia through the North Atlantic Treaty Organization and implement sanctions against Moscow. Ukraine recently received a restructuring of credit, but that can only end in the country losing its public assets to private hands like Greece has just suffered.

A reigniting of revolution or conflicts between Kiev and the country's rebel eastern regions could only add to the unstable international situation, including the growing U.S. vs Russia/China shoulder-shoving.

**Europe and Refugees**
The same can be said for the increasing turmoil Europe is facing with the flooding of war refugees from the Middle East — a result of the U.S.-led West's efforts at endless war in Afghanistan, Iraq, Syria, Libya and beyond.

Refugees arriving in Greece by sea.

The European Union on Sunday called an emergency meeting of ministers to try to cope with the mass migration of hundreds of thousands from war-torn areas. The exodus efforts are seeing hundreds die as they try to flee via land and water.

Nationalists in European countries actively oppose the migrations, affecting national policies and surely will affect future elections and unrest within European borders.

**World Debt**
All of these struggles will prove harder to solve, primarily because the world debt continues to expand at an alarming rate, made clear in Jeff Desjardins's August article "$60 Trillion of World Debt in One Visualization."

Washington and American corporate media have recently spotlighted China's shaky stockmarket as the culprit leading to current market trends. But Desjardins's figures say no, showing world debt as the culprit, with the U.S. holding 29 percent of the global debt and Europe 24 percent, while China holds only 6 percent. Some independent investors like Peter Schiff, CEO of Euro Pacific Capital, say China's not the problem, it's the U.S. Federal Reserve. Others like Michael Pento of Pento Portfolio Strategies say it's both the Fed and China.

Both Schiff and Pento foresee a coming economic crisis which investors might beat only by holding precious metals like gold and silver, which both Russia and China have been mining and buying for a while.

# World War III: The Heat Rises
**Roger Armbrust,** December 7, 2015

In June of this year, we wrote a column entitled "NukeBuild: This Will Not End Well". We discussed how, as international tensions grow, the U.S., Russia, and China possess and are increasing nuclear arms. Today, we see rising conflict and antagonism moving us – not farther away — but closer to confrontation of these major powers into what is becoming World War III.

We base our assessment on these chief factors:

**A Dissolving Global Economy**
We've pointed out in other columns how history shows that, when a nation's economy is deeply struggling, the federal government will often look for an enemy both within and outside its borders, then propagandize those "enemies" to instill fear and promote nationalism – in effect taking the citizenry's minds off the reality of their own struggles, and the government and business community's responsibility for those struggles.

In the United States, the government is controlled by Wall Street's banks and the military industrial complex. This has led the U.S. to expand its endless-war tactics (a) primarily in the Middle East with military invasions, as well as (2) against Russia and Iran through economic sanctions, and (3) China with U.S. saber-rattling primarily regarding America's "exceptionalism" and right to control the world economy and specifically the South China Sea area.

This American view and resulting actions to promote "exceptionalism" have frayed U.S. international relations. We're mired in a Middle East quagmire promoted by Washington's neocons in Congress and the White House who are about to get what they've wanted: a head-to-head confrontation with a nuclear-armed Russia.

This, as you should know if you're paying attention, is taking place primarily in Syria. The U.S. has led an effort to remove the government of Syria President Bashar al-Assad, an ally of both Russia and Iran. America has led a coalition which has invaded Syria's sovereign borders to promote civil war there while arguing it is also fighting the terrorist group The Islamic State of Iraq and Syria (ISIS). This Syrian invasion has included over a year of aerial bombings by American military, and now the mission creep of boots on the ground starting – as Vietnam's invasion began — with only a handful of special forces.

**U.S.-Russian Confrontation**
Washington and Moscow began seriously jousting politically in 2014, when the U.S. backed the overthrow of Ukraine's corrupt, but democratically elected pro-Russian government. Following the right-wing-led revolution, an election saw the pro-European Union oligarch Petro Poroshenko installed as president. Immediately, Ukraine's pro-Russian eastern region of Crimea broke away from Ukraine and was annexed by Russia.

This set Ukraine and the U.S., as well as the European Union due to U.S. pressure, to oppose Russia, with both the U.S. and EU imposing economic sanctions. It also allowed the U.S. to fulfill its effort to find a reason for resurging the North Atlantic Treaty Organization (NATO), formed originally after World War II to oppose then-Soviet Union aggression. With the recent Ukraine government change, the U.S. began moving NATO forces closer to Russia's borders.

Vladimir Putin, Russia's president, has seen his popularity in

Russia grow with the U.S. and EU's economic punishment of his country. He also saw a move to Russia's advantage when Syria's Assad requested Russian military air support for his army in fighting ISIS within Syria's borders.

Putin began coordinating Russian aerial bombings with Syria's army, particularly striking ISIS petroleum convoys close to Turkey's border. Putin also offered to coordinate Russia's efforts with the U.S. coalition as a united fight against ISIS, but Washington refused.

**Turkey Provokes Russia**
The Russia-Syria versus U.S. coalition political fracas escalated into a direct military confrontation in late November, when a Turkish fighter jet shot down a Russian bomber for allegedly violating Turkey air space. The incident also prompted NATO to say it will send military aircraft to support Turkey, which is a NATO member.

The incident gave Putin just what he needed to muster national support for his presidency and efforts at defending Syria from foreign aggression. He has publicly condemned Turkey's actions, and accused Turkey President Recep Tayyip Erdogan of collaborating with ISIS in receiving oil from the terrorist group. Ergodan has denied it.

But Putin has also upped Russia's military involvement in Syria, vowing to protect Russia's naval base on the Syrian coast, and threatening to confront any foreign military aircraft violating Syrian air space.

Syria appears to have seconded Russia's challenge. In a Dec. 7 *Eurasia Review* op-ed, "Syria Tells NATO: Keep Jets Out or Get Shot Down", columnist Finian Cunningham writes:

> *Syria is ready to deploy the fearsome S-300 air-defence system supplied by its Russian ally. The anti-aircraft surface-to-air missiles will give Syria control over its*

> territory and the capability to shoot down any intrusive warplane or missile. NATO warplanes beware!...
>
> ...Translated from Arabic language Alrai Media (thanks to the reliable Fort Russ Russian news site), the senior Syrian officer at the operations room is quoted as saying: 'Soon Syria will announce that any country using the airspace without coordinating with Damascus will be viewed as hostile and [we] will shoot the jet down without warning. Those willing to fight terrorism and coordinate with the military leadership will be granted safe corridors.'

This will prove to become even more of a military mess because, following last month's Paris terrorist attacks, France began bombing in Syria. And last week, Great Britain's Parliament followed Prime Minister David Cameron's recommendation and voted to also bomb, British war planes immediately went to work.

**Russia-China Alliance**
The U.S., seeing itself as the major global military and economic force for decades, has looked for ways to control Eurasia and its energy supplies. It also has sought to stall China's growth to become now the world's Number 2 economic power. China, on the other hand, has consistently accused America of hegemony. And while the U.S. has concentrated on military actions to support its economic leadership, China has been following a policy of non-interference in other nations' internal affairs, choosing instead to cooperate economically, working out trade and infrastructure agreements with countries on every continent.

This has led the U.S. to oppose China in several ways, including keeping it out of the Trans-Pacific Partnership, fighting Beijing's forming the Asian International Infrastructure Bank, and pushing against China-led BRICS's effort to move currencies away from the U.S. dollar.

Roger Armbrust

China and Russia began developing positive relations through BRICS, the organization consisting of Brazil, Russia, India, China, and South Africa. But Beijing and Moscow deeply solidified themselves as allies through two major energy trade agreements over the last couple of years, with Russia beginning to send major supplies of oil and natural gas to China.
This alliance led China to announce support for Russia when the U.S. and EU implemented Russian sanctions last year. And both China and Russia since 2013 have warned against foreign invasions of Syria.

Meanwhile, with the U.S. saber-rattling at the Chinese this year over the South China Sea, for the first time China has released a detailed military policy statement outlining how it plans to increase its military, including nuclear weapons to both defend its own territory and its overseas investments.
If the Syrian conflict continues to escalate, it may take China to offer and lead negotiations in a political settlement and truce. Or it could mean Beijing, if provoked, might decide to join the conflict.

What kind of future do you think that will offer you and your children?

# Will U.S.-Russia Syria Pact Avoid World War?
**Roger Armbrust,** February 22, 2016

The question isn't whether the U.S.-Russia-brokered ceasefire in Syria, announced Monday, will succeed. Considering the quagmire of combatants involved, it probably won't.

The question is whether the U.S. and Russia now appearing to cooperate might stave off an acceleration toward world war. It might, if it further leads to quelling U.S. aggression in the Middle East, and NATO and Washington's neoconservative hawks stopping further actions to incite Russia. Also, problems have developed in Asia, with the U.S. wanting to implement a missile defense for South Korea, bringing warnings from both China and Russia.

Then there's a major problem: dissolution of the global economy. In a world civilization where politicians respond to their failed national economies by creating an enemy and going to war, the time is ripe for World War III.

**First Immediate Problem: Syria**
The U.S. may have a chance to save face in Syria, despite itself. The U.S.-led coalition, bombing the Islamic State of Iraq and Syria (ISIS) and seeking the overthrow of Syrian President Bashar al-Assad, had seen its year-and-a-half invasion of Syria failing. What seems to have turned around the battle against

ISIS has been Russia's entrance in September, at the invitation of Assad.

Putin (r) greets Assad.

By that time, Russia had been fuming from the U.S.-backed overthrow of the Russian-supported, democratically elected corrupt Ukraine government; the incursions of the North Atlantic Treaty Organization toward Russian borders; U.S-European Union economic sanctions on Russia, and Saudi Arabia's forcing lower and lower oil prices – all threats to Russia's security and economy. And in September, Russian President Vladimir Putin seems to have had enough.

As Moscow continued to see ISIS's threat growing on the Syrian regime, Putin decided to take action, and began bombing rebels on Syria's behalf. At the same time, he called on the U.S. and its coalition to join Russia, and coordinate efforts at bombing ISIS. Washington refused, criticizing Moscow's entering the conflict on behalf of Syria's sitting government, which the U.S. wants to replace.

By February, the U.S. could see the war turning in Assad's favor, and has been quietly negotiating with Russia on a ceasefire plan. By today, the two major countries had at least succeeded in agreeing. Assad also had reluctantly agreed, saying he felt rebel groups would use the ceasefire to repossess land areas they had lost due to Russian bombing.

**Second Immediate Problem: Turkey and Saudi Arabia**
Gregory R. Copley, editor in chief of the Defense and Foreign Affairs publications group, said in a TV interview today that Turkey had instigated the Syrian civil war through its support of rebel groups. He predicted that the ceasefire would lead Turkey to further prepare for a ground invasion of Syria.

Turkey, a part of the U.S.-led coalition and a NATO member, has been greatly complicating the Syrian conflict. It has bombed

## The Vital Realities for 2020 and Beyond

Kurdish rebels — who are fighting ISIS — in Iraq and Syria, considering the Kurds a major threat to the Turkish government.

The Turks also shot down a Russian bomber, apparently over Syria though arguing it invaded Turkey's borders. This led to Putin placing economic sanctions on Turkey, and a continuing of ill-will between the two countries. Turkey, meanwhile, has criticized the U.S. for not leading a ground invasion of Syria. Russia has countered that a ground invasion by foreign troops would lead to world war.

Saudi Arabia has also announced intentions to both bomb and ground invade Syria, adding to Riyadh's waging of violent and economic global wars.

Perhaps Russia and the U.S. together will be able to hold both Ankara and Riyadh in check. Or maybe China will have to quietly enter and negotiate with all of them. President Xi Jinping has led China on a foreign policy of noninterference in other countries' internal affairs, preferring to negotiate trade and security pacts on every continent. He recently visited Saudi Arabia, forming trade agreements. Russia, too, recently met with the Saudis, agreeing to try and limit oil production and raise prices.

But the maverick Turkey may be a problem even with Russia, the U.S. and China cooperating. Its volatile, dictatorial president Recep Tayyip Erdogan of late has been angry at both the U.S. and Russia, has threatened to continue attacking the Kurds, and has been pounding a tight fist at home, quelling the press.

Too, getting the Big Three to cooperate on easing the dangerous Middle East situation itself could be volatile. Both Russia and China have been publicly critical of U.S. hegemony. And Beijing and Washington have been quarreling over U.S. interference in the South China Sea.

All these tensions can't help but lead to concern over the

Roger Armbrust

world's major, major problem: the threat of nuclear war, which we've discussed in columns "World War III: The Heat Rises" and "Nukebuild: This Will Not End Well". As gamblers say, "Read 'em and weep."

# A War Criminal Slow Jams the "News"
**Roger Armbrust,** June 13, 2016

Have you noticed how corporate media works to entertain and indoctrinate you with the government's rendition of news rather than the real news? And how they include entertainment talk shows to pad the process?

President Obama "slow jammed the news" on NBC's "The Tonight Show Starring Jimmy Fallon" last week, gab-crooning how he had made the nation better with his administration's Iran nuclear deal, renewed diplomatic ties with Cuba, gave us affordable health care and is supporting the highly criticized Trans-Pacific Partnership (TPP).

Fallon's rap huskily sweet-talked how: "President Obama stimulated long-term growth. In 2008, the country wasn't feeling in the mood. It was too tired, stressed — said it had a headache. Barack lit some candles and got some silky satin sheets. Told the American people, 'Yes, we can.'" Their smooth propaganda bit has received nearly 35 million views online.

*the jive propaganda missed major infractions*

But we don't elect a president to jive propaganda. We elect a president to follow the law and execute his office to help the nation and the world, and not to go against the U.S. Constitution and international law, nor endanger civilization. The dystopian duo's slow jam, however, missed several major infractions during Obama's reign. And they cannot, and should not, be forgotten or overlooked:

1. War crimes for overseeing the droning deaths and wounding of thousands of civilians, including women and children.
2. His waging a battle to punish whistleblowers who reported *illegal* government activity.
3. His Justice Department spied on the press and also intimidated journalists with threats of imprisonment.
4. His NSA spies on everybody.
5. He's continuing the neo-con endless, aggressive wars, causing chaos in the Middle East and leading us closer to major wars with Russia and China.
6. He's supplying weapons to other countries like Saudi Arabia that are murdering civilians.
7. He's leading a historic rebuilding of nuclear weapons.

No doubt presidents like George W. Bush (See our column "A Bush Insider Cites War Crimes Against his President, VP") and Obama would be tried before the International Criminal Court for war crimes, but there's one minor problem: the United States isn't a signatory to the ICC. So the court tries only small-country dictators. How safe and secure that is for the power wielders in the Oval Office and the Millionaire Congress. How unsafe and insecure they've made it for citizens worldwide.

But wasn't the Prez cute standing there with Fallon doing standup on corporate media? And wasn't the audience of cowed faithful — addicted to entertainment and uncaring about the real world — inspiring with its standing ovation?

Perhaps you should consider — when casting ballots for president, vice president and Congress — whether you want connivers who will continue the destructive path of aggressive war and surveillance — or public servants who will take care of our people and our planet.

# After Chilcot Report: Will ICC Try Blair, Bush?

**Roger Armbrust,** July 11, 2016

Will the recent release of the British government's highly incriminating Iraq Inquiry, commonly called the Chilcot Report, create the final shove to force the International Criminal Court (ICC) to try Tony Blair and George W. Bush for war crimes?

### The Report

Sir John Chilcot, a retired British civil servant, chaired a committee of five who, for seven years, reviewed reams of data regarding Britain and Prime Minister Tony Blair's roles in the U.S.-led Iraqi invasion beginning in 2003. Chilcot publicly presented the report which was published July 6.

The panel was damning of Blair's actions on several points regarding the war. Those points included:

- The UK joined the invasion before peaceful options were exhausted.
- Blair deliberately exaggerated Saddam Hussein's threat to the U.S. and UK.
- Blair promised Bush in writing: "I will be with you, whatever."
- The UK military was ill-equipped to invade Iraq.
- Blair ignored warnings of the invasion's aftermath.
- The UK had no post-invasion strategy.

Roger Armbrust

- The UK was lax in tallying Iraqi civilian casualties, wanting instead to "rebut accusations that coalition forces were responsible for the deaths of large numbers" of Iraqis.

You can search the entire Iraq Inquiry here, including Chilcot's statement.

*Will Chilcot Report join ICC's other damning evidence?*

Chilcot's panel made no determination, in fact may have been forbidden to, regarding the legality of the UK's Iraq invasion. But the report is being presented to the International Criminal Court, who will review it.

The question is whether the 2.6 million-word report will join other evidence before the ICC which might lead to trials for Blair and even Bush. That other data is also damning, particularly for Bush.

**The ICC**
The International Criminal Court is a relatively new body, founded in 2002, created by the Rome Statute, a treaty adopted in 1998 which established four core international crimes: genocide, crimes against humanity, war crimes and the crime of aggression.

Authorities this past week have argued that "crime of aggression" prosecution is not available to the ICC, although that's not clear why. They speak vaguely, as in this July 7 report from *The Washington Post*:

> *In theory, one place where world leaders — both current and former — who have committed war crimes could face trial would be the International Criminal Court, established by the Rome Statute in 2002 to investigate and prosecute when states are "unable" or "unwilling" to do so themselves. Unfortunately, the ICC*

> has a mixed record of going after heads of state. It has tended to pursue only African leaders (in part because of independent war-crimes tribunals in other conflict zones) and struggled to get convictions.

> Mark Kersten, a researcher at the Munk School of Global Affairs at the University of Toronto who runs the Justice in Conflict blog, said it is 'very unlikely' that Blair will face charges. 'The ICC cannot investigate or prosecute the crime of aggression, so the invasion of Iraq is out of its remit,' Kersten said. Thus, one of the most popular complaints about Blair's decision to go to war in 2003 — that the war was an 'illegal' act of military aggression — cannot be judged at the ICC. As things stand now, that act can really be sanctioned only by the United Nations Security Council, of which both Britain and the United States are permanent members.

But if the ICC can't prosecute the crime of aggression, deemed the chief crime by the Nazis in World War II, the court can look for the other three areas: genocide, crimes against humanity, and war crimes.

The British law firm Public Interest Lawyers (PIL) went after Blair in 2014, filing a complaint with the ICC. As PIL principal Phil Shiner explained in a Feb. 27, 2014 statement in *The Guardian*:

> ...on 10 January 2014 my firm and the European Centre for Constitutional and Human Rights lodged a formal complaint to the ICC about the systemic abuse of hundreds of Iraqis in the period 2003 to 2008 while being interrogated by UK interrogators. The defence secretaries at the material time knew (or ought to have known) that interrogators were being trained to use, and were using, coercive interrogation techniques that were in flagrant breach of international legal standards. But who insisted the UK had an interrogation capability in Iraq

> that allowed us to punch our weight with our co-illegal aggressors, the US, knowing that a lawful approach to interrogation did not permit the use of such techniques? The complaint to the ICC has been made to explore the potential of criminal accountability for such systemic issues at the very top of the military, civil service and potential chain of command.

**Forceful Continuum**
The PIL's 2014 effort is only a part of the forceful continuum of accusations which should eventually lead to Blair's, and particularly Bush's, prosecutions for Iraqi war crimes. We reported in detail in 2014 of condemnations of Bush in our CFR column "A Bush Insider Cites War Crimes Against His President, VP".

The CFR column included an accusatory statement from Richard Clarke–who served a brief stint as Bush's national coordinator for security and counterterrorism; discussion of former U.S. Congressman Dennis Kucinich's legislation to impeach Bush in 2008, and the results of a 2012 Malaysian trial which convicted Bush, Dick Cheney, and others in the administration of Iraqi war crimes.

Clarke, in an interview on the TV news program "Democracy Now", stated:

> I think things that they authorized probably fall within the area of war crimes. Whether that would be productive or not, I think, is a discussion we could all have. But we have established procedures now with the International Criminal Court in The Hague, where people who take actions as serving presidents or prime ministers of countries have been indicted and have been tried. So the precedent is there to do that sort of thing. And I think we need to ask ourselves whether or not it would be useful to do that in the case of members of the Bush administration. It's clear that things that the Bush

*administration did — in my mind, at least, it's clear that some of the things they did were war crimes.*

We also pointed out in that column that 122 states are parties to the ICC, but the United States and Israel have refused to ratify, recognize or adhere to statutes of the court. Because the U.S. is not a state party to the court, no U.S. official can be tried, unless the alleged crime(s) took place in the territory of a state that has accepted the court's jurisdiction. Iraq is not a state member.

However, in 2006, the ICC's prosecutor reported that he had received 240 communications alleging various war crimes in connection with the invasion of Iraq. Some of those appear to involve the UK, a state party to the ICC, and the country that worked most closely with the U.S. in Iraq. It's possible the prosecutor may find the U.S. complicit in UK alleged war crimes, which would be considered a war crime in itself.

All the added data, including the PIL's complaint, Clarke's accusation, the Malaysia war-crimes trial convictions, and now the UK's Iraq Inquiry are evidence which just might push the ICC to prosecute Blair and Bush. But you can bet it will be a courageous move that will counter great political pressure.

If the ICC does rebuff that pressure and go after Blair and Bush, then we might see that courage even move to try President Barack Obama, who has expanded Bush's efforts, as we described in our column for reality: a world of views: "Obama Widens Carter's, Bush's Global-Rule Policies".

# Obama Widens Carter's, Bush's Global-Rule Policies
**Roger Armbrust,** Thursday, November 17, 2016

To understand President Barack Obama's determination at using military force to assure chaos in the Middle East and to challenge China and Russia – furthering the threat of world war – we need to look back to the Brzezinski Plan under President Carter and the Wolfowitz Doctrine under George W. Bush.

The effort of the exceptionalist neoconservatives within Obama's administration to advance endless war, to economically feed the military-industrial complex, and continue a military reason for NATO's existence are all based on both the Brzezinski and Wolfowitz design to make and maintain the United States as the world's lone superpower.

Zbigniew Brzenzinski, Jimmy Carter's national security advisor from 1977-81, believed that causing the decline of the Soviet Union would assure American global supremacy. Paul Wolfowitz, serving under both Bush administrations, posed a policy that pre-emptive military action would keep at bay any potential foe to American world power.

**Brzenzinski's Design**
We pointed out in a 2012 column for *The Clyde Fitch Report* that Brzenzinski has for decades espoused the need for America to control Eurasia: i.e. the uninterrupted landmass of Europe and Asia. To have this occur, he knew in the late '70s the Soviets

needed to be weakened. He encouraged and got Carter to sign a directive to provide secret support to opponents of Afghanistan's Soviet-supported regime, leading America's chief foe to intervene in Afghanistan in 1979. Brzezinski has called that the "Soviet Union's Vietnam," meaning the aid to the Soviets decline through a military quagmire.

Brzenzinski also has recognized the importance of controlling the flow of energy as the key to power in Eurasia. He reviews this within three paragraphs of his 1998 book *The Grand Chessboard: American Primacy and Its Geostrategic Imperatives*:

*About 75 per cent of the world's people live in Eurasia, and most of the world's physical wealth is there as well, both in its enterprises and underneath its soil. Eurasia accounts for about three-fourths of the world's known energy resources. (p. 31)*
*The world's energy consumption is bound to vastly increase over the next two or three decades. Estimates by the U.S. Department of Energy anticipate that world demand will rise by more than 50 percent between 1993 and 2015, with the most significant increase in consumption occurring in the Far East. The momentum of Asia's economic development is already generating massive pressures for the exploration and exploitation of new sources of energy and the Central Asian region and the Caspian Sea basin are known to contain reserves of natural gas and oil that dwarf those of Kuwait, the Gulf of Mexico, or the North Sea. (p. 125)*

*America is now the only global superpower, and Eurasia is the globe's central arena. Hence, what happens to the distribution of power on the Eurasian continent will be of decisive importance to America's global primacy and to America's historical legacy. (p. 194)*

**Wolfowitz Doctrine**
Wolfowitz was working as an undersecretary of defense for policy in the George H.W. Bush administration, and under Defense Secretary Dick Cheney. By February 1992 Wolfowitz

had initiated, and his deputy Scooter Libby had overseen, preparation of the Defense Planning Guidance for the 1994–99 fiscal years. Less than a month later, it was leaked to *The New York Times*, leading to widespread criticism of U.S. efforts at imperialism.

Here are four of the 46-page document's most inflammatory paragraphs that aroused opposition:

To keep the U.S. as the world's lone superpower:

*Our first objective is to prevent the re-emergence of a new rival, either on the territory of the former Soviet Union or elsewhere, that poses a threat on the order of that posed formerly by the Soviet Union. This is a dominant consideration underlying the new regional defense strategy and requires that we endeavor to prevent any hostile power from dominating a region whose resources would, under consolidated control, be sufficient to generate global power.*

U.S. leadership in a new world order:

*The U.S. must show the leadership necessary to establish and protect a new order that holds the promise of convincing potential competitors that they need not aspire to a greater role or pursue a more aggressive posture to protect their legitimate interests. In non-defense areas, we must account sufficiently for the interests of the advanced industrial nations to discourage them from challenging our leadership or seeking to overturn the established political and economic order. We must maintain the mechanism for deterring potential competitors from even aspiring to a larger regional or global role.*

The U.S. should strive for unilateralism:

*Like the coalition that opposed Iraqi aggression, we should expect future coalitions to be ad hoc assemblies, often not lasting beyond the crisis being confronted, and in many cases carrying only general agreement over the objectives to be accomplished. Nevertheless, the sense that the world order is ultimately backed by the U.S. will be an important stabilizing factor.*

Pre-emptive intervention, i.e. aggressive war:

*While the U.S. cannot become the world's policeman, by assuming responsibility for righting every wrong, we will retain the preeminent responsibility for addressing selectively those wrongs which threaten not only our interests, but those of our allies or friends, or which could seriously unsettle international relations.*

Following the heavy negative reaction to the article, Cheney oversaw the rewriting of the document, watering down the highly aggressive language Wolfowitz and Libby had developed, making the U.S. seem more friendly toward other nations.

After George W. Bush took office in January 2001, the original Wolfowitz plan appears to have been resurrected as the basis of the Bush Doctrine. As you can see from U.S. military actions under Bush and then Obama, recorded on *Wikipedia*, the Wolfowitz neocon attitude and aggressive foreign invasions have been implemented, including:

**War in Afghanistan**
(2001–2014)
*Part of the War on Terror*

**Iraq War**
(2003–2011)
*Part of the Iraqi Insurgency* and *War on Terror*

**War in North-West Pakistan**
(2004–present)
*Part of the War on Terror*

Roger Armbrust

**2011 military intervention in Libya**
(2011, renewed U.S. involvement 2015)
*Part of the Libyan Crisis*

**War on ISIL (Operation Inherent Resolve)**
(2014–present)
*Part of the Iraqi Civil War, Syrian Civil War, Second Libyan Civil War, Boko Haram insurgency, and the War on Terror*
**Location**: **Iraq**, **Syria**, **Libya** and **Nigeria**

**War in Afghanistan**
(2015–present)

**Yemeni Crisis**
**Yemeni Civil War (2015–present)**
(***This column originally ran*** in reality: a world of views)

# Saudis Wage Violent/Economic Global Wars
**Roger Armbrust,** February 18, 2016

We've written often of our frustration with the United States pursuing endless war and creating chaos in the Middle East. Meanwhile, recent years have shown Saudi Arabia's kingdom advancing with global aggressive war — either violent or economic — detrimentally affecting every continent. Its vicious effort has even led now to negatively harm the kingdom's economy, leading to efforts at austerity. To deflect Saudis' attention from their internal problems, King Salman bin Abdulaziz Al Saud ramped up the war effort this week, threatening to send U.S.-supplied air power and troops into Syria, further complicating the complex, globally dangerous conflict there.

The Saudis' violent aggression has occurred on three main fronts: (1) the inhumane, bloody assault on Yemen; (2) both funding and fighting the murderous Islamic State of Iraq and Syria (ISIS), and (3) the Sunni-led government's beheading of a popular Shia cleric, inciting volatile response in the Middle East and raising international alarm.

Meanwhile, the Saud royalty has created a global economic malaise by manipulating the price of oil, forcing it lower and lower through glutting the market with continued high production to protect market share. This has caused fiscal woes worldwide, especially among nations monetarily dependent on selling oil, ranging from the United States and Canada to Russia and Venezuela.

The Saudis' effort, actually with schizoid cooperation from Washington, can only catapult the growing trudge toward world war.

**Violent Aggression in Yemen**
Yemen, a poor Middle East country (income per capital of $2,500) and a Saudi neighbor, has been caught up in a war between the government and rebel Houthis for over a year. In March 2015, a Saudi-led coalition – with arms, planes and logistic support supplied by Washington – have conducted airstrikes, allegedly on Houthi positions, but also killing civilians, and destroying infrastructure including water supplies and ports. Riyadh believes the Houthis are backed by Iran, and considers Iran an enemy.

A month after the bombing began, the United Nationscondemned the attacks and requested they cease so the UN could send aid and humanitarian personnel. Last month, UN Secretary-General Ban Ki-moon publicly chastised the Saudis for bombing a Yemeni hospital operated by Medecins Sans Frontieres (Doctors Without Borders, or MSF).

On Sunday *The New York Times* reported Human Rights Watch was accusing the Saudis of firing "American-made cluster munitions, banned by international treaty, in civilian areas of Yemen, and said their use may also violate United States law."

An *Associated Press* report Tuesday night revealed:

*The U.N. humanitarian chief warned Tuesday that a 'humanitarian catastrophe' is unfolding in Yemen, exacerbated by increasing restrictions on efforts to respond to the staggering needs of millions of people including the diversion of a U.N. aid ship by Saudi-led coalition forces.*

*Stephen O'Brien painted a grim picture of the war-ravaged*

*country: more than 35,000 casualties since March 2015 including over 6,000 deaths; at least 7.6 million people 'severely food insecure;' more than 3.4 million children now out of school; and nearly 600 health facilities and over 1,170 schools unfit for use because of the conflict.*

*O'Brien's briefing to the U.N. Security Council, requested by Russia, was the first focusing on the humanitarian crisis sparked by the country's civil war.*

## Funding and Fighting ISIS

Like Riyadh and Washington's schizoid relationship with the murderous assault on Yemen, Saudi Arabia appears to have its own internal violent contradictions regarding ISIS. On the one hand, the Riyadh government has joined with the U.S. since September 2014 in fighting ISIS. On the other hand, Riyadh has publicly discouraged but allowed Saudis to privately funnel support to the radical Muslims who, like the Saud family, are Wahabbis, i.e. ultra-conservative followers of Sunni Islam. Sunni Islam is the world's largest religious faith. Wahabbism denounces the Shia faith, the second largest sect of Islam.

The Saudis are foes of Shia governments in Iran, Iraq, and Syria. Iran and Iraq are members with Riyadh in the Organization of PetroleumExporting Countries (OPEC) and three of the world's top 10 oil producers. While OPEC members, they also compete for global market share, thus placing them at both religious and economic odds.

Washington, more in love with Arabian oil and weapons sales than logical foreign policy, has looked away from Riyadh's bloody contradiction, allowing it to help continue Middle East chaos. Besides, it allows the Saudis to be U.S. allies in opposing Syria's Shia-led government ofBashar al-Assad. But it also led Washington to basically ignore Riyadh's helping ISIS in Iraq.

## A Religious/Political Beheading

On January 1, Riyadh greatly upped the ante in the Wahabbi

vs Shia confrontation by beheading — along with 46 others — Sheikh Nimr al-Nimr for "terrorism". Riyadh obviously considered him an enemy of the state. But his death set off a regional firestorm. As UK's *The Guardian* reported:

*The Iranian government and religious leaders across the Middle East have condemned Saudi Arabia's execution of a prominent Shia cleric and warned of repercussions that could bring down the country's royal family.*

*In a serious escalation of religious and diplomatic tensions in the region, councils and clerics in Iran, Yemen and Lebanon said the killing of Sheikh Nimr al-Nimr would prompt widespread anger.*

**Oil and Global Economic War**
Riyadh's refusal to curb oil production, at first, was largely seen as an effort to destroy the oil-fracking industry in the United-States, and Washington has appeared limp in opposing that. The American fracking industry took on deep debt, and has needed oil prices to maintain at $50-$60 a barrel to survive. But, with the Sauds glutting the market, prices have fallen to currently $20-$30, threatening the shale industry in the U.S.

But the Saudi effort has also greatly harmed major oil producers like Russia, Venezuela, Nigeria and Mexico, along with others. Indeed, the world's economy has now been gouged.

This week, in a public relations ploy at seeking a solution, Russia and Saudi Arabia met in Qatar along with Venezuela. They agreed to freeze production at January levels if other oil producers would agree. They may not.

That goes particularly for Iran, who has just seen decades of sanctions lifting, allowing it again to sell oil worldwide, threatening Riyadh's and others' share of the take. It also means, while oil prices are killer low for everyone else, Iran can now make money on oil at quantities it couldn't produce and sell for years, meaning an extra 500,000 barrels added to its 2.9 million barrels a day.

Will this end with Riyadh getting serious about curbing production and raising prices, easing others' plight? Or will it mean the king getting serious about invading Syria, bringing that regional conflict, already resembling 1914, even closer to world war? While Russia and the U.S. actually seem to be seeking a stalemate in Syria...for the moment, at least...Riyadh and Turkey appear intent on confusing the issue and increasing the bloodshed. And Russia's prime minister has warned of world war should foreign ground troops invade Syria.

Is there a solution? Perhaps China, who wants to peacefully trade with everybody, is powerful enough to step in and bring reason. It seems to have been trying. Chinese President Xi Jinping visited Saudi Arabia and Iran, as well as a trip to Egypt, in late January in efforts at good will and trade.

But, for now, the whole sad Middle East affair looks bleak indeed, and leads us to quote the words of the late John Lennon:

*Nobody told me there'd be days like these...Strange days indeed...*

*(Originally published in reality: a world of views)*

# In Vietnam and U.S., Millions Still Affected by Agent Orange

**Roger Armbrust,** Friday, November 18, 2016

April 30, 2015 marked the 40-year anniversary of the fall of Saigon, bringing an end to the Vietnam War. Four decades later, the U.S. spraying of Agent Orange for 10 years there, still affects the health of as many as 3 million Vietnamese. Health problems range from cancer to birth defects.

U.S. military veterans and their offspring also remain affected, with the federal Department of Veterans Affairs, as recently as March 10, 2015, placing on its website an article headlined "10 Things Every Veteran Should Know About Agent Orange".

**Background**

Agent Orange, also called Herbicide Orange (HO), is produced by mixing two herbicides: 2,4,5-T and 2,4-D. Manufactured for the U.S. Defense Department primarily by Monsanto Corporation and Dow Chemical, Agent Orange's 2,4,5-T reportedly "was contaminated with 2,3,7,8-Tetrachlorodibenzodioxin (TCDD), an extremely toxic dioxin compound. In some areas, TCDD concentrations in soil and water were hundreds of times greater than the levels considered safe by the U.S. Environmental Protection Agency.[5][6]"

The U.S. military used Agent Orange for a major defoliation program (Operation Ranch Hand) in Vietnam from 1961-1972.

# The Vital Realities for 2020 and Beyond

According to history.com:

*U.S. aircraft were deployed to spray powerful mixtures of herbicides around roads, rivers, canals and military bases, as well as on crops that might be used to supply enemy troops. During this process, crops and water sources used by the non-combatant peasant population of South Vietnam could also be hit. In all, Operation Ranch Hand deployed more than 19 million gallons of herbicides over 4.5 million acres of land.*

By 1979, four years after Saigon's fall and the war's close, a class-action lawsuit was filed on behalf of U.S. veterans who served in Vietnam for health issues resulting from Agent Orange. By 1984, seven major chemical companies reached an out-of-court settlement in the suit, agreeing to pay $180 million to veterans or their next of kin. That amount was raised later to $240 million including interest.

A group of Vietnamese citizens filed a class-action lawsuit against more than 30 chemical companies in 2004, but it was thrown out of two courts.

**Current Results**
As far as detrimental effects on the Vietnamese, history.com notes:

*In addition to the massive environmental impact of the U.S. defoliation program in Vietnam, that nation has reported that some 400,000 people were killed or maimed as a result of exposure to herbicides like Agent Orange. In addition, Vietnam claims half a million children have been born with serious birth defects, while as many 2 million people are suffering from cancer or other illness caused by Agent Orange.*

A report on Germany's Deutsche Weille Television stated that as many as 3 million Vietnamese are still suffering from results of Agent Orange. The report specifically showed a couple with two children suffering from birth defects. The father had been exposed to Agent Orange as a boy.

Also today, in an interview on Chinese America TV (CCTV), New York University professor Marilyn B. Young, author of The Vietnam Wars, 1945-1990, said that Agent Orange is the major problem Vietnam still faces from America's presence there.

The news reports noted that in 2012, the U.S. and Vietnam began a toxic cleanup effort to reduce soil contamination levels.

In its March 2015 article, the VA cites the following 10 points veterans should be aware of regarding Agent Orange, following each point with paragraphs of more specific information:

1. **Agent Orange was a herbicide and defoliant used in Vietnam.**
2. **Any Veteran who served anywhere in Vietnam during the war is presumed to have been exposed to Agent Orange.**
3. **VA has linked several diseases and health conditions to Agent Orange exposure.**
4. **Veterans who want to be considered for disability compensation must file a claim.**
5. **VA offers health care benefits for Veterans who may have been exposed to Agent Orange and other herbicides during military service.**
6. **Participating in an Agent Orange Registry health exam helps you, other Veterans and VA.**
7. **VA recognizes and offers support for the children of Veterans affected by Agent Orange who have birth defects.**
8. **Vietnam Veterans are not the only Veterans who may have been exposed to Agent Orange.**
9. **VA continues to conduct research on the long-term health effects of Agent Orange in order to better care for all Veterans.**

10. **VA contracts with an independent, non-governmental organization to review the scientific and medical information on the health effects of Agent Orange.**

(*This column originally ran on* reality: a world of views.)

# Vet Colonel Scathes Gulf Military Policy, Prez Hopefuls
**Roger Armbrust,** April 9, 2016

A retired Army colonel – who is also a Vietnam veteran, military historian and best-selling author — has issued a clear, concise condemnation of America's four-decade foreign policy in the Middle East, as well as ominous criticism of presidential candidates Donald Trump, Hillary Clinton and Ted Cruz.

Andrew J. Bacevich, a 20-year Army veteran and now a professor emeritus of international relations and history at Boston University, is author of the new book *America'sWar for the Greater Middle East: A Military History*. He was interviewed Friday, April 8, on the TV program "Democracy Now" about the premise of his book, and also his view of the current presidential hopefuls.

**Endless Gulf Wars**
Concerning Middle East involvement, Bacevich said the U.S. has a "failed" policy which has "abused" the American military. In his book, he observes:

*From the end of World War II to 1980, virtually no American soldiers were killed in action while serving in that region. Within a decade, a great shift occurred. Since 1990, virtually no American soldiers have been killed in action anywhere except in the Greater Middle East. President [Jimmy] Carter neither intended nor foresaw that transformation — any more than European statesmen in the summer of 1914 intended or foresaw the horrors they were unleashing. But he, like they, can hardly be absolved of responsibility for what was to follow.*

## Carter-Bush-Clinton-Bush-Obama

"Democracy Now" host Amy Goodman played three brief clips quoting three presidents — George H.W. Bush, George W. Bush, and Barack Obama — all stating "we will prevail" in the Middle East. She asked Bacevich, "Have we prevailed in any way?"

Bacevich responded:

*Well, we haven't. And I have to say, those are exquisitely chosen clips, because they really do illustrate what's the point of my book. And that is that we have been engaged militarily in the Greater Middle East, large parts of the Islamic world, for going on four decades. We've engaged in innumerable interventions—large, small, brief, protracted—and we have yet to come anywhere close to achieving our aims. Whether we define our aims as restoring stability or promoting democracy or reducing the prevalence of anti-Americanism, it's not happening. And arguably, our military efforts are actually making things worse.*

In his interview, Bacevich concisely described the four-decade evolution of America's futile Gulf policy:

*...prior to the beginning of the Cold War, the United States was not a great military power. We raised forces from time to time to deal with some particular issue, but it was in the wake of the Cold War that we, as a nation, decided on a permanent basis to maintain a large military establishment.*

*For the first several decades of that Cold War, the United States had two priorities. We were willing to fight for Western Europe. We were willing to fight—did fight—in East Asia. We were not willing to fight for the Middle East. That changes in 1980, specifically a particular moment in January of 1980, when President*

Roger Armbrust

*Jimmy Carter, in his State of the Union address, promulgates what's known as the Carter Doctrine...*

*...Carter himself had no understanding of the implications that would flow from that statement. What happens, on an immediate basis, is that the national security bureaucracy now redefines its priorities and begins to orient itself toward the possibility of armed intervention by U.S. forces in the [Middle East] region. And over the course of the next 10 years, that process begins: [Ronald] Reagan sending peacekeepers into Lebanon, the initial jousting with Colonel Gaddafi in Libya, support for Saddam Hussein, of all people, in what I refer to as the first Gulf War—that's the Gulf War of 1980 to '88, pitting Iraq against Iran, with the United States coming to the aid of Iraq.*

*So, Carter starts the process of militarizing U.S. policy, which, over time, deepens, becomes more frequent, becomes more ambitious and becomes more costly, bringing us to where we are today in 2016, where we continue to hear these speeches by presidents insisting — insisting that we will prevail — when obviously we have not.*

Bacevich's view basically coincides with our analysis stated in our Oct. 18, 2015 *reality* column headlined "Obama Widens Carter's, Bush's Global-Rule Policies". In that column we detailed the Brzezinski Plan under President Carter and the Wolfowitz Doctrine under George W. Bush.

**Presidential Candidates as Dangerous Hawks**
**Cruz-Trump-Clinton**
Bacevich expressed grave concern about the hawkish views of presidential candidates Trump and Cruz on the Republican side and Clinton on the Democratic. He described Trump as having an infantile personality unfit for the role of commander in chief, and slapped Cruz for surrounding himself with "Islamophobes":

*I have a five-year- old grandson, who I love dearly, and he's a wonderful boy. He also has a tendency to blurt out whatever happens to be passing through his mind. And it seems to me that Donald Trump, who is not five years old, suffers from the same sort of inclination. And it suggests that he would be an enormously dangerous commander-in-chief. And I think we all recognize people say things on the campaign trail that may not actually reflect their intentions were they to be in office, but there does come—there are moments when the gap between what's being said and what ought to be done by any responsible person, when that gap is so broad that the rhetoric itself, I think, becomes a disqualifying factor.*

*But let me quickly add, it's not clear to me that Senator Cruz, who is the apparent alternative, is, by any inclination, any better. And if you take a look at the people Cruz is surrounding himself with as foreign policy advisers, that, to my mind, is deeply troubling...we've got Islamophobes. We've got General—retired Lieutenant General Boykin, who, for all practical purposes, sees the war for the Greater Middle East as an exercise in Judeo-Christian jihad. I mean, he is keen to go slay the Muslims and, clearly, views Islam itself as the enemy.*

Of Clinton, Bacevich stated:

*...Secretary Clinton is an unreconstructed hawk. Now, in terms of the rhetoric, she comes across as more reasoned than the Republican opposition, but the fact of the matter is, if we elect her to be our next commander-in-chief, we are voting for the continuation of the status quo with regard to U.S. national security policy, and specifically U.S. national security policy in the Greater Middle East. So, for people for whom that is an important issue, who want to see change in U.S. policy, she's not going to be the vehicle for change.*

Bacevich's statement was in response to Goodman's quoting Sen. Bernie Sanders, Clinton's Democratic opponent, who criticized the former Secretary of State as having a pro-war stance. Other than that, Bacevich did not discuss Sanders. Nor did he

Roger Armbrust

speak of third-party candidates. But Bacevich did explain his own stance on supporting the renewal of a military draft:

*I think that one of the unintended consequences of ending the draft, creating a professional military, was to create a gap between the military and society. Now, we don't acknowledge that gap. Matter of fact, we deny the existence of that gap by all of the rhetorical tributes that are paid to the troops and the obligation that we all have to, quote-unquote, "support the troops."*

*The reality, I think, is that when it really comes down to it, the American people don't pay much attention to how the troops are being used. And because they're not paying attention, the troops have been subjected to abuse. That is to say, they've been sent to fight wars that are unnecessary. The wars have been mismanaged. The wars go on far longer than they ought to.*

*And we respond by letting people in uniform be the first to board airplanes. And I think, frankly, that that is disgraceful and that it actually ought to be one of the things that gets discussed in a presidential campaign, but tends not to, sadly.*

We expressed a similar frustration regarding the American public's lack of concern for our troops in a 2012 column in *The Clyde Fitch Report*: "Memorial Day: Recalling and Caring for Our Constant Brave".

Goodman asked Bacevich, who lost a son serving in Iraq in 2007, "What do you want these presidential candidates—what do you want to hear from them? What do you want them to say to you?"

Bacevich answered:

*What they ought to say to us, not simply to me because of my personal circumstances—what they ought to say is:*

'I understand that we, as a nation, have been engaged in this war for going on four decades now, and I have learned something from that experience. I have taken on board what the United States tried to do militarily and what it actually ended up doing and what the consequence is that resulted. And here's what I've learned, and here's how I'm going to ensure, if you elect me commander-in- chief, that we will behave in ways that are wiser and more prudent and more enlightened in the future.'

In other words, they have to look beyond simply the question of how many more bombs are we going to drop on ISIS. That is a secondary consideration. They have to have some appreciation of the history, that I try to lay out in this book.

*(This column originally ran in* **reality: a world of views***.)*

**Economic Revolution**

# Solving the Decade of Our Discontent
February 27, 2011

**By Roger Armbrust**
***Special to the Clyde Fitch Report***

On Feb. 24, in a New York Times op-ed, a powerful Saudi prince took a hard look at the current Middle East turmoil and possible reform solutions. One can't help but compare his list of specific problems to those in the U.S., which can only lead to concerns about what American turmoil might lay ahead over the next decade. And that includes for artists.

The op-ed author isn't just any Saudi prince. The Times identified Alwaleed bin Talal bin Abdulaziz Al-Saud as "a grandson of the founding king of modern Saudi Arabia," and also "the chairman of the Kingdom Holding Company and the Alwaleed bin Talal Foundations." Having built a fortune, he's considered a financial rather than a political power in the Saud family.

The prince reviewed what analysts see as the major reasons for the revolution spreading across the Middle East, dividing them into two main categories: (1) "policies of autocratic regimes that had become oblivious to the need for fundamental political reform," and (2) "dire economic and social problems that for decades have been afflicting much of the Arab world, most particularly its young."

Roger Armbrust

America's population of 308.7 million is suffering as a result of these two categories combined. Americans have expressed deep concern both in polls and at the polls, giving their previous and present presidents and Congress low ratings, and voting to change the majority in the U.S. House and close the majority gap in the Senate. The growing number of independent voters, and the sweeping in of a number of Tea Party candidates to the House, are signs of voter discontent with the federal government — its destroying the nation's economy by exploding the national debt; its lack of monitoring financial institutions and Wall Street; and its devaluing the dollar, leading to losses of jobs and homes.

Our economic malaise doesn't appear ready to end any time soon. Doug Elmendorf, director of the Congressional Budget Office, predicted this last week in looking at fiscal years from 2011 to 2021:

> *Unfortunately, it is likely that a return to normal economic conditions will take years, and even after the economy has fully recovered, a return to sustainable budget conditions will require significant changes in tax and spending policies.*

For a fast-food nation like America, craving comfort quickly, it's highly doubtful a slow march will do. It's highly likely the American revolt will grow.

Look at this paragraph from Prince Alwaleed bin Talal's op-ed and compare these Middle East issues to those in the U.S.:

> *The majority of the Arab population is under 25, and the unemployment rate for young adults is in most countries 20 percent or more. Unemployment is even higher among women, who are economically and socially marginalized. The middle classes are being pushed down by inflation, which makes a stable standard of living seem an unattainable hope. The gap*

*between the haves and the have-nots is widening. The basic needs for housing, health care and education are not being met for millions.*

The U.S. population numbers may be different, and the unemployment rate among America's young may not be as high. But people under 20 years of age make up 27.3 percent of our nation's population, a population that more than tripled in the 20th century, according to the U.S. Census Bureau.

As for the more than 14 million unemployed Americans, by mid-2010 some 31 percent of them had been without work for a year or more. If "normal economic conditions" won't return for years, as the CBO director predicts, it's tough to see employment opportunities improving significantly.

That's particularly true for full-time jobs which include health and retirement benefits. Even when economic conditions seemed to be good previous to the 2007-08 fiscal meltdown, corporations had for years downsized full-time workers in favor of part-timers — sometimes even the same employees — so they wouldn't have to pay for benefits.

Nor does America's enduring unemployment problem chiefly affect the young. It's hammering the family's primary breadwinner, too. The federal Bureau of Labor Statistics, in its October 2010 report, showed workers 25 to 54 years old made up 58 percent of the unemployed. That group may not have the energy and high ideals of the young, but when adults can't support their families, they can not only become enraged, but they will tend to become organized, either nonviolently or violently.

The Tea Party is one immediate example of that. Republicans have been in the news recently with efforts to bust unions, and one can bet that unions won't take it lying down. They may even find ways to seek coalitions with the angry unemployed who aren't union members.

Roger Armbrust

This anger with the federal government is also a primary cause for an increase in American "hate groups." As CNN reported on Feb. 23, "The number of radical right groups in America — including hate groups, 'Patriot' groups and nativist groups — increased in 2010 for the second year in a row, according to a report by the Southern Poverty Law Center." The report documented 1,002 hate groups operating in the U.S.

The Law Center cited the following reasons for the rise:

> *resentment over the changing racial demographics of the country, frustration over the government's handling of the economy, and the mainstreaming of conspiracy theories and other demonizing propaganda aimed at various minorities.*

Could the predicted years of sick economy lead to a decade of American discontent that may boil over into actual revolution as is occurring in the Middle East? If those countries used the Internet to stir up and organize revolt, then could that happen in this country where over 77 percent of the population has Internet access?

You may note that some Middle East governments cut off Internet access in an effort to quell revolutionary activity. You may also note that Congressional legislation appears from time to time, and has recently, to authorize a similar, stateside cut-off under certain conditions. Last summer, Sen. Joe Lieberman sponsored just such a bill, basically giving the president power to "kill" Internet access in an emergency.

So, prepare yourself for what points to a coming decade of our discontent. Artists have already seen efforts to stop public funding on the federal and state levels for arts groups and projects. Now seems just the right time to get organized, get educated and get active.

The prince, in his Times op-ed, suggests there's still time to cure the Mideast maladies:

## The Vital Realities for 2020 and Beyond

*...we can succeed only if we open our systems to greater political participation, accountability, increased transparency and the empowerment of women as well as youth.*

That also goes for all artists, from painters to poets to playwrights to filmmakers and beyond.

# PBS "Frontline": Yeoman's Effort at Solving Financial Crisis Puzzle

**Roger Armbrust,** May 2, 2012

The Public Broadcasting System's "Frontline" news program last night ended its four-hour exhaustive, detailed effort to connect the bones of America's mammoth financial-meltdown skeleton: "Money, Power, and Wall Street." Overall, it was a yeoman's effort, piecing together a chronology to the economy's collapse and the major factors involved. The producers also lined up an extensive gallery of players ranging from Wall Street execs, bankers, politicians, lawyers, and economists involved in the quagmire.

The news broadcast took pains to simplify a financial network that endlessly pushes to expand in complexity and opaqueness, control the economy and government, and avoid regulation. The program also strove to clarify the major reasons for the meltdown.

Basically, "Frontline" identified the same fault lines laid out by the Financial Crisis Inquiry Commission, the 10-member government-appointed panel that investigated and reported on the meltdown's causes.

The commission listed 10 conclusions, including **widespread**

## The Vital Realities for 2020 and Beyond

**failures in financial regulation and supervision; dramatic failures of corporate governance and risk management at many systemically important financial institutions; a combination of excessive borrowing, risky investments, and lack of transparency; government being ill-prepared and inconsistent in its response; collapsing mortgage-lending standards, and massive marketing of over-the-counter derivatives.**

The program could have spent more time with the commission's chairman, Phil Angelides, former California state treasurer. He seemed to be one of the few interviewees without a direct stake in the financial-political-legal ramifications of the meltdown mess, even though his panel was surely political. In other words, his brief snippets of interview just seemed to make objective sense.

The other interviews, for the most part, possessed hedges, as investment types, politicians, and administrative officials constantly performed to "inform" while covering their posteriors. The absence of interviews with the major players-George W. Bush, his treasury secretary Henry Paulson, Barack Obama and his treasurer Timothy Geithner-kept the program from cresting, shielding them from direct accountability to the public.

But the extensive report showed that both Bush and Obama proved lightweights in facing the Wall Streeters and bankers, and that Geithner, former president of the Federal Reserve Bank of New York, remains a cohort of Wall Street.

As does Congress, who has avoided any major effort at reforming a financial system mired in greed, manipulation, and void of ethics-which, come to think of it, is a pretty good description of Congress itself. "Frontline," when describing efforts at financial-reform legislation, constantly referred to Wall Street's lobbyists killing or stifling bills. But lobbyists, under the Constitution, don't have the responsibility for writing, amending and approving legislation. Congress has that. If Congress gives that

Roger Armbrust

up to lobbyists, then voters need to protect themselves from such cowards by kicking them out of office.

The program, in seeking some reasonable solution to the meltdown mess, did seem to find a common recommendation from economists and lawyers: separate the banks from being involved in both securities trading and regular banking services-basically as banks had to perform before being given a free hand in the '90s. That's when Bill Clinton, his treasury secretary Robert Rubin, and Congress scrapped the Glass-Steagall Act, the post-1929 Stock Market Crash legislation meant to protect the public's bank investments from speculation.

Perhaps the "Frontline" report's most poignant moment: interviews with young, former Wall Street employees-intelligent, highly educated, sensitive-who decided to abandon the Greed Breed and join Occupy Wall Street. One scene even showed them meeting together, sincerely attempting to draw up suggested Congressional legislation which might bring true reform.

That brief segment, for any aware audience, should inspire citizens to get organized, get educated, and get active.

The link to Frontline's "Money, Power and Wall Street": http://www.pbs.org/wgbh/pages/frontline/money-power-wall-street/

The Financial Crisis Inquiry Commission's site: http://fcic.law.stanford.edu/

An overview of the Glass-Steagall Act: http://en.wikipedia.org/wiki/Glass%E2%80%93Steagall_Act

# Congress, Finance Law and Your Personal Economic Future
**Roger Armbrust,** July 27, 2012

In the past week, three occurrences brought signals of what you can do to protect your personal economic future. But you'll have to remember that your president, U.S. senators and Congress members are not leaders. They're followers. And you're going to have to tell them what you want...and hold their feet to the political furnace. Which, of course, means you'll need to get organized, get educated, and get active.
The three occurrences:

1. Sandford Weill, creator of the banking giant Citibank, basically said last week he was wrong. The nation needs to break up the big banks he helped foster and return to the two separate systems: commercial banks and investment banks. In other words, Congress needs to bring back legislation comparable to the Glass-Steagall Act which regulated the financial industry, foiled greedy speculation, and for decades avoided another Great Depression.

Following the historic stock market crash of 1929, research showed that much investment in the bubbling market came from borrowed money. It also involved banks providing "trash mortgages," according to investment banker/commentator James G. Rickards, i.e. mortgages which banks knew couldn't be paid back. Banks then bundled those mortgages into securities and sold them. Does that banking method sound familiar? As in the economic meltdown of 2008.

To insure that the crash of '29 wouldn't recur, Congress created Glass-Steagall in 1933. It mandated separating commercial banks-which operate through taking customer deposits and providing loans-from investment banks that deal in stocks, bonds and securities.

That act stood, and so did the U.S. economic system, until 1999, when Congress and President Bill Clinton-at the behest of the big banks—scrapped it for the Gramm-Leach-Bliley Act. That law repealed Glass-Steagall's separation of commercial and investment banks. After signing the Gramm legislation, Clinton said, "The Glass-Steagall Act is no longer relevant."

But it *was* still relevant. In less than a decade, banks had repeated their trash-mortgage bundling of securities, leading to the meltdown of the world economy that we're still dealing with today.

The Bush Administration, under Treasury Secretary Henry Paulson, hurriedly designed a multi-billion-dollar TARP bailout for the banks which Paulson deemed "too big to fail." Congress approved it. Neil Barofsky, former special inspector general for TARP (SIGTARP), just came out with a book in which he blames both Paulson and current Treasury Secretary Timothy Geithner for a "bias toward the banks" which basically gave the banks money, and has helped only 20 per cent of the homeowners it was supposed to help. Burofsky said Geithner told him the bailout was designed to "foam the runway for the banks" rather than help the public.

TARP is expected to lose $32 billion to $70 billion in public monies, according to Burofsky.

Will Congress create a new form of Glass-Steagall and the president sign it? You'll have to make them.

2. Congressman Ron Paul's "Audit the Fed" legislation passed the House by a vote of 327-98 this past week. The bill calls for the Government Accountability Office to audit the Federal Reserve's monetary policy and deliberations.

It's basically an effort to give taxpayers some control over the independent agency that prints and distributes money to banks. Paul and other Fed critics have complained that the agency has printed trillions of new dollars and made them available to the banks, but that the banks either hoard or spend the money, but don't make it available to citizens who need it for everything from home mortgages to small businesses.

The Fed, of course, has defied any effort to force transparency on it. Late last year, it came out that the Fed in 2008 had secretly loaned banks $7.7 trillion more than reported.

Investment banker Rickards also pointed out last week that the Fed's manipulation (lowering) of interest rates is costing savers $500 billion a year. It actually displaces the money from investors, who lose it through lowering of rates, to the banks which use the monies for their own benefit.

Democratic opponents of the Paul bill warn it will place the free-dealing Fed at the mercy of politicians. The bill now goes to the Senate, and Sen. Harry Reid, the Democrats' leader, has said he won't let the legislation come up for a vote. So it seems dead for this session.

But this is an election year, and if you want to protect yourself and your children from our money-printing and distributing institution that seems to favor the banks over citizens, you need to get your Congressional candidates to commit to it.

Will Congress eventually create and pass Federal Reserve-monitoring legislation and the president sign it? You'll have to make them.

Roger Armbrust

3. The Tax Justice Network issued a report showing that 92,000 people (0.001 per cent of the world's population) have stashed at least $21 trillion in hidden assets in offshore tax havens. The independent research network equaled the sum to both the U.S. and Japanese economies combined.

The July 45-page report said the hidden amount of untaxed funds could be as high as $32 trillion. Much of the data analyzed in the report comes from the World Bank, International Monetary Fund (IMF), Bank for International Settlements (BIS), and the United Nations.

James N. Henry, the study's author, states:

> *The very existence of the global offshore industry, and the tax-free status of the enormous sums invested by their wealthy clients, is predicated on secrecy: that is what this industry really "supplies" as it competes for, conceals, and manages private capital from all over the planet, from any and all sources, no questions asked.*
>
> *We are up against one of society's most well-entrenched interest groups. After all, there's no interest group more rich and powerful than the rich and powerful, who are the ultimate subjects of our research.*

If Congress would decide to pursue and tax this vast wealth, it would keep our lawmakers from looking to tax you more. And it could protect you from their efforts to abuse your Social Security trust fund, cut America's Medicare program, and penalize the poor, elderly and homeless. They might even look for ways to help our college students out of their $1 trillion debt, and Americans' $1 trillion credit-card debt, both of which provide wealth for America's bankers.

So far, regulators have shown slight results at finding and bringing in some of this money. *The New York Times*' Mark

## The Vital Realities for 2020 and Beyond

Scott reported in April that, worldwide, "countries have collected about $18.7 billion in additional taxes from more than 100,000 wealthy individuals... The situation has left private banks scrambling to bolster their risk management practices and educate wealthy clients on the new regulatory environment."

As you can see, that's far short of taxing all the $21-32 trillion, so there's room for more heavy enforcement.

Scott also noted:

> *Several European allies reached an agreement with the United States in February to help enforce the Foreign Account Tax Compliance Act, which requires that virtually every financial institution in the world report any accounts held by Americans. Many wealthy clients who previously had not worried about revealing all their international assets to home authorities are taking advantage of tax amnesty programs in countries like the United States and Britain.*

U.S. federal regulators will only make a determined push to find and collect taxes on the trillions in offshore funds, or before the money makes it there, if Congress and the president demand it. One problem: nearly half of the Congress are millionaires. So is President Obama. So is Mitt Romney. So is Ron Paul.

Will Congress create shark-teeth legislation to really bite into these offshore tax havens, and will the president sign it? Will they push for strict enforcement of the Foreign Account Tax Compliance Act? You'll have to make them.

# Iceland Lets Banks Fail, Sees Economy Blossom
**Roger Armbrust,** January 28, 2013

When it comes to handling an economic collapse, Iceland is not the U.S. When the worldwide economy melted in 2008-as America bailed out Wall Street-Iceland let its major banks fail, tossed bankers in jail, and has seen its economy rise.

That was the word this past week from Ólafur Ragnar Grímsson Iceland's president. He was interviewed by *Al Jazeera* television news at the World Economic Forum in Davos, where the globe's political and financial elite rub elbows, tap wine glasses, and laugh about the rest of us.

But Grímsson wasn't laughing; he was calmly making sense, saying that Iceland now is recovering with economic growth and "very little unemployment. We didn't follow the prevailing orthodoxy of the Western world in the last 30 years. We established currency controls, let the banks fail, provided for the poor, and didn't introduce austerity measures on the scale you're seeing in Europe."

Asked if he thought letting banks fail would work for the rest of Europe, Grímsson replied:

> *I think it would work for the rest of Europe. Why do you consider banks to be the holy churches of the modern*

> *economy? Why are private banks not like airlines and telecommunications companies, allowed to go bankrupt if they've acted in an irresponsible way? The theory that you have to bail out banks is about bankers enjoying for their own profit or success, and letting the ordinary people bear the failure through taxes and austerity. People in enlightened democracies aren't going to accept that in the long run.*
>
> *One thing we learned: Icelandic banks, like British and American banks, have become high tech companies, hiring engineers, mathematicians and computer scientists. When they failed, the innovative sectors-the IT sector, the high tech sector-blossomed, and have done better in the last three years. The lesson is, the financial sector, even successful, is in fact bad news if you want to be competitive in innovation and technology.*

You can see Grímsson's three-minute interview *here.*

Grímsson's dialogue didn't get into three other hard legal facts:

First, by 2010, Icelandic bankers began going to jail, and finding themselves as defendants in billion-dollar lawsuits. More about that *here*.

Second, a European court ruled just today that Iceland acted responsibly by refusing to repay billions of euros to Britain and the Netherlands for bailing out depositors in a failed Icelandic bank, Landsbanki.

*Reuters* reports:

> *After the collapse four years ago of Iceland's top lenders during the credit crunch, the British and Dutch governments stepped in to repay savers in the online "Icesave" account run by Landsbanki and wanted Iceland to pay them back directly.*

Roger Armbrust

> *Iceland did not comply, triggering a row between the governments and potentially complicating the island's bid to join the European Union.*
>
> *But the court of the European Free Trade Association (EFTA) bloc found Iceland did not break depositor protection laws by refusing to return the money.*

Third, Iceland also forgave mortgage debts, which you can see *here*.

That hasn't been the American experience, where the federal government has bailed out the big banks-with little of that money going to help homeowners-and refused to prosecute bankers for obvious criminal activity.

The Justice Department's chief investigator of bankers' wrongdoing even indicated in a *PBSFrontline* interview last week that he was concerned that prosecution would negatively affect the banks and the nation's economy, meaning to hell with the law and the American taxpayer. You can read a portion of that interview and see the *Frontline* segment here.
To view the full *Frontline* program, entitled "The Untouchables," look here.

# Will UK Finally Jail Banksters? US Next?
**Roger Armbrust,** April 29, 2013

Last July, *CFR* reviewed how governments were responding to bankers who profit through criminal fraud, and ruin others' economic lives. We led with Iran and four death sentencesfor billion-dollar bank fraud. In all, 39 persons in Iran were tried for fraud, with four sentenced to hang, two to life in prison, and others with jail sentences ranging to 25 years.

In January, we reported how Iceland let its major banks fail, tossed bankers in jail, and has seen its economy rise.

Which brings us to last week, and the *Financial Times*' report that Britain's banking commission is considering a new law to jail bankers "who behave recklessly." (Leave it to the Brits to be polite even when describing cannibals of capital.)
The proposed law would call for both imprisonment and also holding bankers personally liable for catastrophic financial losses. Notes *FT*:

> One member told the Financial Times: "Banks benefit from a public subsidy, in that they know they will be bailed out if they fail. I think we want to see a sense of personal responsibility to match that."

The commission is also considering recommendations to

"remodel" the banking sector, including splitting commercial banking from investment activities. Says *FT* of the proposals:

> *One [proposal] is to enforce what one member called an "internal Glass-Steagall split", which would require banks to separate their trading functions from the rest of their operations.*
>
> *Under this system, riskier trading activities would be overseen by a separate chief executive, with the bank's overall CEO in charge of making sure that governance is upheld across the group.*

The US Congress approved the Glass-Steagall Act in 1933 as a shield to protect the nation against another Great Depression by limiting affiliations of commercial banks and securities firms. Congress and President Clinton scrapped Glass-Steagall through 1999's Gramm-Leach-Bliley Act. Within nine years, a world economic meltdown had occurred. In 2008, Clinton argued that the financial crisis had occurred primarily because of banks merging with securities firms. Two years later, the American Bankers Association challenged that view.

The Financial Crisis Inquiry Commission, the 10-member government-appointed panel that investigated and reported on the economic collapse's causes, listed 10 conclusions for the worldwide meltdown. They included **widespread failures in financial regulation and supervision; dramatic failures of corporate governance and risk management at many systemically important financial institutions; a combination of excessive borrowing, risky investments, and lack of transparency; government being ill-prepared and inconsistent in its response; collapsing mortgage-lending standards, and massive marketing of over-the-counter derivatives.**

Will the US follow the UK banking commission's lead in jailing banksters? Don't bet on it.

## The Vital Realities for 2020 and Beyond

Former Treasury Secretary Timothy Geithner

Congress approved a new law, the Dodd-Frank Wall Street Reform and Consumer Protection Act of 2010, aimed at regulating the financial sector. But little has occurred to truly implement penalizing lawbreaking bankers. And attempts have been made to reintroduce Glass-Steagall, but the Obama Administration has opposed those.

The White House has also been reluctant to pursue criminal actions against banks. The Justice Department has said publicly it feared prosecution of executives with major banks would disrupt the international economy. One of the most horrible examples of this occurred last December when Assistant Attorney General Lanny Breuer signed off on a settlement deal with HSBC. The British banking behemoth had admitted to laundering billions of dollars for Colombian and Mexican drug cartels. The bank had also broken important banking laws including the Bank Secrecy Act and the Trading With the Enemy Act.

Neil Barofsky, a former New York prosecutor and special inspector general for the federal TARP funds, said the Justice Department was ready to prosecute HSBC execs, but Treasury Secretary Timothy Geithner, a friend of Wall Street, blocked the effort.

Congress has also been reluctant to shackle Wall Street and the banking industry. And probably won't until the public has had enough, then gets organized, gets educated, and gets active in initiating real change in bankers' control over Washington.

# Austerity as Failure and Killer
**Roger Armbrust,** May 21, 2013

Governments worldwide, still suffering from the global economic collapse of 2008, have made various attempts at implementing austerity.

What is austerity? Basically, it's governments cutting their budget deficits during collapsing economic times. They implement either drastic spending reductions, tax increases, or both. Republicans in the U.S. Congress have led efforts at austerity. And in Europe, the International Monetary Fund, nations' lender of last resort, has demanded austerity from European Union nations like Greece and Spain whose economies have dissolved.

But over the last month, authoritative voices have been decrying efforts at austerity. A dramatic turn came in late April when two Harvard professors-often cited by politicians and conservative columnists as the prophets of austerity-published an op-ed in *The New York Times*, basically saying conservatives had misread them and misused their research. In that piece, Carmen M. Reinhart, a professor of international finance, and Kenneth S. Rogoff, a public policy and economics professor, said:

> The politically charged discussion, especially sharp in the past week or so, has falsely equated our finding of a negative association between debt and growth with an unambiguous call for austerity.

> *We agree that growth is an elusive goal at times of high debt. We know that cutting spending and raising taxes is tough in a slow-growth economy with persistent unemployment. Austerity seldom works without structural reforms – for example, changes in taxes, regulations and labor market policies – and if poorly designed, can disproportionately hit the poor and middle class...*
>
> *...In short: many countries around the world have extraordinarily high public debts by historical standards, especially when medical and old-age support programs are taken into account. Resolving these debt burdens usually involves a transfer, often painful, from savers to borrowers. This time is no different...*

That painful transfer from savers to borrowers has been abusively clear in the US, where the Federal Reserve has addictively continued to artificially keep interest rates low-a torture to regular-citizen savers-while obsessively print more paper money going to banks and Wall Street, the big borrowers and sellers of bonds back to the Fed. Other central banks around the world have also geared up this process.

**"Backfired"**
A week after Reinhart and Rogoff published their op-ed, Robin Bew, the chief economist for the influential London international-affairs news weekly *The Economist*, flatly said Europe's effort at austerity "has backfired." In a May 2 email to subscribers headlined "Europe's austerity dilemma," Bew contended:

> *With the euro zone mired in recession and unemployment at record highs, the debate over the wisdom of fiscal austerity has intensified. Many now believe that the "austerity first" approach has backfired, exacerbating the economic downturn. Could these doubts prompt a shift towards more pro-growth policies? While some modest policy adjustments seem possible at the margins-for example, countries may get*

Roger Armbrust

> more time to reduce their budget deficits-we believe that the extent of any change is likely to be limited. For all the talk about the need to promote economic growth as the cure for Europe's debt problems, expect the status quo to continue with only a few exceptions.

During the past week, the press has dwelt on a just-released book by two scholars which charges that austerity is literally a killer of humans. David Stuckler, an Oxford senior researcher in the economics of health, and Sanjay Basu, an assistant professor of medicine and epidemiologist at Stanford University, have written *The Body Economic: Why Austerity Kills*.

The authors' research examines how financial meltdowns have affected people's daily lives from the Great Depression of the 1930s, to post-Communist Russia in the '90s, to the US foreclosure crisis beginning in the late 2000s.

**Suicides, Jobs, Homes and Healthcare Loss**
Among a wealth of data, the book reveals that the 2008 crisis led to more than 10,000 additional suicides and a million extra cases of depression across the U.S. and Europe since governments started introducing austerity programs. In the US, over five million Americans have lost access to healthcare due to job losses. In the UK alone, austerity has forced 10,000 families into homelessness due to cuts in housing benefits.

Stuckler cites Greece as the most extreme case. In an interview with UK's newspaper *The Guardian*, he says:

> There [Greece], austerity to meet targets set by the troika is leading to a public-health disaster. Greece has cut its health system by more than 40%. As the health minister said: "These aren't cuts with a scalpel, they're cuts with a butcher's knife."

> [Worse, those cuts have been decided] not by doctors and healthcare professionals, but by economists and

*financial managers. The plan was simply to get health spending down to 6% of GDP. Where did that number come from? It's less than the UK, less than Germany, way less than the US.*

If *The Economist*'s Robin Bew is correct, and the power elite simply continues the status quo, don't expect anything to change unless average citizens get organized, get educated, and get active. Only that will make their lawmakers break from their current practice of serving the financial industry, the multi-national corporations, and the military-industrial complex that would rather profit from nations involved in endless war rather than serving their citizens by assuring a solid economy that truly encourages jobs, inspires human creativity, and provides caring medical services.

# A Journalist's Concern about the Clintons
**Roger Armbrust,** February 17, 2014

Back in Arkansas in the mid-1970s, I moved from a job as city hall reporter for the old Arkansas Democrat (which later would buy the Pulitzer Prize-winning Arkansas Gazette) to handling political affairs for the Metropolitan Chamber of Commerce.

I wasn't happy at the Chamber. I had a boss (J. William Perry) who was dedicated, and I learned a lot about the economy and insider politics from him. But I remained an independent journalist at heart, always mistrustful of many of the business executives and their efforts to manipulate the Chamber organization for their own benefit. I admired my boss for not allowing it.

During those years, as journalist and Chamber politico, I watched Bill Clinton operate as the state's attorney general, then his early days as governor.

I remember, after his first election as governor, going into Rhea Drug in what's now called Historic Hillcrest, looking at the magazine rack, and seeing the cover of *Life* magazine: a smiling Bill with his name and below it "America's youngest governor." I thought, "Now it begins."

I suppose everybody in the state who came in contact with him, and understood politics, thought the same thing. He had it all:

looks, intelligence, down-to-earth almost boyish friendliness, and yet a straightforward, serious presence when discussing serious issues.

I once watched him "work a room" as governor—a packed gathering at a meeting, perhaps 100 people. When he walked in, folks flowed to him. Clinton would shake hands with one person, keep his blue eyes on him or her, and listen intently, then respond. Others would crowd around, try to maneuver behind the person he was speaking with; attempt to edge in, hoping he would make eye contact. But the young governor's eyes wouldn't waiver, nor be disturbed by the movement around him. He'd focus on the conversation, then move to another individual and home in. He did that for perhaps half an hour or more before moving away to the dais to speak.

There were times I would run into him and speak briefly. He always seemed to say exactly what he thought and felt, and so did I. Only once, just before he was elected governor, did I meet Hillary—at a private political gathering. Bill did most of the talking, then would look at her to see if she concurred. She usually did, but might add a constructive note.

**The President**
In 1979, I moved to the Northeast, New Jersey and then New York, watching the Clintons from afar, but always having hope that the beautiful, intelligent couple would fulfill themselves and really help the country. I was surprised to see him announce to run against a sitting president, George H.W. Bush, who had just crushed Saddam Hussein's forceful effort to control oil beyond Iraq's borders. I was thrilled when he took Bush on in a debate shared with Ross Perot, hammering him for criticizing Arkansas and its people. And surprised again when he pulled off the election.

While he served as president, I was pleased that he had helped dissolve the debt, and was little concerned with the Monica Lewinsky affair, except to think it was unloving and damaging to his family, politically stupid, and stifled any chance for Congress and the president to actually accomplish something good for the nation during impeachment ...and admired him for basically keeping us out of any prolonged foreign invasions like Vietnam.

What I didn't realize at the time was that he was signing two bills that would: (1) turn the nation's information and entertainment system over to a handful of moguls, and (2) open the American and world economy to dissolution by the wolves of Wall Street.

The Telecommunications Act of 1996 in time turned a widespread competition of radio, TV, filmmaking, book publishing, newspaper and other news and entertainment sources into a half-dozen stale media giants, huge on profits, but sapped of creativity and hungry journalism and its resulting vital information.

In 1999, he succumbed to the banking industry, signing the Gramm-Leach-Bliley Act,which repealed two vital provisions of the Banking Act of 1933. Those were known as the Glass-Steagall Act, which separated commercial banks from securities firms. Congress's legislation and Clinton's signature turned the public trust in banks caring for citizens' checking and savings accounts and home mortgages over to Wall Street's gamblers. Glass-Stegall was created to prevent that, because Congress had seen that Wall Street's greed in combining mortgages and bad securities had led to the Great Depression. Repeal of Glass-Stegall in 1999 would lead to that Wall Street repetition, and to the global meltdown in 2008, which the world has yet to recover from.

**The Senator and Secretary**
The Clintons are both brilliant politicians, which I don't consider a compliment. And yet if I saw them face-to-face after all these years, I'd probably smile, a sucker for their appeal and for having witnessed their long struggle.

Hillary appears simply to be brilliant even beyond politics, and rock-tough. She moved from a rather quiet confidante of her husband in his early political career to an active participant after he had lost and regained the governorship, and proved a visible mainstay of his presidential campaign.

She also compiled an extraordinary resume with her legal and political activity ranging from the Nixon impeachment inquiry, to the White House, and to serving as U.S. Senator and Secretary of State. In a nation that for centuries attempted to stifle women politically and economically (and appears on state levels to try it again), she has worked tirelessly, moved forward, and developed a record that would indicate she deserves to become the first president who happens to be a woman.

Yet here are some basic concerns:

1) She spent six years on Wal-Mart's board of directors. This close tie to an employee-stifling multinational corporation, and its opposition to unions, is a minus. Will she oppose the proliferation of multinationals, which control the Millionaire Congress and Millionaire President? Or just continue business as usual?
2) She wrote a book called "It Takes a Village," (1996), a vision for the children of America. Yet she has remained silent on the CIA's drone bombing of innocent children and adults in Middle Eastern villages while she was Secretary of State. You can call that being faithful to the Obama administration. But it's an appalling affront to humanity.
3) She voted for America's invasion of Iraq. Will she continue America's foreign invasions in support of the military-industrial complex if she becomes president? And if she says "no," do you think she'll mean it?
4) She has been noncommittal on the National Security Agency's abuse of surveillance powers and the roiling debate over it. Will she allow government to continue treating the entire American public, and even foreign leaders, as guilty until proven innocent, which is what

Roger Armbrust

      the NSA's universal gorging of individuals' data and abuse of liberty truly is?

**5)** Did she support Bill Clinton's signing of the 1996 Telecommunications Act and the 1999 Gramm-Leach-Bliley Act? Does she believe the Dodd-Frank Wall Street Reform and Consumer Protection Act has really reformed Wall Street and protected consumers? Will she push to jail top bank executives when they again endanger the economy and ruin people's lives?

For you rabid Clinton supporters, take heart. We'll be asking these hard questions about all other candidates, too.

Meanwhile, as always, *Peculiar Progressive* encourages you: If you seek change in your society, don't depend on politicians to do it. You need to get organized, get educated, and get active to make it happen.

# Russia, China Forsake the Dollar, Pressing U.S., EU

**Roger Armbrust,** May 26, 2014

This past week, Russia and China completed two major deals, striking a defiant blow against U.S. and European Union efforts to punish Moscow with economic sanctions:

First, Russia signed a long-term contract to supply China with natural gas, expanding the two major countries' cooperation on energy. Second, Moscow's and Beijing's chief banks agreed to move away from the U.S. dollar as the international reserve currency, further inflaming the growing global currency wars.

On May 21, *The Washington Post* reported:

> The 30-year [natural gas] deal was announced after meetings in Shanghai between [Russian President Vladimir] Putin and Chinese President Xi Jinping. It is worth an estimated $400 billion, Alexei Miller, chief executive of the Russian energy giant Gazprom, told Russian reporters.

The gas agreement grows the energy relationship between the two giant countries. *Peculiar Progressive* has reported in earlier columns how Russia in 2011 had agreed to begin shipping oil to China, as much as 300,000 barrels a day.

Roger Armbrust

What seemed to receive less notoriety last week in the U.S., but was well publicized internationally: the U.S. dollar has taken a hit from Russia and China. As Aljazeera America reported on May 20:

> *In a symbolic blow to U.S. global financial hegemony, Russia and China took a small step toward undercutting the domination of the U.S. dollar as the international reserve currency on Tuesday when Russia's second biggest financial institution, VTB, signed a deal with the Bank of China to bypass the dollar and pay each other in domestic currencies...*
>
> *..."Our countries have done a huge job to reach a new historic landmark," Putin said on Tuesday, making note of the $100 billion in annual trade that has been achieved between the two countries.*

Following the West's conquering Nazi Germany and Japan in the mid-1940s, the dollar became international transactions' reserve currency, i.e. a single, reliable form of money which countries worldwide can hold for conducting business.

A small crack in that process occurred in 1971, when President Richard Nixon cancelled America's gold standard—no longer using gold as the globally accepted support for the printed paper dollar. The rumbling of international currency wars began following the 2008 world economic meltdown, when the U.S. Federal Reserve began the massive printing of fiat currency, and the world's other central banks began to follow suit.

As the U.S. and European Union recently have struggled economically, they have seen the rise of united economic efforts outside their influence, primarily BRICS—the acronym for an association of Brazil, Russia, Iran, China and South Africa. The BRICS countries have continually expanded cooperation in trade areas, and look to become more involved in global affairs.

## The Vital Realities for 2020 and Beyond

Recently, the U.S. and EU seemed to believe their backing the overthrow of the corrupt, but democratically elected government in Ukraine—a pro-Russian regime—might bring NATO closer to Russian borders and somehow destabilize Russian, and therefore BRICS, power. The North Atlantic Treaty Organization is the Western-backed military organization, created primarily to guard against Russian or Chinese aggression. Ukraine, a former member of the Soviet Union, sits on the northeastern border of Russia.

The U.S. tried to increase this destabilizing effort by getting China to support the West's sanctions against Russia. These came following Moscow's backing Crimea's recent separation from Ukraine and its new right, pro-Western government this year. But China–already receiving oil from Russia, plus heavy involvement in other BRICS trade activities–didn't bite.

China's central bank, in fact, had issued a memo months ago recommending it turn away from the dollar in all its oil transactions, depending instead on its own yuan. BRICS, too, has been looking at stepping away from Western funding sources like the International Monetary Fund, and setting up its own lending exchange among its BRICS member countries.

*Peculiar Progressive* also pointed out in a recent column how the West, rather than storing gold, had been selling it to Russia. Russia, in the meantime, and China have both been mining and storing even more gold. Russia is also the world's major oil producer, and a chief gas producer and supplier, including to European countries. All this seems to point to Moscow setting itself up with BRICS for stabilizing its member countries as the world continues to struggle back from the 2008 global economic tragedy.

Another harmful blow hit the EU in its European Parliament elections this weekend—a blacklash by voters against unification. As *The New York Times* reported today (Monday):

Roger Armbrust

*Members of the European political elite expressed alarm on Monday over the strong showing in European Parliament elections by nationalist and anti-immigrant parties skeptical about European integration, a development described by the French prime minister as an "earthquake."*

*In France, Britain and elsewhere, anti-immigrant parties opposed to the influence of the European Union emerged in the lead. In France, the National Front won 26 percent of the vote to defeat both the governing Socialists and the Union for a Popular Movement, the center-right party of former President Nicolas Sarkozy. In Britain, the triumph of the U.K. Independence Party, or UKIP, which won 28 percent of the vote, represented the first time since 1910 that a nationwide vote had not been won by either the Conservatives or Labour.*

This follows a strong EU effort at austerity—governments' attempts to stabilize economic struggles through higher taxation, cuts in services, or both.

The U.S., still struggling economically, has seen efforts at austerity by Republicans in Congress. With mid-term elections coming in November, we'll see how voters respond to those efforts, as citizens are saddled with a nearly trillion-dollar credit card debt, over a trillion-dollar student loan debt, a national debt of $12.5 trillion (held by the public), and national infrastructure needs of $2.3 trillion.

Meanwhile, voters in the struggling Ukraine this weekend elected a pro-Western billionaire, Petro O. Poroshenko, as president. Russia, choosing to maneuver, said it was willing to work with him.

# Economic Meltdown Zombies: They're Baaaack!
**Roger Armbrust,** June 23, 2014

The 2008 global economic meltdown led to a deluge of lost homes, dissolved jobs, suicides, deaths of citizens who couldn't afford health care, and broke governments ruining more lives through attempts at austerity. *The Economist* published a recent column citing that we're just now experiencing the true magnitude of the Ongoing Global Depression that government and Big Media timidly refer to as the Great Recession.

Analysts examining reasons for the tragic worldwide crash basically agreed on two major culprits: the $600 trillion (at the time) derivatives market and subprime lending—two devastating zombie creations of Wall Street's wolves, backed by Washington's jackals.

Well, recent reports from several sources these days agree: the two stalking zombies are back, feeding their hunger.

**Derivatives, Lending and Betting**
What is a derivative? It's a special contract that *derives* its value from an underlying asset. A form of risky financial gambling. For example (to simplify a complex process), in 2006, a bank might provide a $500,000 mortgage to someone with little or no credit. Then the bank might purchase $1 million in insurance on that mortgage, a bet to make money if the

homeowner reneged. That $1 million investment *derived* from the underlying asset: the home. Then other, larger investments (bets) would *derive* from that, probably from other banks or investors. Sound insane? Yep.

The insanity can be seen in two simple figures: according to The World Bank, the global domestic product (GDP), or underlying assets, in 2007 was $54.3 trillion. But the over-the-counter derivatives market was over $600 trillion. Wall Street and Washington knew that couldn't last. And it didn't. In 2006, the housing bubble burst, and by 2008, the global economy had melted. But Wall Street's wolves made a lot of money, including buying up competitive banks who had placed the wrong bets.

What's worse, these derivatives, sold over the counter, are non-transparent: the public can't see what the Wall Street wolves are doing with derivatives. This thanks to Congress, which in 2000 passed the Commodity Futures Modernization Act (CFMA), and President Bill Clinton signed it.

The federal Financial Crisis Inquiry Commission—the panel assigned to analyze what happened in the 2008 worldwide economic meltdown—heavily criticized this law. The commission said flatly:

> *The enactment of legislation in 2000 to ban the regulation by both the federal and state governments of over-the-counter (OTC) derivatives was a key turning point in the march toward the financial crisis.*

If governments can't regulate the gambling Wall Street wolves, guess who gets devoured?

Mayra Rodríguez Valladares, managing principal at MRV Associates, a capital markets and financial regulatory consulting and training firm in New York, last month warned that the wolves are back. In a May 13 article in *The New York Times*, she stated:

> *Despite slow economic growth in the United States and most of Europe still in or hovering around recession, global derivatives markets are 20 percent larger than in 2007. The Bank for International Settlements announced late last week that the global derivatives market is about $710 trillion...Higher volumes are a strong indication that derivatives players' operational risk is rising...*

> *...Not only is the enormous size of these portfolios of concern, so is the fact that less than 5 percent of the portfolios are regulated and transparent exchange-traded products. The rest is in far more lucrative, opaque over-the-counter products.*

Others agree with her, including *Forbes*, who saw it a year ago, and *Financial News*, which discussed it in late May.

## Scrapping Glass-Steagall and Your Shield

A second major reason that led to the global meltdown originated in Congress a year before it passed the CFMA of 2000. The Financial Services Modernization Act of 1999, also signed by Clinton, removed the Glass-Steagall Act of 1933. From after the Great Depression until 1999, Glass-Steagall had separated commercial banks from securities firms. It protected your checking and savings accounts and home mortgages from the Wall Street gamblers.

After signing the FSMA, also called the Gramm-Leach-Bliley Act for the legislators who formed it, Bill Clinton said, "The Glass-Steagall law is no longer appropriate." He couldn't have been more wrong. Just as Wall Street's wolves had done before the Great Depression, they began betting customers' money by combining securities with bad mortgages until the bubble burst, making great sums while the rest of America and the world suffered, and continues to suffer.

The wolves' freedom allowed them to make big bucks with subprime lending: i.e., making loans to people who won't be able to pay the money back. What better way for wolves to devour profits than bet on the loans through derivatives, then, add to profit by repossessing the property and selling it again?

Of course, the subprime racket is also back, this time victimizing businesses. *Bloomberg* reported this in its May article "Wall Street Finds New Subprime With 125% Business Loans":

> From an office near New York's Times Square, people trained by a veteran of Jordan Belfort's boiler room call truckers, contractors and florists across the country pitching loans with annual interest rates as high as 125 percent, according to more than two dozen former employees and clients. When borrowers can't pay, Naidus's World Business Lenders LLC seizes their vehicles and assets, sometimes sending them into bankruptcy.
>
> Naidus isn't the only one turning to subprime business lending. Mortgage brokers and former stock salesmen looking for new ways to make fast profits are pushing the loans, which aren't covered by federal consumer safeguards. Goldman Sachs Group Inc. (GS) and Google Inc. are among those financing his competitors, which charge similar rates...
>
> Subprime business lending — the industry prefers to be called "alternative" — has swelled to more than $3 billion a year, estimates Marc Glazer, who has researched his competitors as head of Business Financial Services Inc., a lender in Coral Springs, Florida. That's twice the volume of small loans guaranteed by the Small Business Administration.

Business as usual in the Wall Street lair. But the Millionaire Congress and Millionaire President will stop that by bringing back Glass-Steagall or enforcing current laws and regulations prohibiting predatory lending. Right? Don't bet on it.

Oh, the federal Justice Department slaps a bank's hand from time to time. But in the U.S., we don't execute finance crooks like they do in Iran for ruining people's lives, or imprison them like Iceland. We fine them, so they can pay with clients' money. And meanwhile, the Federal Reserve keeps printing money to buy the banks' bonds, and they continue risky investments rather than help consumers with those funds.

Bottom line: If you want to protect your homes, businesses, and bank deposits, you might want to get organized, get educated, and get active in forcing Congress to bring back Glass-Steagall. That would be a good start. Because a bad ending again seems to be looming.

# BRICS Forms Funds, Defying U.S., IMF, and World Bank
**Roger Armbrust,** July 21, 2014

Brazil, Russia, India, China and South Africa together represent 40% of the world's population and 25% of the global gross domestic product (GDP). Total trade among the countries is $6.14 trillion, or nearly 17 percent of the world's total.

These are the three major reasons they formed BRICS, an association to promote cooperation among the five emerging economies. Another major reason has been to oppose U.S. hegemony and to find a way to challenge the global financial dominance of America and its ruling lenders: the International Monetary Fund and the World Bank.

BRICS took a major step in forcing its challenge last week. It formed two multi-billion-dollar funding structures to promote cooperative economic development independent of the West. The first is the New Development Bank, started with $50 billion and expected to quickly expand to $100 billion. The second is a crisis lending fund of $100 billion, called the Contingent Reserve Arrangement.

Western media hasn't been excited about covering this event. Even *The New York Times* buried a story deep in its World section last week.

But Nobel-prize-winning economist Joseph Stiglitz vocally understood the importance of the BRICS move. He said last Thursday on the progressive TV program *Democracy Now*:

> *It's very important in many ways. This is adding to the flow of money that will go to finance infrastructure, adaptation to climate change — all the needs that are so evident in the poorest countries. It [also] reflects a fundamental change in global economic and political power. The BRICS countries today are richer than the advanced countries were when the World Bank and the IMF were founded. We're in a different world — but the old institutions haven't kept up...*

> *...there have been a lot of changes in the global economy. And a new institution reflects the broader set of mandates, the new concerns, the new sets of instruments that can be used, the new financial instruments, and the broader governance. Realizing the deficiencies in the old system of governance, hopefully, this new institution will spur the existing institutions to reform. And, you know, it's not just competition. It's really trying to get more resources to the developing countries in ways that are consistent with their interests and needs.*

**Effort to Replace the U.S. Dollar**
The new bank and fund are also sharp picks BRICS will use for chipping away at the U.S. dollar's dominance as the world's reserve currency. Since the 2008 global economic meltdown, some economists have called for replacing the dollar with the Chinese yuan. And Chinese policymakers have been quietly seeking to slowly make that a reality.

China is a major holder of U.S. debt in the form of bonds, and its central bank has recommended trading in oil with yuan rather than dollars while it looks for more ways to make the yuan a more acceptable currency worldwide.

It took a major step recently through a historic agreement with Russia to purchase Russian natural gas—a growing effort by China to move away from burning coal, which has led to major pollution problems. Russia and China agreed to fulfill the energy contract with yuan and rubles, not U.S. dollars.

But this was more than a single major business deal. It was a symbol to the world, and particularly to the BRICS fellow countries, that BRICS unity could lead to major trade benefits.

**China as Global Leader**

Also, China President Xi Jinping appears to really be pushing to grow China's image as an economic and political leader. And Simon Baptist, chief economist and Asian regional director for *The Economist* magazine's intelligence unit, commented on this last Thursday:

> *China is in the midst of a serious economic and political transition and both are having global impact. Over the past decade or so the growth rate in China, with strong government control, has been amongst the fastest in the world. This has led to a marked shift in the attitude of many governments across Asia, Africa and Latin America, which have grabbed the opportunity to have a role model justifying a government-led approach.*

Xi's effort has led to BRICS agreeing to headquarter the New Development Bank in Shanghai. And he hasn't limited the idea just with BRICS for a development bank to oppose Western financial control. Xi proposed a $50 billion Asian Infrastructure Investment Bank when he was visiting Southeast Asia last October.

He also made a major speech last week where he addressed not only BRICS, but the rest of South America, encouraging a growing economic and political alliance. In that speech, he spoke generally of hegemony, not mentioning any specific country; but BRICS and other South American countries understood he was referring to the United States. Most of those countries are primed to find ways to oppose the U.S., its dollar, and the IMF and World Bank for their efforts at financial control. Add to that growing information of U.S. efforts through the National Security Agency's spying on those countries.

The IMF also has become a villain to struggling countries because of its demand for austerity to lower debt, but now also seen as a plot for privatizing public utilities and lands—a primary effort toward oligarchic rule of a nation.

The China-BRICS-and-Beyond train has been slow-moving. But its current activity is showing growing power in its economic engine. And, while its countries also have their own internal struggles, they're all well aware that the old warhorse U.S. and its efforts at empire have led to a nation of discontent, married to its policy of endless war, and American citizens being saddled with a nearly trillion-dollar credit card debt, over a trillion-dollar student loan debt, a national debt of $12.5 trillion (held by the public), and national infrastructure needs of $2.3 trillion. And a banking industry creeping back into financial practices that led to the 2008 global economic tragedy.

How can you turn this around? As always, *Peculiar Progressive* recommends you get organized, educated and active politically, and push your President and Congress toward national bank and media-conglomerate reform, and global cooperation rather than hegemony.

# Economic Meltdown Zombies II
**Roger Armbrust,** August 4, 2014

Just over a month ago, *Peculiar Progressive* warned you about Wall Street sneaking back into its old evil ways that led to the 2007 global economic meltdown: voraciously marketing derivatives and gouging poor-credit consumers with subprime loans.

While in the early 2000s, the large subprime loans were for mortgages, recent reports show the Wall Street wolves had turned more to small businesses.

Now add to the mix increases in subprime lending for automobiles and credit cards—a further sign that Wall Street is moving America, and the world, back toward another economic tragedy.

The numbers aren't as large as the fat meltdown of 2007, when we had been sold on the idea of a booming economy, which wasn't. But the reality is the current economy still sucks, as does employment and salaries for employees who aren't chief executives. And, if you ever blew soap bubbles from a little plastic ring as a kid, you know another reality: some bubbles may be gigantic, and some may be miniscule...but they all pop. And a factual poor-economy bubble may just pop faster than a false surging-economy bubble.

What will certainly add to the problem: Banks are taking those subprime auto loans and credit-card contracts and bundling them into securities, just like the pre-meltdown days.

## The Vital Realities for 2020 and Beyond

They're selling those securities to pension funds and insurance companies, just like the pre-meltdown days.

So we're seeing the Wall Street wolves—through these combined efforts with subprime small business loans, auto loans, and credit cards to consumers with no earning power—further feed the dangerous derivatives industry through bundling with securities. And investors, caught in a zero-interest market, are craving to find profits anywhere they can...meaning they'll take greater risks to make money. And these bundled products—that derive (and are therefore called "derivatives") from subprime loans—are risky indeed.

**The Analyst and Numbers**
William White, a Canadian economist famous for predicting the 2007 global economic meltdown, was interviewed today (Monday August 4) on the TV financial news show *Boom Bust*. White, now chairman of the Economic Development and Review Committee at the Organisation for Economic Co-operation and Development (OECD) in Paris, said today's economy is "a black box" where "there are a lot of things that can go wrong."

White specifically cited concern over looming debts.

"In the crisis of 2007, debt was allowed to build up," he said. "Unfortunately the current debts of the G20, as a proportion of GDP, are 30% higher than 2007."

He noted that both household debt and government debt worldwide are "huge." As for the U.S., he cited wage stagnation and zero interest rates as reasons that households had to take on debt, in efforts to make ends meet.

That household debt can only increase with banks' current hyper-hawking of subprime auto loans and subprime credit cards.

You can immediately see the rising problem in a July 19 *New York Times* article ominously headlined "In a Sub-Prime Bubble for Used Cars, Borrowers Pay Sky-High Rates." That article reports:

> Auto loans to people with tarnished credit have risen more than 130 percent in the five years since the immediate aftermath of the financial crisis, with roughly one in four new auto loans last year going to borrowers considered subprime — people with credit scores at or below 640.
>
> The explosive growth is being driven by some of the same dynamics that were at work in subprime mortgages. A wave of money is pouring into subprime autos, as the high rates and steady profits of the loans attract investors. Just as Wall Street stoked the boom in mortgages, some of the nation's biggest banks and private equity firms are feeding the growth in subprime auto loans by investing in lenders and making money available for loans.
>
> And, like subprime mortgages before the financial crisis, many subprime auto loans are bundled into complex bonds and sold as securities by banks to insurance companies, mutual funds and public pension funds — a process that creates ever-greater demand for loans.

The article also explained that the ratings agency Standard & Poor had warned against growing losses due to subprime auto loans. But the article said:

> Despite such warnings, the volume of total subprime auto loans increased roughly 15 percent, to $145.6 billion, in the first three months of this year from a year earlier, according to Experian, a credit rating firm.

Research shows that the subprime credit-card push from banks began as far back as 2011 (as did subprime auto loans). *The New York Times*, in an April 10, 2012 article, explained:

> *Credit card lenders gave out 1.1 million new cards to borrowers with damaged credit in December, up 12.3 percent from the same month a year earlier, according to Equifax's credit trends report released in March. These borrowers accounted for 23 percent of new auto loans in the fourth quarter of 2011, up from 17 percent in the same period of 2009, Experian, a credit scoring firm, said.*

Where does that put American households today? USA Today reported July 29:

> *More than a third of the country is in trouble when it comes to paying debts on time; 35% of Americans have debt in collections, according to a study out Tuesday from the Urban Institute, which analyzed the credit files of 7 million Americans.*
>
> *That means the debt is so far past due that the account has been closed and placed in collections. This typically happens after the bill hasn't been paid for 180 days. It also means the debt has been reported to credit bureaus and can affect someone's credit score.*
>
> *The 77 million Americans with debt in collections owe an average of $5,200. That includes debt from credit card bills, child support, medical bills, utility bills, parking tickets or membership fees.*

That's debt in collections. Overall, Americans' credit card debt is $1 trillion. Add to that an over $1 trillion college-loan debt, a national debt of $12.5 trillion (held by the public), and national infrastructure needs of $2.3 trillion, the economy is shaky.

Still, the major problem worldwide remains Wall Street's ravenous growth in derivatives. *Peculiar Progressive* earlier reported that the Bank of International Settlements (BIS) issued a report stating great concern over the derivatives

Roger Armbrust

market, now over $700 trillion, much greater than its $600 trillion at the time of the 2007 global economic crash.

The EOCD's White, who is a former economist for the BIS, said he concurred with the report's concern.

# The Sanctions Mess, Energy and You
**Roger Armbrust,** September 15, 2014

First, let's filter past all the suicidal political gestures leading toward World War III, and examine what's at the basis of this growing schism of East and West:

Economics, natural resources, and consumption. That's right. Not democracy. Not human rights. Primarily we're talking about energy—what makes a country's economy run and its people survive. Essentially we're talking about oil, natural gas, and atomic energy. How to get it and how to control it.

A paragraph of quick review: *Peculiar Progressive*has cited energy as the third (behind water and food) of our globe's five vital realities. In 2012, we wrote about how President Carter's national security adviser, Zbigniew Brzezinski, had written about how the U.S. had to control Eurasia to be the world's lone super power. In other words, control the access to energy in Eurasia. We also wrote about how President Obama called Brzezinski a genius in foreign relations.

According today to Pepe Escobar, the far-traveling journalist for *Asia Times*, America under Obama appears to still be trying to implement the Brzezinski Method and control Eurasia, now with the help of the European Union. They're hoping to corner Russia through supporting the Ukraine revolt and new right-wing government, and use NATO as a force to intimidate Russia. Escobar believes this is actually splitting Europe and Asia. And he makes sense.

**Sanctions Lead Russia to Look East**
Energy currently is high and deep on the minds of policymakers in the U.S., European Union (EU), Russia and China...the major players in the sanctions war allegedly over Ukraine. While the EU and U.S. are only yelping about Russia, and not including China in the mix, reality shows the Great Dragon to be heavily involved. And energy is the main reason.

When the Ukraine revolt broke early this year, we wrote of how the EU opposing Russia could lead to Russia cutting off its vital supply of natural gas and oil to Europe. The EU and Russia didn't really talk about it then. But now the possibility of a cutoff is becoming clearer to Europe. The EU recently agreed to find new sources of energy as insurance for a potential end to Russia's supply.

On Sept. 1, *Reuters*' story "Europe drafts emergency energy plan with eye on Russia gas shutdown" explained:

> *The European Union could ban gas exports and limit industrial use as part of emergency measures to protect household energy supplies this winter, a source told Reuters, as it braces for a possible halt in Russian gas as a result of the Ukraine crisis.*

> *Russia is Europe's biggest supplier of oil, coal and natural gas, and its pipelines through Ukraine are currently the subject of political maneuvering – not for the first time – as Europe and Moscow clash over the latter's military action in Ukraine.*

Will this also hurt Russia? Yes, in its immediate economy. But we've written about Russia's recent historic contracts with neighbor China for oil and natural gas. And this, along with the

## The Vital Realities for 2020 and Beyond

EU's growing sanctions on the Big Bear, could prove the major impetus for a real separation of East and West as Russia turns away from its economic cooperation with Europe. Instead, it would concentrate on the East, not only China, but India and other Asian countries.

As for China, it appears to be welcoming the growing cooperation with Russia. Quartz, a New York-based business-news outlet, on Sept. 1 published the story headlined "As the West tries to punish Moscow, China touts growing energy ties with Russia." That story noted:

> This past weekend, leaders from Beijing and Moscow met in the Russian capital for the 11th "China-Russia Energy Cooperation Committee.
>
> China's first vice premier Zhang Gaoli, one of the country's seven most powerful men, was there. He told China's state-run media that Beijing would "devote consistent and unswerving efforts to establishing a strategic partnership of energy cooperation with Russia."
>
> Zhang then flew to Yakutsk, Siberia to attend a ceremony today marking the opening of the $5 billion "Sila Sibiri" (Power of Siberia) gas pipeline that will ship Russian gas to China, possibly as soon as 2017. Russian President Vladimir Putin will also be there. Construction of the 4,000 kilometer (2,485 mile) pipeline will employ thousands of Russians."

Martin Henneke of The Henley Group, a Hong Kong-based division of a British-listed wealth management firm, said in a TV interview today (Monday) that he considered Russia and China as the world's "two major equity markets." That falls in line with a Sept. 2 story from moodys.com stating "Russian oil and gas producers poised to benefit from China energy deals."

Also consider this: The recent news that BRICS, the cooperative international body consisting of Brazil, Russia, China, India, and South Africa, formed a bank fund to oppose the West's International Monetary Fund and World Bank—and that Russia and China have made it clear they want to replace the U.S. dollar as the international reserve currency. It seems obvious that any continued effort by the EU and U.S. to challenge Russia could bring China, and perhaps other nations, into the conflict. Which so far has been peaceful. But may not stay that way, as we noted in our column "Hurtling Toward World War III."

**The Tipping Point**
U.S. and EU sanctions on Russia, and Moscow's response with a few smaller shutoffs, may hurt Europe and irritate America. But has anyone in the major media conglomerates looked at how Russia might truly hurt the U.S. with retaliatory sanctions yet unknown? Haven't seen it from the biggies, but a finance researcher and a former assistant Treasury Secretary under Ronald Reagan have looked at the possibilities.

Marin Katusa, Casey Research's chief energy investment strategist, in a TV interview last week emphasized this: 20% of American homes run on nuclear power. Half of those are powered by utilities who receive nuclear fuel from Russia.

Which leads to this question: Should Russia really get frustrated and stop delivering that fuel, thus shutting off power to 30 million Americans, would that lead Washington's military-industrial complex to advance to a hot war?

Then there's Paul Craig Roberts, who helped create Reaganomics in the '80s. In his Sept. 14 column entitled "Washington's War Against Russia," he opined:

> My conclusion is that the purpose of the sanctions is to break up and undermine Europe's economic and political relations with Russia. When international relations are intentionally undermined, war can be the result. Washington will continue to push sanctions against

> Russia until Russia shows Europe that there is a heavy cost of serving as Washington's tool.

Later in the column, he added:

> A Russian response to Washington would be to stop selling to the US the Russian rocket engines on which the US satellite program is dependent. This could leave the US without rockets for its satellites for six years between the period 2016 and 2022.
>
> Possibly the Russian government is worried about losing the earnings from gas and rocket engine sales. However, Europe cannot do without the gas and would quickly abandon its participation in the sanctions, so no gas revenues would be lost. The Americans are going to develop their own rocket engine anyhow, so the Russian sales of rocket engines to the US have at most about 6 more years. But the US with an impaired satellite program for six years would mean a great relief to the entire world from the American spy program. It would also make difficult US military aggression against Russia during the period.

How do you think Washington's military-industrial complex, including the spying-conscious National Security Agency (NSA), would respond to that?

As always, we urge you to get organized, educated, and active, so you can demand your Congressional representatives take care of this nation, rather than continually lead it into wars we never seem to win. Or, in the case of World War, a conflict no one will win.

# Geneva Warns of Greater Global Economic Crisis
**Roger Armbrust,** September 30, 2014

A second major global report in two months foresees current record-high debt worldwide leading to another economic meltdown tragedy, but worse than in 2007-2008.

That's the view from an international panel of senior academic and finance-industry economists. Their late September study, referred to as The Geneva Report, was released this week. It has been commissioned and published by the International Centre for Monetary and Banking Studies.

*Peculiar Progressive* discussed an earlier report with a similar warning from the Bank of International Settlements earlier this year. That column is here.

The Geneva Report, early within its 125 pages, stated:

> *Contrary to widely held beliefs, the world has not yet begun to delever [from 2008's crisis] and the global debt-to-GDP [gross domestic product] is still growing, breaking new highs...At the same time, in a poisonous combination, world growth and inflation are also lower than previously expected, also – though not only – as a legacy of the past crisis...Moreover, the global capacity to take on debt has been reduced through the*

*combination of slower expansion in real output and lower inflation.*

The report argues that developed economies like the U.S. and Europe have "been on a declining path since the 1980s". But it added that "output growth has been slowing since 2008 also in emerging markets, most prominently China."

The bottom line: all the world's economies, except perhaps for Germany, are in trouble. Economists have been citing problems with the world's central banks pushing interest rates lower and lower, hoping it would spur borrowing, investment, and job growth. At the same time, the central banks have been devaluing their currencies by printing more and more of them. The process has seemed to work for the big banks, but not for the citizenry, leading to growing personal debt and a dissolution of the middle class.

Economist and investor Jim Rickards, author of "Currency Wars" and "The Death of Money", has said that, in the U.S., the result has been this: the Federal Reserve has basically been printing money and giving it to Wall Street. The low interest rates have shortchanged savers, who can't make any money on their savings. He said last year that the result was a transfer of $500 billion in wealth from savers to the big banks.

Other officials, like Sheila Bair, former chair of the Federal Deposit Insurance Commission, have argued this: the Obama administration should prosecute Wall Street executives who caused the 2008 crisis through bundling toxic securities and nontransparent derivative sales, and throw them in jail. But Obama would prefer to settle on large monetary fines, costing bank shareholders, but leaving the Wall Street wolves free and their banks to keep profits.

As *Peculiar Progressive* has reported through this year, that policy has allowed Wall Street to continue its parasitic practices. We've shown that in columns, here and here.

Roger Armbrust

Worldwide, the European Union, the International Monetary Fund, and the Millionaire Congress in the U.S. have pushed toward austerity. *Peculiar Progressive* has shown how austerity has led to tragedies ranging from deaths to poverty in a column here.

What can you as a citizen do about all this? In America, you've a November election coming up. Get organized, get educated as to your candidates and their economic stances, and get active in electing someone who will do something to truly help America. More specifically, public executives and legislators who will make derivatives transparent, bring back the federal Glass-Steagall Act, and realistically begin to reduce Americans' $1 trillion credit card debt, over $1 trillion college-loan debt, a national debt of $12.5 trillion (held by the public), and fixing our national infrastructure needs of $2.3 trillion.

# As U.S. Austerity Deepens, Prepare for Revolution
**Roger Armbrust,** November 10, 2014

If politicians, with their pabulum "debates" leading to 2/3 of eligible voters not voting, and newscasters with their pabulum "analyses" think Americans (who are growing angrier) are going to lie down and be throttled by austerity from the newest Millionaire Congress...they'd better start paying attention.

*Peculiar Progressive*, during the deafening campaigns, heard both "debates" and news reports repeating over and over: the Republicans feverishly connecting their opponents with Everything Obama, and the Democrats howling about out-of-state billionaire money coming in their states to defeat them.

We watched Friday night's pabulum "analysis" on the *PBS News Hour*, with conservative *New York Times* columnist David Brooks and liberal syndicated columnist Mark Shields echoing the limited thought process of the pabulum campaigns. They stressed Obamacare and immigration...as if that's all that really matters to Americans. They seemed to agree that nothing would continue to get done if Congress and the president didn't, as Brooks said, start small — "Let's try kindergarten." — meaning little pieces of legislation that might make the Millionaire Politicians look good.

Roger Armbrust

In none of the Congressional campaigns we heard this year, nor from the mouths of Brooks and Shields Friday night, did anyone admit or offer solutions for what is really torturing Americans:

1. **The over $1 trillion college loan debt, which is frustrating our young, and even abusing our elderly.**
2. **The $1 trillion credit card debt, which is increasing as banks turn more to subprime lending, not only for credit cards, but auto loans, and, yes, mortgages.**
3. **The $12.5 trillion debt (owed by the public). That's the federal government's figure. Some analysts claim it's as high as $17 trillion.**
4. **The $2.3 trillion estimated need for U.S. infrastructure.**
5. **The gluttonous growth of the nontransparent (as in secret) derivativesinvestment industry, considered the chief cause for the economic meltdown of 2007-08. International banking analysts are expressing consistent concern that the derivatives racket, at a then-high of over $600 trillion in 2007, is currently over $700 trillion. Analysts are also extremely wary of the growing private debt worldwide.**
6. **The Millionaire Congress, Millionaire president, military industrial complex, Wall Street, and media conglomerate's endlessly pushing the racket of endless war. It's sucking the budget of any chance to fund solutions to America's true needs, but instead sends money to the weapons industry and the bankers who back it.**
7. **The 750,000 active military and veterans suffering from TBI (Traumatic Brain Injury) and PTSD (Post-Traumatic Stress Disorder), the tragic brain injuries caused by military conflict and leading to a continuing plague of suicides.**

8. **The skewed employment figures from government, ignoring the fact that 50 million Americans are on food stamps, 7 million Americans want full-time jobs but can't find them. And while part-time jobs are being created, the country's seeing no increase in incomes (except for top execs) and no benefits for part-time workers (many working two jobs or more) and their families.**
9. **A bubble stock market, fed not by executives investing in their corporations to create real jobs with rising employee incomes and benefits, but buying back their companies' stocks to enrich their own incomes.**
10. **The conservative assault on state and local levels against women and minority rights.**
11. **The now-turned America from a democracy to an oligarchy.**

Shields reached in his holster of accusatory sayings, chiding that if Americans don't vote, they can't complain. That's a 20th century pabulum quip.

This is the 21st century, and we are seeing a vastly frustrated electorate, increases of citizens' protests worldwide as governments attempt to continue austerity that is keeping people unemployed, and literally killing citizens who can't get health care.

This is the 21st century, where in the last two weeks 1 million people protested austerity in Rome, thousands protested police brutality in France, violent protests broke out in Brussels, hundreds of thousands have protested in Greece and Spain. Even seemingly financially sound Germany is witnessing a week of transportation strikes.

This is the 21st century, where in America, the U.S. military is arming local police departments, who are being trained no longer to befriend citizens, but control and contain legal protests while wearing armor and carrying assault rifles.

Roger Armbrust

It may not be clear yet to the cowed, politically ignorant American millions that they themselves are preparing to ignite, that they're growing closer to mirroring the revolutions of the Middle East and those escalating efforts in Europe and Hong Kong. But the American federal and local governments know it.

And it's time for you to know it. Click on the links to this column and connect the dots. And recall how this nation has a nearly 250-year history of revolution, either violent or peaceful, started by revolting against a violent, repressive dictatorial British regime.

*Peculiar Progressive* wishes all this wasn't happening, that the younger generation could take hold of their power and make government and the military-industrial complex respond to them before they're too beaten down through surveillance, intimidation, propaganda and debt. That a Gandhi would rise and challenge government with a peaceful revolution.

But we don't see that. We see government actions ready to physically challenge Constitutional civil protest. And government, banks and big business cooperating in destroying the middle class and miring Americans in debt.

We even saw it coming and expressed it in a *Peculiar Progressive* column in 2011: "Solving the Decade of Our Discontent". We wrote in 2012 about candidates refusing to discuss the Five Vital Realitiesfacing America. And they are, indeed, vital realities. It's a column in which we specify how to **peacefully** take your government back from the oligarchs, maybe. In 2013, we wrote about "Austerity as Failure and Killer".

That's why we've recommended for years that you get organized (you can't do it alone), get educated, and get active. In this vital jousting for your and your children's freedom, it's now your Constitutional move.

# China Tightens Bonds with Russia, India
**Roger Armbrust,** May 17, 2015

In the last two weeks, China has actively solidified economic, political and military ties with both Russia and India – two of its five partners in the BRICS coalition which also includes Brazil and South Africa. All five are considered to be "newly developing" countries economically.

The recent increases in solidarity with Moscow and New Delhi also push forward President Xi Jinping's vision for his new Silk Road Economic Belt and 21st Century Maritime Silk Road, establishing modern land and sea trade routes linking Asia, eastern Europe and Africa. The two projects have become simply known as "One Road, One Belt".

Russia borders China to the north, India borders Xi's nation to the south. The three countries total 39% of the world's population. Their growing cooperation represents a strong counter to the United States' aggressive efforts to control the world's economy and energy resources, particularly in Eurasia.

China over the last couple of decades has moved into competition with the U.S. for becoming the global economic leader. It's done this with heavy industrialization and aggressive exporting. It's brought great economic gain, but has caused grave domestic pollution problems, primarily with air and water. Xi's administration is altering that approach now, looking to clean up pollution and create the "New Normal," a national policy concentrating on farming and production of goods to sell at home to China's 1.35 billion citizens, which includes a growing middle class.

Xi's domestic efforts also include legal, human rights, and corporate reform. But he's also keeping a strong hand over dissent and Internet freedom. And he has been particularly visible in traveling globally, pushing on every continent to stress China's policy of noninterference in other countries' political affairs, while also making trade alliances and offering financial support for helping countries in Asia, Africa and Latin America build infrastructure – a sharp contrast to the U.S. foreign policy of aggressive military actions and surveillance in other countries. He's pointed in speeches to this contrast between China's cooperation and America's "hegemony".

The visit by China's leader over the last biweek to Russia, and hosting India's Prime Minister Narendra Modi continue Xi's efforts at pushing for a new Asia that will lead the world in the 21st Century, a mission both he and Modi have said they share.

**Russia Trip**
Xi spent May 8-10 in Russia, starting with standing next to Putin at Moscow's military parade commemorating the 70th anniversary of the end of World War II. He brought with him China's honor guard, which marched in the parade for the first time in history. He helped decorate war veterans, while Russia and China had also recently held joint military drills.

Putin and Xi's meetings also included public statements of their nations' mutual support, and cover a broad spectrum. According to a news report from Germany's international broadcaster *Deutsche Welle*:

*During Xi's latest trip to Russia, experts say, a joint statement is expected to be inked on strengthening the China-Russia partnership and advocating cooperation. According to the Chinese*

*Foreign Ministry, the two nations will also sign a number of cooperative documents in areas including energy, aerospace, taxation, finance and investment.*

Reports also said that Putin and Xi's meetings led to rail and port projects. According to Reuters:

*China Civil Engineering Construction Corporation (CCECC) said it had agreed with Russian firm Tuva Energy Industrial Corporation LLC (TEIC) to consult on and help source funds from Chinese institutions for projects including a 410 km (255 miles) track across the central southern part of Russia from Elegest to Kuragin.*

*The other projects comprise a railway line connecting the Tuvan Republic, in the same area of Russia, to western China, and a port project in eastern Russia.*

Xi's trip to Russia broadens his and Putin's relationship, strengthened over the last couple of years by major agreements of Russia to supply China with oil and natural gas, and Xi's statement earlier this year that China would financially support Russia if American and European sanctions over Ukraine began to deeply hurt Moscow. Russia seems to have ridden through the worst from the sanctions, so far.

**Modi Comes to China**
India's prime minister came to China last week for cooperative talks and the signing of $22 billion in investment and trade agreements, and to find ways to help reduce India's $48 billion trade deficit. He also wanted to discuss concerns about China's activities in the South China Sea, and its recent investment of $46 billion in power generation and other projects with India's arch rival Pakistan.

China also had its own list of wants and concerns regarding India. *The Associated Press* notes:

Roger Armbrust

*China is looking to India as a market for its increasingly high-tech goods, from high-speed trains to nuclear power plants, while India is keen to attract Chinese investment in manufacturing and infrastructure. With a slowing economy, excess production capacity and nearly $4 trillion in foreign currency reserves, China is ready to satisfy India's estimated $1 trillion in demand for infrastructure projects such as airports, roads, ports and railways...*

Beijing is also concerned about India's improving relations with Japan and the U.S. — China's chief rivals for influence in Asia. Xi's desire to build a strong personal bond with Modi can be seen as an attempt to ensure China ranks high in his affections and improve coordination on regional and international issues.

Modi's visit is a continuum of India-China cooperation expanding from Xi's visit to India which led to $20 billion of Chinese investment into India trade and infrastructure.

India is also a major player in the BRICS New Development Bank, to be based in Shanghai and directed by an Indian banker. In March, Putin signed a bill through which Russia ratified that bank agreement. We wrote about the formation of the BRICS controversial investment efforts last year for *The Clyde Fitch Report*.

India is also involved, along with leading European nations, with China's new Asian Infrastructure Investment Bank, which we wrote about here. Modi also made clear to Putin last year that Russia would remain India's chief defense supplier.

# Greece's Debt Battle: What's the Real Story?
**Roger Armbrust,** July 5, 2015

Greece's voters on Sunday, celebrating democracy, rejected the country's creditors and their dictatorial efforts to mire the nation in austerity – a no-win situation keeping Greece from reducing unemployment and building the economy.

The hardnosed Troika – the name the creditor European Commission, European Central Bank, and International Monetary Fund hate to hear themselves called – has been refusing to let Greece revise its debt repayment plan, agreed to by a previous government, not Alexis Tsipras's Syrizaparty which took control in January. Among other dictates, the Troika has refused to let Greece tax corporations, and demands that suffering pensioners – whose payments have already been reduced by 40 percent – must see deeper cuts.

The question is this: Why would Germany, with the EU's most solid economy, and the country basically controlling the relationship with Greece, not want the seat of democratic civilization to get a restructured plan — one that would allow Athens to begin growing a depressed economy with 25% unemployment (higher among youth) and gradually pay off its debt? After all, it was the West's debt forgiveness to Germany following World War II that allowed Berlin to rebuild and again become an economic power in Europe.

Roger Armbrust

The most forceful voice *Peculiar Progressive* has heard consistently answer that question is Paul Craig Roberts, a former Assistant Treasury Secretary under Ronald Reagan and one of the brain trust behind Reaganomics. He says simply that the EU (primarily Germany) and international banks want to force Greece into a position where it must sell its public assets, i.e. privatize the natural resources that belong to the Greek people.

That sounds logical. It's an effort that Wall Street and major corporations are attempting globally, e.g., Nestle's effort to privatize water worldwide for profit. It's an effort suspicioned in new international trade agreements such as the Trans-Pacific Partnership, except Washington and the corporations are forcefully attempting to keep their plot secret. In the case of Greece, it's the EU's plotting.

What will happen next? Here's the way the seasoned Roberts sees it in his column published following Sunday's Greek vote. It happens to coincide in what we were seeing in our column on Greece back in February, which was the entry into the fray by Russia and China. Says Roberts:

> As the Greek banks are closed and evidently cannot reopen without a resolution of the issue, EU inflexibility would force Greece to leave the euro and return to its own currency in order to reopen the banks. This would not require Greece's departure from the EU as the UK and one or two other EU member states have their own currencies. However, most likely the EU and Washington and Washington's Japanese, Canadian, and Australian vassals would attack the new Greek currency and drive its value in exchange markets to such a low value that Greece could not import and wealth held in Greek currency would be worthless abroad.
>
> An inflexible EU creates conditions for Russia and China to act. These two powerful nations have the means to finance Greece and to bring Greece into the economic

> *relationships established by these two countries and by the BRICS.*

That, of course, would send Washington's neoconservatives both in the White House and Congress into fits. Obama has been consistently attempting to find ways to control the EU and NATO, crush Russia's economy and egg it into war, and stifle China's growing role as the globe's economic leader, even saber-rattling against Beijing.

*Peculiar Progressive*, therefore, sees the Greek vote leading to the possible unraveling of the European Union, which we wrote about here, including Greece receiving overtures from Russia. The problem is this: a uniting of Greece with Russia and China could move Washington closer to igniting a military confrontation. And since the U.S., Russia and China all have enough nuclear weapons to send Earth into fireworks that can be seen from distant galaxies, it could be the world's final conflict.

Roberts is a bit more optimistic. We'll end with his column's closing view:

> *The Greek drama is far from over. Pray that the Russian and Chinese governments understand that rescuing Greece is the start of the process of unravelling NATO, Washington's mechanism for bringing conflict to Russia and China. The One Percent have Italy and Spain targeted for looting, and eventually France and Germany herself. If the Greek people rescue themselves from the clutches of the EU, Italy and Spain could follow.*
>
> *As Southern Europe departs NATO, Washington's ability to create violence in Ukraine is diminished as the world realigns against the Evil Empire.*
>
> *Washington's power could suddenly diminish, thus saving the world from the nuclear war toward which Washington's neoconservatives are pushing.*

# Greece, Others Falling to Predator Creditors
**Roger Armbrust,** July 20, 2015

Greece has shockingly agreed to another unsustainable financial bailout meant to pay off previous bailouts rather than receive money to help the Greek citizens suffering from austerity. Only now it's worse. Greece is preparing to give up its citizens' vital resources and assets such as water and energy to foreign multinational corporations or oligarchs.

What should Greece do, that *Peculiar Progressive*thought the communist Greek Prime Minister Alexis Tsipras would do but didn't? Walk away from the predator creditors' demands, refuse to pay the debts, and move on.

This isn't a new idea. David Stockman, who was Ronald Reagan's budget director — and often fought with Reagan, criticizing his tax cuts — publicly called in February for Greece to do just that:

> For its part, Greece stands at a fork in the road. Syriza can move aggressively to recover Greece's democratic sovereignty or it can desperately cling to the faltering currency and financial machinery of the Euro zone. But it can't do both...
>
> ...Indeed, the crony capitalist corruption and

> *craven appeasement of the banks and financial markets that have become the modus operandi there are inexorably destroying the EU and single currency. By fleeing the euro and ECB with all deliberate speed, therefore, the Greeks will give-up nothing except the opportunity to be lashed to the greatest monetary train wreck ever recorded.*

Also, Paul Craig Roberts, a former Assistant Treasury Secretary under Reagan and one of the brain trust behind Reaganomics, basically has said that the EU (primarily Germany) and international banks want to force Greece into a position where it must sell its public assets, i.e. let foreign multinationals privatize the natural resources that belong to the Greek people. And he added earlier this month that Washington has an even more greedy cause in play:

> *Washington has a higher interest than the interests of the US financial interests who purchased discounted sovereign debt with a view toward profiting from a deal that pays 100 cents on the dollar. Washington also has higher interest than the interests of the European One Percent intent on using Greece's indebtedness to loot the country of its national assets. Washington's higher interest is the protection of the unity of the EU and, thereby, NATO, Washington's mechanism for bringing conflict to Russia.*

Roberts also foresees greedy money eventually going after other European sovereign nations, saying, *"The One Percent have Italy and Spain targeted for looting, and eventually France and Germany herself."*

Interesting, eh, to see two Republican economic stalwarts opposed to private money overtaking the public and its assets?

Why Greece's Tsipras, an active communist politico since high school, would succumb to the predator creditors is puzzling

Roger Armbrust

indeed. Perhaps he's stalling so Greece can eventually walk away from the debt and join BRICS, which we thought we saw coming this spring. Or, and it wouldn't be the first time we've seen a politcian go bad, perhaps he's worked out a deal with the predator creditors to secure himself and his family financially. Let's hope this suspicion never proves fact.

**What Greece is Attempting to Sell**
Whatever his reasoning, with his capitulating to the predator creditors' demands Tsipras has deepened his people's burdens to austerity, and now having to sell the country's major sources for providing services and national income. Here's what *The Washington Post* listed as the major assets on the auction block:

Athens Water Supply and Sewerage Company (will sell 61 percent of shares); Public Power Corporation (7.5 million of Greece's 11 million population subscribe to the service); Hellenic Petroleum (2/3 of Greece's refinery capacity, with 35 percent of company up for auction); Athens International Airport ("Greece is holding on to 25 percent of shares in the airport, which was opened in 2001, but the development fund is selling off 30 percent of shares. The rest are held by private corporations and several families.")

Other resources the Post lists in the top ten sale offerings include four thermal springs; 15 boutique hotels; 90 percent of Hellenic Post, the nation's post office system with 750 outlets; Peace and Friendship Stadium; Egatia Odos Motorway, "670 kilometers (416 miles) of scenic Greek byway".

Meanwhile, Greece's people are captive to debt payments totalling 280 billion euros through 2054, according to the *Wall Street Journal*. The *Journal* has itemized the debt-payment schedule here.

**Who's Set to Follow Greece?**
Earlier this month the British newspaper *The Guardian* cited a recent report from The Jubilee Debt Campaign, a coalition of UK

national organizations and local groups calling for the poorest countries' unjust and unpayable debts to be cancelled. The report listed 20 other countries suffering their own debt crises.

The in-danger debtor countries include, besides Greece: EU countries Ireland, Portugal and Spain. The rest of the 20 countries involved in current government external debt crises, as well as 14 other nations "at high risk of government external debt crisis" are listed in the *Guardian* story here.

Also, on July 16, *Vox*, a general interest news site, published a chart showing Greece as only one of a number of countries "being strangled by the euro". You can find that chart here.

These countries all have the potential to fall prey to the predator creditors who keep pulling the governments deeper into unsustainable debt, leading to the nations giving up their natural resources and assets: in other words, the slow, or not so slow, privatizing of the world into the hands of The One Percent and their crony multinationals.

# Unsustainable: Debt Rising for Students, Individuals
**Roger Armbrust,** August 3, 2015

Following the U.S. general elections last November, *Peculiar Progressive* complained of 11 major issues facing the country that candidates avoided discussing during their campaigns. The first two issues dealt with citizens' personal debt:

- **The over $1 trillion college loan debt, which is frustrating our young, and even abusing our elderly**
- **The $1 trillion credit card debt, which is increasing as banks turn more to subprime lending, not only for credit cards, but auto loans, and, yes, mortgages.**

The student and personal debt continue to grow as we move through 2015.

**Student Loan Debt**
The national student loan debt now stands at over $1.2 trillion, according to an Aug. 2 article by The Motley Fool, a very serious multimedia financial-services company despite its bring-a-smirk name. Other sources see it higher.

The class of 2015 graduated with an average student debt of $35,051, according to *MarketWatch*, calling it "the most student debt in history," adding:

## The Vital Realities for 2020 and Beyond

*That's about $2,000 more than their peers who graduated in 2014, though the share of students graduating with debt remained roughly the same as last year at about 70%.*

*A combination of stagnant wages, declining federal and state funding to schools on a per-student basis, and rising tuition has meant that families 'have only two real choices' when it comes to paying for college: borrow more or try to send their kids to a cheaper school, said [Edvisors.com publisher Mark] Kantrowitz.*

The Motley Fool points out the student loan debt is not only high, it's confusing. And it can mire graduates into a debt cycle foiling efforts at marriage and homebuying, or even renting:

*Student loans are different from many other forms of debt, with special rules and programs having to do with repayment options, loan consolidation, and even how they're treated in bankruptcy...*

*...Starting in 1976, loans offered by the federal government or non-profit colleges and universities had to be repaid, no matter the circumstances. This made sense, as these organizations were often loaning the money out at lower interest rates than one could find on the open market, backed by private companies.*

*Starting in 1984, private loans for student tuition were added to the list of non-dischargeable debts. This means that even if you file for bankruptcy, your student loan lender can have your wages garnished from your paycheck until the loan is paid off in full.*

Back in February, James McAndrews, Executive Vice President and Director of Research for the Federal Reserve Bank of New York, stressed the rising problem that student loan debt was creating for the U.S. economy:

Roger Armbrust

> *Student loans seem like a good part of the solution, but over the past decade our reliance on loans for funding higher education has increased and we are learning that they have many problems and implications we had not sufficiently understood or considered...*
>
> *... between 2004 and 2014, the total student debt in the US tripled from $364 billion in 2004 to $1.16 trillion in 2014... Between 2004 and 2014, the number of borrowers increased by 92 percent from 23 million borrowers to 43 million. In the same period, average debt per borrower increased by 74 percent, from about $15,000 to $27,000.*

That brings us to over midway through 2015, where that $27,000 average student loan debt has increased to over $35,000. With no relief in sight. A truly abusive position which the federal government, banks, and higher tuitions have forced on our young people.

Is there a solution? Yes. There are countries that offer free higher education, so their young people can graduate and immediately begin contributing to the economy rather than be stifled by debt. The press has begun to write about those, such as articles in Salon, and Wikipedia gives you an overview of free education globally. Also at least two announced presidential candidates — the Green Party's Jill Stein and socialist Democrat Bernie Sanders — have free higher ed in their platforms.

**Personal Debt**
Meanwhile, the monster scaring economic analysts globally is the rising worldwide private debt which could lead us into another global economic meltdown. Analysts were grumbling over it as far back as March 2014, as you can see in this analysis on *Daily Ticker*.

*Peculiar Progressive* showed international debt concerns in columns here, here, and Wall Street's continuing manipulation of credit here.

## The Vital Realities for 2020 and Beyond

For an overview on the growing problem in U.S. personal debt, check out the U.S. National Debt Clock at www.usdebtclock.org. Its figures are garnered from federal agencies including the Treasury Department, Congressional Budget Office, and U.S. Census Bureau.

Looking at the clock on Aug. 3, we see personal U.S. debt at $16.9 trillion. Mortgage debt at $13.5 trillion. Student loan debt now closing in on $1.4 trillion (real-time total via the Federal Reserve). Credit card debt at $904 billion. Personal debt per U.S. citizen: $52,622. Median income: $28,868.

Good night, and good luck.

# Oligarchs, Central Banks and Our Sinking Economy

**Roger Armbrust,** January 26, 2016

In the ski resort of Davos, Switzerland this past week, the global oligarchs and their lessers gathered to gab about the sinking global economy at the World Economic Forum.

We can best define "global oligarchs" by looking at the global-inequality report — "An Economy for the 1%" — Oxfam America released just before the Davos gathering. Oxfam America is a part of Oxfam, an international confederation of 17 organizations working in some 94 countries worldwide, seeking solutions to global poverty and injustice.

The Oxfam report emphasized:

- In 2015, just 62 individuals had the same wealth as 3.6 billion people – the bottom half of humanity. This figure is down from 388 individuals as recently as 2010.
- The wealth of the richest 62 people has risen by 44% in the five years since 2010 – that's an increase of more than half a trillion dollars ($542 bn), to 1.76 trillion.
- Meanwhile, the wealth of the bottom half fell by just over a trillion dollars in the same period – a drop of 41%.

You can bet that the Big 62 or their reps were rubbing elbows at Davos with multinational corporate heads and politicians.

## The Vital Realities for 2020 and Beyond

Reports from Davos showed much talk about four major areas of concern in the global economy: (1) the "volatility" of the Chinese economy; (2) plunging stock markets; (3) sinking oil prices, and (4) debt crisis in the emerging markets, led by BRICS (Brazil, Russia, India, China, and South Africa).

*Peculiar Progressive*, however, sees global private and public debt as the real, long-term problem, spurred by the world's central banks colluding to hold interest rates down. For example, Jim Rickards, author of the books *Currency Wars* and *The Death of Money*, complained in 2014 that the Federal Reserve's zero interest rates had led to a transfer of $500 billion from American savers to Wall Street banks. That, along with decades of stagnant incomes and recent lack of full-time employment for U.S. workers, has led to dependence on credit to make ends meet, and the dissolution of the middle class.

We wrote in 2014 about William White, who predicted the 2008 global financial meltdown, expressing grave concern about the growing worldwide private and public debt. White is former chief economist for the Bank of International Settlements, and currently chair of the review committee for the Swiss-based Organisation for Economic Cooperation and Development (OECD). He was interviewed last week before Davos by the UK's *Telegraph*, in which he warned of even deeper concerns about the growing global debt. Summarizing White, the *Telegraph* reported:

> Mr. White said Europe's creditors are likely to face some of the biggest haircuts. European banks have already admitted to $1 trillion of non-performing loans: they are heavily exposed to emerging markets and are almost certainly rolling over further bad debts that have never been disclosed.
>
> The European banking system may have to be recapitalized on a scale yet unimagined, and new "bail-in" rules mean that any deposit holder above the guarantee of €100,000 will have to help pay for it...

> ...Mr. White said stimulus from quantitative easing and zero rates by the big central banks after the Lehman crisis leaked out across east Asia and emerging markets, stoking credit bubbles and a surge in dollar borrowing that was hard to control in a world of free capital flows.
>
> The result is that these countries have now been drawn into the morass as well. Combined public and private debt has surged to all-time highs...

**What's the Answer?**

We believe White and his committee from The Group of Thirty (G30) in Washington, DC have provided the logical long-term solution in an October 2015 report: "Fundamentals of Central Banking: Lessons from the Crisis". The G30 is an international body of financiers and academics who examine economic/financial issues and their consequences. In its executive summary, the report observes:

> ...the ultimate resolution of crises that have their roots in excessive credit creation and debt accumulation often can only be accomplished through arms of government other than the central bank...
>
> ...Supportive actions by central banks can be useful, but there are serious risks involved if governments, parliaments, public authorities, and the private sector assume central bank policies can substitute for the structural and other policies they should take themselves. The principal risk is that excessive reliance on ever more central bank action could aggravate the underlying systemic problems and delay or prevent the necessary structural adjustments.

So there you have it: Our political policymakers have continuously passed the responsibility buck to unelected manipulators in the central banks; and politicians have "kicked the can" down

## The Vital Realities for 2020 and Beyond

the road for making any legislative reform to take care of their citizens and national and global economies.

So, do you see how important the coming 2016 November elections are, at every level of government? And particularly in the U.S. for electing a Congress who must take responsibility for basic economic reform policies?

Following the 2014 November national elections, we wrote a column listing 11 major economic areas where Congress has let us down. You can read those in the column, "As Austerity Deepens, Prepare for Revolution".

Currently Congress consists of a majority of millionaires who cater to Wall Street and the military-industrial complex, encouraging the racket of endless war and debt growth. They won't change our democracy-turned-oligarchy. Only a citizen-led revolution at the polls might do it. So you'll have to get organized, educated to issues, and active to see America become a nation with a sound economy for you and your children.

# This is the Economic Plan All Candidates Need
**Roger Armbrust,** March 11, 2016

Just a reminder: elections this year don't occur only for U.S. president. A plethora of other important elections are taking place nationwide for federal, state and local offices. And, at every level, any politician worth his or her salt better have an economic plan to help all the people.

In late February, the Brookings Institution — the Washington think tank respected by both conservatives and liberals — issued such a general plan for most of the population: "Remaking Economic Development – The Markets and Civics of Continuous Growth and Prosperity". Its author: Amy Liu, VP and Director of Brookings' Metropolitan Policy Program.

Liu's plan is designed for U.S. cities and metro areas, where most people live and most jobs are created. As the plan states:

> **The goal:** To put a regional economy on a trajectory of higher growth (growth) that increases the productivity of firms and workers (prosperity) and raises standards of living for all (inclusion), thus achieving deep prosperity—growth that is robust, shared, and enduring.

She lists five "action principles": (1) set the right goals; (2) grow from within; (3) boost trade; (4) invest in people and skills; (5) connect place, i.e. local communities and regional opportunities.

We're specifically interested in Number 4: invest in people and skills. This means more than just appropriating money. It also means creating an environment for young people to be educated in the pursuit of happiness: growing creatively, leading them to choose companions, partners and work that enlarge their given skills and therefore benefit the community.

In short, every human needs to keep pursuing education and growth throughout life, whether college, trade schools or self-education. This author welcomes a book by Dr. Tony Armstrong: *Educating Angels: Teaching for the Pursuit of Happiness*. It's published by Parkhurst Brothers, Publishers, where I worked as editor a few years earlier. Dr. Armstrong's book offers a guide to respecting students and guiding them to discover happy, productive lives.

We're also concerned about how newly elected officials and community leaders might apply specifics to a portion of Brookings' general goal: raising the "standards of living for all (inclusion)". Here are just three specific areas where voters should challenge candidates to work and raise standards of living:

1. Removing from our young the burden of college loan debt, now at over $1 trillion. It's affecting the young's ability to invest in homes and new families, and causing a destructive wear on psyches.
2. Turning corporate greed away from buybacks of stock to raising employee incomes and benefits, which have been stagnant or fallen in recent decades. And creating full-time jobs which lead to increased production and company growth, rather than part-time jobs which filter any profit to executives and stockholders, and not sharing it with employees.
3. Repairing and sustaining infrastructure, thus avoiding

Roger Armbrust

> major tragic problems like the lead-poisoning of water in Flint, Michigan and other areas.

These are only three of America's many problems, major ones we outlined following the November 2014 elections in our column, "As U.S. Austerity Deepens, Prepare for Revolution". As you read it, consider which issues directly affect you, your family and others in your community.

We need candidates and public officials who value the worth of the individual and community over the worth of the corporation and career. And we need an electorate who demands it of their elected officials.

Consider these points as you get organized, educated and active yourselves – positively affecting the outcome of this year's November elections. Oh, and vote!

# How Hillary Must Change, for Us
**Roger Armbrust,** August 8, 2016

If Hillary Clinton does indeed become America's next president, she must change the course she has been traveling in three major areas: (1) an economy benefiting Wall Street's wolves, (2) endless war which could lead to world war, and (3) pushing for a police state. Her history shows she won't want to change, in fact may feel she can't change in this oligarchy called America. But she must for us, the people. And only you, the voter, can make her change.

**The Economy Benefiting Wall Street's Wolves**
The millionaire candidate has reaped millions financially from Wall Street, including obscene sums for speeches to big-money audiences, and she won't reveal those speech transcripts. It's difficult to see her stepping away from the Wall Street wolves and their money factory, but she must break from them if she is going to govern and care for the American people.

This includes keeping her husband, former President Bill Clinton, away from any say involving the economy. She said during her summer campaign she was going to rely on him on economic matters. That would be a mistake.

Why? Because it was President Clinton's ties to Wall Street which led him to sign the two harmful pieces of legislation which

Roger Armbrust

led to the 2008 global meltdown: the Gramm-Leach-Bliley Act, which scrapped the economically vital Glass-Steagall Act; and the Commodity Futures Modernization Act of 2000 which quelled federal and state governments from regulating the $600 trillion over-the-counter derivatives industry.

The Glass-Steagall Act had been created following the Great Depression. It separated commercial banks, which handled checking and savings accounts and home mortgages, from the Wall Street wolves and their investment gambling which led to the Depression. After signing Gramm-Leach-Bliley, Clinton stated that Glass-Steagall "is no longer relevant." He couldn't have been more wrong.

Wall Street continues sucking trillions through derivatives. And it also has returned in recent years to the parasitic practice of subprime loans. Subprime mortgages helped cause the 2008 meltdown. Now Wall Street is not only involved in subprime mortgages, but has spread into subprime small-business loans, subprime auto loans, subprime credit cards, and subprime college-student loans. We've written in-depth about these issues here, here, and here.

Hillary Clinton's love for Wall Street includes close ties to major corporations, such as Walmart, on whose board she served for six years. It also means her flipflop on major trade agreements like the Trans-Pacific Partnership – which she favored before her candidacy, then has opposed as a candidate – will see her flip again as president and support the TPP and TTIP with Europe. Critics shout that both these secret trade agreements are more the creation of corporate forts than trade pacts, giving corporations powers that transcend nations' powers.

You might notice that the National Democratic Party in its platform did not include opposition to TPP, a clear sign of where Mrs. Clinton is going. We've written about TPP and TTIP here and here.

## Endless War Leading to World War

We've written in detail about President Obama's continuum of endless war ranging from killing innocents with drones to expanding previous presidents' efforts at world rule. See our column "Obama Widens Carter's, Bush's Global-Rule Policies".

Mrs. Clinton has been an ally in these global-rule policies. And she has been a stalwart supporter of Obama's "Asian Pivot," the U.S. effort to send 40% of America's military to encircle Eurasia as a threat to both Russia and China. In fact, she wrote about it in 2011 in a column headlined "America's Pacific Century".

This is a major problem. Russia and China are not Vietnam, Afghanistan, Iraq or Syria. They're ancient civilizations like the smaller nations, but they are not the smaller nations. They are major world powers who will not accept invasion nor threats of invasion and war, nor efforts to control their seas.

No doubt they've read Mrs. Clinton's column on the Asian Pivot. And both Russia and China continue to respond to it.

Russia and China have also seen Obama begin a 30-year, $1 trillion rebuilding of America's nuclear arsenal. It has led those two countries to expand their nuclear capabilities. We wrote about this in our column "Nukebuild: This Will Not End Well".

We've also written about Andrew J. Bacevich, a retired Army colonel, Vietnam veteran, military historian, academic and best-selling author who has hammered the U.S. four-decade Middle East military policy. He has expressed grave concerns about Mrs. Clinton, calling her a hawk. And when someone with Bacevich's credentials warns of the Democratic candidate's neo-con war obsession, you should listen. You can read that column here.

If you read the column, you'll also see Bacevich has no stomach for Trump either, comparing his personality to that of a "five year old".

## Police-State Push

We wrote in late March of Hillary Clinton wanting to push America into a deeper police state in our column "Hillary Joins the Police-State Parade".

In her nomination acceptance speech, and other speeches, she prefers the politically acceptable term "security". But such a generality is dangerous, and can easily move to more surveillance, more militarizing of police, and less freedom for Americans.

So there it is. We see the direction Hillary Clinton has been traveling. She won't change this direction — or even if she might want to, the oligarchy, and its puppet Millionaire Congress, won't let her — unless you get organized (you can't do it alone), get educated to these issues, and get active in letting her know she needs to change course, for our own good, and the good of the world.

Of course, you could greatly help the cause at the November polls by cleaning the millionaires out of Congress and replacing them with public servants who really mirror the U.S. public, like John Adams called for in his landmark paper "Thoughts on Government".

# At Davos & UN, Xi Firms China's Global-Leader Status

**Roger Armbrust,** January 23, 2017

China President Xi Jinping last week took center stage at two international gatherings: Davos and the United Nations. His speeches there helped solidify China's calculated effort to establish itself as a global economic and political leader.

Davos, sponsored by the Swiss-based World Economic Forum, gathers the globe's business, political, and academic shakers to "shape global, regional, and industry agendas". It's been a trademark of the West's control of the world economy. Xi's arrival was the first appearance by a Chinese leader, and his giving the keynote address symbolizes the West's understanding of China's established international economic influence.

Xi's Davos speech repeatedly emphasized "economic globalization" and international cooperation, a sharp contrast to Donald Trump, who at the week's end would take the oath of office as the new President of the United States. Trump's rhetoric and first actions as president have stressed American nationalism and opposition to globalization. Without naming names, Xi alluded to Trump in his Davos speech, stating:

> We should commit ourselves to growing an open global economy to share opportunities and interests through opening-up and achieve win-win outcomes. One should

> not just retreat to the harbor when encountering a storm, for this will never get us to the other shore of the ocean. We must redouble efforts to develop global connectivity to enable all countries to achieve inter-connected growth and share prosperity. We must remain committed to developing global free trade and investment, promote trade and investment liberalization and facilitation through opening-up and say no to protectionism. Pursuing protectionism is like locking oneself in a dark room. While wind and rain may be kept outside, that dark room will also block light and air. No one will emerge as a winner in a trade war.

Xi followed his Davos speech with an address at the UN's European headquarters in Geneva. Speaking on China's place in international affairs, Xi became more specific, including China's goal for relationships with other countries, including the U.S.:

> We will build a circle of friends across the whole world... We will strive to build a new model of major country relations with the United States, a comprehensive strategic partnership of coordination with Russia, a partnership for peace, growth, and reform among different civilizations and a partnership of unity and cooperation with BRICS countries.

But at the UN, Xi also alluded to the U.S., contrasting China's goals with any "hegemon":

> Trade protectionism and self-isolation will benefit no one...Big countries should treat smaller countries as equals instead of acting as a hegemon imposing their will on others...

> ...We always put people's rights and interests above everything else and we have worked hard to develop and uphold human rights. China will never seek expansion, hegemony or sphere of influence.

## China's Economic Evolution

In recent decades, China built an industrial base that has thrust it into a global economic leadership role. Its economic progress, according to the World Bank, allowed China to lift "more than 600 million people out of poverty between 1981 and 2004." China's population is 1.2 billion, or about one-seventh of the globe's people.

Notes the World Bank in its China profile:

> *Rapid growth and urbanization have been central to China's poverty reduction in the past 25 years, as have a number of reforms, including the opening of the economy to global trade and investment. Even as the overall level of poverty has dropped, inequality has increased, and remaining poverty has become concentrated in rural and minority areas.*

> *The government has implemented a series of programs to identify and reach those who have not reaped the full benefits of China's rapid growth. Prior to 1990, China's poverty reduction program depended primarily on single-year and single-sector projects that were not capable of overcoming poverty in the worst-affected areas. In addition, the statistical system used to assess where the poor were located was limited.*

This economic growth also has led to dire environmental problems, including both air and water pollution. Xi's administration has made major efforts to solve those, but it will take years to accomplish. They've begun to turn away from coal, signing major contracts with Russia for supplying China with oil and natural gas. And Xi's administration has also pushed for sustainable energy projects, leading Beijing to a world leadership role in green energy. This, in turn, led to Xi joining President Obama last year in signing the Paris Climate Accord, the world's major effort to combat climate change.

Meanwhile, Xi has spent the last couple of years on a global quest for cooperative economic development. He has visited continents from Africa to South America to Europe, arranging trade and security pacts. And he has stressed infrastructure construction, specifically in Africa and South America, where Chinese companies can come in and help countries build highways, railroads, and businesses to increase jobs for local citizens and trade advantages with China.

While doing this, Xi has preached how China will not interfere with a country's internal affairs, and opposes any efforts at hegemony.

Xi has also led China in an ambitious global plan for economic development: The One Belt, One Road Initiative. Its two main components are the land-based "Silk Road Economic Belt" (SREB) and oceangoing "Maritime Silk Road" (MSR). The area covers primarily Asia and Europe, comprising about 60 countries. Different projects are springing up within this. The latest was seen this past week in the UK, when the first train from China arrived in London.

**U.S. vs China**

This Chinese economic growth has been welcomed by U.S. industries who have experienced large sales with China, ranging from Boeing planes, to iPhones, to U.S. corn.

But China's success has not been welcomed in Washington. Obama has concentrated on trying to carry on the U.S. hegemonic effort to keep America as the world's lone superpower, including finding ways to control Eurasia, the connected landmass of Europe and Asia. This means having to try and control Russia and China.

Obama tried to implement the "Asian Pivot", hoping to limit China trade by excluding Beijing from the now-failed Trans-Pacific Partnership. He opposed China's efforts to form the Asia International Infrastructure Bank; but China was able to bring countries, including the U.K. and others in Europe, together to form the bank.

Obama also tried saber rattling, including challenging China over control of the South China Sea. China has responded by tightening its bond with Russia; the two nations now cooperate in military drills in those waters.

Trump has consistently castigated China while basically praising Russia's leader Vladimir Putin. Time will tell if Trump can influence the China-Russia bond. But don't look for China to back down from any U.S. threat. Beijing has come too far. It's preaching peace and cooperation, but it also has made clear it's prepared to meet any American challenge.

**Surveillance Versus Freedom**

# Will the U.S. Indict the Wikileaks Leader?
January 27, 2011

**By Roger Armbrust**
**Special to the Clyde Fitch Report**

Although the U.S. government would undoubtedly love to find an American felony law which WikiLeaks founder Julian Assange has broken — then extradite, try, convict and jail him — it appears that time has not yet arrived.

According to a Congressional Research Service (CRS) report issued last month, government precedent has been *not* to prosecute anyone in Assange's journalistic position for having leaked classified information publicly.

"Leaks of classified information to the press have only rarely been punished as crimes, and we are aware of no case in which a publisher of information obtained through unauthorized disclosure by a government employee has been prosecuted for publishing it," explains legislative attorney Jennifer K. Elsea in her Dec. 6 CRS report, "Criminal Prohibitions on the Publication of Classified Defense Information." "There may be First Amendment implications that would make such a prosecution difficult, not to mention political ramifications based on concerns about government censorship."

Roger Armbrust

Since Assange is an Australian activist and journalist, Elsea further points out,

> **"To the extent that the investigation implicates any foreign nationals whose conduct occurred entirely overseas, any resulting prosecution may carry foreign policy implications related to the exercise of extraterritorial jurisdiction and whether suspected persons may be extradited to the United States under applicable treaty provisions."**

According to *The New York Times*, Attorney General Eric Holder has stated that the government is conducting "a very serious, active, ongoing investigation that is criminal in nature" regarding Assange. President Obama ordered that last summer, when WikiLeaks began releasing classified Pentagon documents regarding the U.S. invasions of Afghanistan and Iraq.

But more recently, that dramatic stance has lessened as U.S. officials softened their view of the seriousness of Wikileaks' revelations. Times reporter Elizabeth Bumiller wrote in October that U.S. Defense Secretary Robert M. Gates had sent an Aug. 16 letter to Sen. Carl Levin, chairman of the Senate Armed Services Committee, diffusing the threat of the WikiLeaks Pentagon-document revelations.

In his letter, Gates told Levin, "...the review to date has not revealed any sensitive intelligence sources and methods compromised by this disclosure."

Times blogger Robert Mackey recapped the Bumiller report in his Jan. 19 post where he wrote about the State Department also judging WikiLeaks' other mass release of diplomatic cables as basically unharmful to security. Mackey wrote that an unnamed Congressional aide told Reuters the leak "was embarrassing but not damaging."

Those two news reports would deem to dampen any Obama Administration efforts to go after Assange in court or have him extradited to the U.S. When added to precedence cited by attorney Elsea in her CRS review, a government case would seem even weaker.

But that's just so far.

If other cables or documents are published, the government would study them to see if the WikiLeaks founder or others might be culpable. Elsea's CRS report lists possible specific statutes which might apply, including the federal Espionage Act.

Assange, meanwhile, has his own problems overseas. He has been arrested in England, and is fighting extradition to Sweden on a warrant for alleged sex offenses. The timing of the arrest seems to smack of a family of Big Brothers seeking to down the Little Guy Who Roared. Time will tell if Assange has committed crimes or been set up.

Meanwhile — despite the U.S. government now playing it down — Assange's actions with WikiLeaks have created a hot plate that's scorching authority worldwide, causing governments and freedom advocates to examine their responsibilities in the age of digital information flow.

We've come a long way technologically since 1971, when Daniel Ellsberg stooped over a cranky copy machine, snailing out piles of the Pentagon Papers to sneak to the press. In 2010, Assange was able to globally distribute thousands of documents to limitless viewers by basically clicking a mouse.

Yet the struggle for freedom of information hasn't changed. It's only become more complex. During the Vietnam War, the government's attempt to quell the public release of the Pentagon Papers saw a defiant effort by America's major newspapers. When the U.S. Supreme Court, at President Nixon's behest,

Roger Armbrust

ordered The New York Times to cease publishing the Ellsberg-leaked documents, other papers took up the cause and printed them. After 15 days, the high court ordered the Times could again begin publishing them.

With the WikiLeaks releases, news organizations picked up the information. But the situation became more complicated, and volatile, via the Internet. When British police arrested Assange, and a Brit court denied him bail, Wikileaks supporters internationally began digitally tossing bugs into a number of corporate websites, either shutting out those attempting to do business, or slowing access to a crawl Eventually, Assange was allowed bail.

The cyber attacks on the corporate sites by WikiLeaks supporters must have the Obama Administration considering what might happen should the U.S. extradite Assange, or prosecute anyone else involved in the leaks. Would such action ignite another round of cyber attacks on American businesses, which have been struggling through two years of a tanked economy that's been scraping out of its abyss? Could the earlier cyber attacks have only been a test run, with plans for a larger assault in the offing? Could the primary barrage have inspired other digital guerillas to come down from the hills and join the WikiLeaks efforts? This past week Al Jazeera released information about leaked cables from several sources regarding negotiations between the Palestinians and Israel, a sign that the WikiLeaks activities could be inspiring similar efforts from other whistleblowers.

This international spread of leaks could be creating the potential for an even more complex conflict in controlling the flow of information, even a long cyber war.

Such an occurrence would no doubt provide the government fuel to take dictatorial control of the Internet, which is a threat that digital democracy advocates have already been fighting

# The Vital Realities for 2020 and Beyond

against for years. Note the net-neutrality controversy currently taking place in Washington.

What could be looming for us, from 2011 on, is a decade of real digital revolution, involving the public's right to know and to freely communicate ideas and opinions.

Then again, what more could government expect? After a decade in which the Bush Administration and Congress invaded Afghanistan for gas and oil (see "Obama, Congress and Our Afghan Reality"), lied about weapons of mass destruction to invade Iraq, allowed Dick Cheney's Halliburton to rake in billions of dollars off those two quagmires, scrapped habeas corpus by establishing Guantanamo and a network of secret torture-prisons, ignored regulation of the finance industry leading to a world economic meltdown, and the Obama Administration and a new Congress following in many of those footsteps, government surely knew some world citizens still craving freedom would revolt. And the cyber eggheads outside government would prove the most dangerous at efforts to shutting down the military-industrial complex.

If you've any question how far we've come toward Orwell's Big Brother existence, check out online Frontline's "Are We Safer" which aired Jan. 18 on PBS: a look at the National Security Agency's ever-growing terrorism-industrial complex.

Seeing that could tell us that the struggle for freedom may be too late. Or it may just be beginning. As great legal cases, the press, art, literature, theater and films often remind us, it all depends on the individual's spirit.

# Forming America: John Adams' Thoughts on Government
**Roger Armbrust,** May 4, 2012

In the sweltering Philadelphia spring of 1776 — before the signing of the Declaration of Independence, and after Massachusetts' John Adams had established himself as a leader in the Second Continental Congress — he wrote down his letter/essay *Thoughts on Government: Applicable to the Present State of the American Colonies.*

Delegates from other colonies had approached Adams requesting these thoughts. They were responding to efforts back home to form state constitutions.

Adams wrote just under 3,000 words, a powerful philosophy which would lead the forming of several state documents and the Constitution of the United States. Within those words, he actually profiles and analyzes America's federal government today-first, what it should be, and second, what it really is.

First, Adams stresses:

> ...the form of government which communicates ease, comfort, security, or, in one word, happiness, to the greatest number of persons, and in the greatest degree, is the best.

Happiness. It's a keyword his friend Thomas Jefferson also used in finalizing the Declaration of Independence, the Congress's announcement to the world of an American Revolution that had already begun: "...endowed by their Creator with certain unalienable Rights, that among these are Life, Liberty and the pursuit of Happiness."

Adams notes that, to provide Happiness for its people, a government must possess "virtue": "All sober inquirers after truth, ancient and modern, pagan and Christian, have declared that the happiness of man, as well as his dignity, consists in virtue," says Adams in his letter/essay.

But then Adams quickly contrasts those requirements for good government to what existed at the time, and certainly flagrantly exists in our government today:

*Fear is the foundation of most governments; but it is so sordid and brutal a passion, and renders men in whose breasts it predominates so stupid and miserable, that Americans will not be likely to approve of any political institution which is founded on it.*

But we Americans today have approved it, primarily by not educating ourselves to the basics of good government and a solid economy. And therefore we have let our federal government envelop us with such fear for our security and welfare, we seem helpless and prostrate before a military-industrial complex engaged in endless war, oligarchy, and media conglomerates that corroborate in dictatorial population control and crimes against humanity. We have a federal government that would rather invade foreign countries with aggressive war and build corporate empire than assure its own citizens' economic and personal health, education, and individual freedom.

Just look at America, from the last six years' lowest public opinion polls for presidents and Congress, to the state of the depressed economy, to the breedings for revolution rising in the Occupy Wall Street movement nationwide, to the growing police state's response to it.

The degrading of America has been caused by men and women we have admitted to the presidency, Congress, and the laws they've approved allowing massive corporate, police, and military control. If you don't believe this, look at the causes of the economic meltdown; the over-aggressive police response to the Occupy movement; the massive proliferation of security cameras throughout the nation; spread of a nationwide federal surveillance operation through Homeland Security; the president's recent signing of a defense appropriations bill which includes authority for the military to arrest and hold American citizens without trial; and a new law allowing for populating our country's skies with unmanned drone planes designed for surveillance, war and killing.

Adams emphasizes in his *Thoughts*:

> *The principal difficulty lies, and the greatest care should be employed, in constituting this representative assembly. It should be in miniature an exact portrait of the people at large. It should think, feel, reason, and act like them.*

Does that sound like *your* Congress, made up of a majority of millionaires? Does that sound like *your* presidents who talk a good game of democracy but continue to move forward in effort to unravel individual rights and build empire? Does that sound like *your* banks and corporations which continue to merge to control markets, increase profits while holding down wages and attempting to limit or end employee benefits? These are not imaginations. Just read and heed, but you'd best be paying attention to writings and voices not under the major media's control. You can start with the links below.

And you'd best follow John Adams' and his cohorts' lead in pressing for a *free* America, if not for your own good, at least for the happiness of your children and future generations.

## The Vital Realities for 2020 and Beyond

In other words, get organized, get educated, and get active.

John Adams' *Thoughts on Government*: http://oll.liberty-fund.org/?option=com_staticxt&staticfile=show.php%3Ftitle=592&chapter=76854&layout=html&Itemid=27

The economic meltdown: http://www.pbs.org/wgbh/pages/frontline/money-power-wall-street/

The Occupy Movement: http://topics.nytimes.com/top/reference/timestopics/organizations/o/occupy_wall_street/index.html

Security cameras, drones, surveillance: http://voices.yahoo.com/cameras-phone-taps-drones-oh-my-10374303.html

Drones in the U.S.: http://www.texasobserver.org/cover-story/send-in-the-drones

Homeland Security and top-secret America: http://projects.washingtonpost.com/top-secret-america/

# Homeland Security Aims at Internet Control
**Roger Armbrust,** May 5, 2012

With the blessing of Barack Obama, the federal Department of Homeland Security (DHS) is planning to eventually take control of the Internet, according to an DHS counsel. Such a move by government logically would end citizens' Constitutional right to freedom of expression, including limiting them to sharing only government-approved information.

Bruce McConnell, a senior cybersecurity counselor with DHS, reported to a cybersecurity gathering last Wednesday in Washington that DHS will establish "institutions" on the Internet to govern it, including working with other nations to determine what content is "proper." McConnell led his presentation by explaining that Obama has instructed HLS to protect the Internet because it is a "civilian" agency.

Americans should voice two major concerns to their Congressional representatives regarding this DHS plan: (1) when government establishes an "institution," it basically means it plans to become entrenched and take control; (2) government deciding what content is "proper" is called censorship, and, again, is opposed to the U.S. Constitution.

McConnell, in speaking on a three-person panel covering "Cybersecurity Across the Atlantic," also noted that Internet control should be a "public-private partnership," adding that DHS has successfully worked with Internet Service Providers (ISPs) in the past, thus indicating they would continue that process.

Which leads to a third major concern citizens should voice immediately to their U.S. senators: the Republican-controlled House just over a week ago approved the **Cyber Intelligence Sharing and Protection Act** (**CISPA**). The proposed law will basically force technology and manufacturing companies to share Internet traffic information with the federal government.

Big business, including Facebook and the U.S. Chamber of Commerce, support the legislation as a means of protecting against cyber threats. Microsoft had supported it, but turned against it in late April, citing privacy concerns. Internet privacy and civil liberty advocates oppose the bill, saying it will allow government intrusion of individual Internet freedoms.

The Electronic Frontier Foundation, an international digital rights advocacy and legal group, has criticized CISPA:

"CISPA would allow ISPs, social networking sites, and anyone else handling Internet communications to monitor users and pass information to the government without any judicial oversight," said EFF Activism Director Rainey Reitman. "The language of this bill is dangerously vague, so that personal online activity – from the mundane to the intimate – could be implicated."

In opposing CISPA, the American Civil Liberties Union-a legal nonprofit whose sole purpose is to defend Americans' Constitutional rights-has offered this logical alternative to CISPA in an official release:

*Rather than seeking more access to Americans' private information in the name of cybersecurity, the government should be doing all it can to encourage private entities and government agencies to address security fundamentals. It simply does not make sense to undermine our freedoms in the pursuit of complex, expensive, and intrusive security policies when the most basic measures are not being implemented properly.*

The ACLU noted, "According to a comprehensive forensic analysis by the U.S. Secret Service, Verizon, and the Dutch National High Tech Crime Unit, 96 percent of otherwise successful cyber-attacks could have been avoided simply by using existing best practices and good cyber hygiene. Even the CIA's Chief of Information Assurance has said that up to 90 percent of cybersecurity problems could be countered using due diligence. Yet, only 58 percent of North American corporations have a cybersecurity plan in place, and only 31 percent plan to increase spending on security."

It's not clear as of this writing when the Senate might vote on CISPA. And DHS's McConnell indicated the agency's working with other nations and private companies to take over the Internet was only in the planning stage. Obama, while pushing DHS to "protect" the Internet, reportedly opposes CISPA.

So now's the time for anyone concerned about continuing Internet freedom to get organized, get educated, and get active. And for Americans to contact their senators and oppose CISPA, then encourage all of Congress to stifle the administration's effort to censor and control the Internet via DHS.

Here's the link to last week's panels on Transatlantic cybesecurity: http://www.c-span.org/Events/Conference-Looks-at-Ways-to-Strengthen-Transatlantic-Cybersecurity/10737430366/

An article on Microsoft's about-face regarding CISPA: http://news.cnet.com/8301-33062_3-57423580/microsoft-backs-away-from-cispa-support-citing-privacy/

The ACLU's release on CISPA: https://www.aclu.org/blog/national-security-technology-and-liberty/cybersecurity-legislation-and-common-sense-still

The EFF's alert on CISPA: https://www.eff.org/deeplinks/2012/04/cispa-national-security-and-nsa-ability-read-your-emails

Facebook defends its pro-CISPA stance: http://www.pcmag.com/article2/0,2817,2403036,00.asp

# July 4: Our Independence Versus Today's Emergency Powers

**Roger Armbrust,** July 2, 2012

When Thomas Jefferson formed our Declaration of Independence in 1776, he did so to attack King George III of England's dictatorship over the American colonies, and to state Americans' opposition to and separation from England's oppression and possession.

Jefferson accused the king of "the establishment of an absolute Tyranny over these States. To prove this, let Facts be submitted to a candid world."

He went on to list 27 offenses, engaging accusatory active verbs-such as "has obstructed," "cutting off," "depriving," "abolishing," "has abdicated," "has plundered"-in such a forcefully progressive column of charges that any reasonable human would concur that, indeed, the king was a tyrant and the colonies must break free.

And so we have progressed to America today. Which leads to this question: In America today, when can our country's chief executive–with Congress's concurrence–most likely become a tyrant? It would appear to occur if the President of the United States ever takes possession of all authorities granted under the National Emergencies Act, passed and signed in 1976.

## The Vital Realities for 2020 and Beyond

Presidents have declared limited states of emergency before and since that time. We have been under a limited, but ongoing, emergency since the Sept. 11, 2001 attacks on New York and Washington. George W. Bush declared a limited national emergency on Sept. 14, and then extended it yearly. Barack Obama has annually continued the national emergency declaration regarding terrorism on September 10, 2009, on September 10, 2010, and on September 9, 2011.

The Congressional Research Service (CRS) has analyzed the National Emergencies Act on various occasions. The latest updated analysis appears to have been prepared and submitted for Congress on Aug. 30, 2007 by CRS's Harold C. Relyea, a specialist in American national government. Simply titled "National Emergency Powers," the report describes the vast authorities allowed the president during declared emergencies. It also cites Congress's power in regulating the president.

The 25-page study notes four aspects to an emergency condition: (1) "sudden, unforeseen, and of unknown duration;" (2) "dangerous and threatening to life and well-being;" (3) "in terms of governmental role and authority...who discerns this phenomenon?" and (4) requires immediate action that is not always "according to rule."

Presidents have jumped at the chance to solidify their dictatorial powers during times they determined to be national emergencies. And the CRS report notes the startling vastness of these powers:

> *Under the powers delegated by such statutes, the President may seize property, organize and control the means of production, seize commodities, assign military forces abroad, institute martial law, seize and control all transportation and communication, regulate the operation of private enterprise, restrict travel, and, in a variety of ways, control the lives of United States citizens. Furthermore, Congress may modify, rescind, or render dormant such delegated emergency authority.*

Roger Armbrust

While extending the national emergency from 2009 through Sept. 9, 2012, Obama has approved—with Congress's voted support or unopposing observance—a number of actions extending his and the federal government's powers. Here are four of the major ones:

1. In May 2011, he signed a law extending for four years the controversial counter-terrorism search and surveillance powers at the heart of the Patriot Act.

"The provisions allow authorities to use roving wiretaps to track an individual on several telephones; track a non-US national suspected of being a "lone-wolf" terrorist not tied to an extremist group; and to seize personal or business records or "any tangible thing" seen as critical to an investigation," according to *Agence France-Presse*. "The law had drawn fire from an unusual coalition of liberal Democrats and Republicans tied to the arch-conservative 'Tea Party' movement, who say it grants the government too much power and infringes on individual liberties."

2. On Dec. 31, 2011, he signed the National Defense Authorization Act, allowing the military to place anyone, including American citizens, under worldwide indefinite detention without charge or trial.

"The statute is particularly dangerous because it has no temporal or geographic limitations, and can be used by this and future presidents to militarily detain people captured far from any battlefield," according to Anthony D. Romero, executive director of the American Civil Liberties Union (ACLU).

3. On March 16, 2012, he signed an executive order on "National Defense Resources Preparedness."
Edwin Black in *The Huffington Post* says that the order "renews and updates the president's power to take control of all civil energy supplies, including oil and natural gas, control and

restrict all civil transportation, which is almost 97 percent dependent upon oil; and even provides the option to re-enable a draft in order to achieve both the military and non-military demands of the country."

Texas Congresswoman Kay Granger, in her March 30 newsletter, states:

> *This order gives an unprecedented level of authority to the President and the federal government to take over all the fundamental parts of our economy – in the name of national security – in times of national emergency.*
>
> *This means all of our water resources, construction services and materials (steel, concrete, etc.), our civil transportation system, food and health resources, our energy supplies including oil and natural gas – even farm equipment – can be taken over by the President and his cabinet secretaries. The Government can also draft U.S. citizens into the military and force U.S. citizens to fulfill "labor requirements" for the purposes of 'national defense.' There is not even any Congressional oversight, only briefings are required.*
>
> *By issuing this as an Executive Order the President puts the federal government above the law, which, in a democracy, is never supposed to happen.*

4. In early May, with Obama's blessing, the federal Department of Homeland Security (DHS) indicated it's planning to eventually take control of the Internet, according to a DHS counsel. Such a move by government logically would end citizens' Constitutional right to freedom of expression, including limiting them to sharing only government-approved information.

Bruce McConnell, a senior cybersecurity counselor with DHS, reported to a cybersecurity gathering in Washington on May 2 that DHS will establish "institutions" on the Internet to govern it, including working with other nations to determine what content is "proper." McConnell led his presentation by explaining that Obama has instructed DHS to protect the Internet because it is a "civilian" agency.

"We hold these truths to be self-evident," Jefferson said in our Declaration, "that all men are created equal, that they are endowed by their Creator with certain unalienable Rights, that among these are Life, Liberty and the pursuit of Happiness.– That to secure these rights, Governments are instituted among Men, deriving their just powers from the consent of the governed."

If you feel the continuing activation of government powers listed above will secure your life, liberty, and pursuit of happiness, then…as you were. If you consider them an infringement, then it would be wise to get organized, get educated and get active. And demand your president, U.S. senators and Congress members do their jobs, move away from growing government control, and protect our nation's freedoms.

# Obama Expands His Power over Internet, Media
**Roger Armbrust,** July 14, 2012

The White House, through a recently signed order, has given the executive branch emergency control of America's communications including the Internet and media outlets. It's the president's second executive order in five months which binds more citizens' freedoms under federal government emergency authority.

What's the unstated significance of these two orders involving "emergency preparedness?" President Barack Obama placed the nation under a year's limited emergency last September, an extension of yearly limited emergencies since 2001 based on America's worldwide "war on terror." So, since we're under a state of emergency, it would seem he could activate the orders and take emergency control at any time.

Obama on July 6 ordered that emergency control of communications would occur under an executive committee made up of "heads of the Departments of State, Defense, Justice, Commerce, and Homeland Security, the Office of the Director of National Intelligence (DNI), the General Services Administration, and the Federal Communications Commission, as well as such additional agencies as the Executive Committee may designate. The designees of the Secretary of Homeland Security and the Secretary of Defense shall serve as Co-Chairs of the Executive Committee."

Roger Armbrust

The Secretary of Defense would "oversee the development, testing, implementation, and sustainment of NS/EP [national security/emergency preparedness] communications that are directly responsive to the national security needs" of the White House.

The Secretary of Homeland Security would oversee communications at every level of government throughout the nation. The secretary's other duties also include power to "maintain a joint industry-Government center that is capable of assisting in the initiation, coordination, restoration, and reconstitution of NS/EP communications services or facilities under all conditions of emerging threats, crisis, or emergency."

Homeland Security also will exercise authority over telecommunications, wireless and "next generation" service.

In May, a Homeland Security attorney indicated that the department was planning to eventually take control of the Internet. Such a move by government logically would end citizens' Constitutional right to freedom of expression, including limiting them to sharing only government-approved information.

Bruce McConnell, a senior cybersecurity counselor with DHS, reported to a cybersecurity gathering in Washington on May 2 that DHS will establish "institutions" on the Internet to govern it, including working with other nations to determine what content is "proper."

Under the most recent executive order, the Commerce secretary would oversee radio spectrum. The Federal Communications Commission would control radio and television broadcasting.

Deep within the 2,231-word order, Obama states, "With respect to the Intelligence Community, the DNI [Director of National Intelligence], after consultation with the heads of affected agencies, may issue such policy directives and guidance as the DNI deems necessary to implement this order. Procedures or other guidance issued by the heads of elements of the Intelligence Community shall be in accordance with such policy directives or guidelines issued by the DNI."

In March, Obama signed an executive order on "National Defense Resources Preparedness."

Edwin Black in *The Huffington Post* says that the order "renews and updates the president's power to take control of all civil energy supplies, including oil and natural gas, control and restrict all civil transportation, which is almost 97 percent dependent upon oil; and even provides the option to re-enable a draft in order to achieve both the military and non-military demands of the country."

The president indicates in the orders that the department functions he outlines are designated by law. Also, Congress has provided the president with vast powers under the National Emergencies Act.

The question: Why has Obama decided to activate these executive orders as he approaches the end of his four-year term, since he's placed the nation under a limited emergency from his first year in office?

Obama evidently doesn't announce the orders, or take questions. He simply and quietly signs the orders. Presidential custom. The nation's chief executive always has the power of the "bully pulpit," but when it comes to taking control over freedoms, he may not always want to use it.

# Senate Bill Supports President's Effort to Control the Internet

**Roger Armbrust,** July 24, 2012

The U.S. Senate will vote this week on the Cybersecurity Act of 2012, which would strengthen President Obama's attempt to control the Internet, primarily through the departments of Homeland Security (DHS) and Defense.

The bill even includes an effort at international Internet control. It also sets up, deep in the legislation's wording, "cybersecurity exchanges" for monitoring the Internet.

Obama earlier this month signed an order giving the executive branch emergency control of America's communications including the Internet and media outlets. It was the president's second executive order in five months which binds more citizens' freedoms under federal government emergency authority.

Under the president's emergency order, the secretaries of Homeland Security and Defense would co-chair a multi-department committee overseeing the Internet and media.

The Senate's Cybersecurity Act further secures the president's order regarding the Internet.

The Senate bill provides for a National Cybersecurity Council comprised of representatives from the Departments of Commerce, Defense, Homeland Security, Justice "and other appropriate" federal agencies "with responsibilities for regulating the security of covered critical infrastructure." The Secretary of Homeland Security will chair the council "and will coordinate with owners and operators of critical infrastructure."

The bill mentions that private businesses could be verified as cybersecure under the monitoring process. Business participation would be voluntary, and Constitutional rights allegedly would be protected. But we've seen little actual effort from the executive or legislative branches in recent years in following through on these protections.

The bill instructs the council "to identify categories of critical cyber infrastructure only if a cyber attack to that infrastructure could reasonably result in: (1) interruption of lifesustaining services sufficient to cause a mass casualty event or mass evacuations; (2) catastrophic economic damage to the United States; or (3) severe degradation of national security."

(If the president's control over the Internet protects us from "catastrophic economic damage to the United States" the way the president and Congress shielded us from the economic meltdown of 2008, then we'll be in good hands.)

Businesses "voluntarily" involved in being federally verified as secure "will be entitled to several benefits including: (1) liability protections from any punitive damages arising from an incident related to a cybersecurity risk where the owner is in substantial compliance with the cybersecurity practices at the time of the incident; (2) expedited provision of security clearances to appropriate personnel employed by the certified owner; (3) priority technical assistance on cyber issues; and (4) receipt of relevant realtime cyber threat information."

(You may recall telephone companies, under security legislation, receiving federal liability protections for tapping Americans' phones. Also, "priority technical assistance" and "receipt of relevant realtime cyber threat information" sounds like a subtle threat: Any business that won't cooperate "voluntarily" will be left waiting for assistance and won't receive cyber threat information in time.)

The bill further calls for efforts at obtaining international cooperation in cybersecurity, instructing Homeland Security and the Secretary of State to communicate with foreign owners and operators of "information infrastructure." It further calls for DHS and the State Department to "coordinate with international governments and owners of such information infrastructure regarding mitigation or remediation of cyber risks."

In May, a Homeland Security attorney indicated that the department was planning to eventually take control of the Internet. Such a move by government logically would end citizens' Constitutional right to freedom of expression, including limiting them to sharing only government-approved information.

Bruce McConnell, a senior cybersecurity counselor with DHS, reported to a cybersecurity gathering in Washington on May 2 that DHS will establish "institutions" on the Internet to govern it, including working with other nations to determine what content is "proper." McConnell led his presentation by explaining that Obama has instructed DHS to protect the Internet because it is a "civilian" agency.

The proposed Senate legislation also calls for consolidating several DHS cybersecurity functions under a new "National Center for Cybersecurity and Communications (NCCC or the Center). The Center would be headed by a Director appointed by the President and confirmed by the Senate. The Director would be responsible for managing Federal efforts to secure, protect, and ensure the resiliency of cyber networks in the United States."

The bill further requires the new director to "facilitate

cybersecurity information sharing of both classified and unclassified cybersecurity information with other Federal agencies, the private sector, state and local governments, and international partners. Information shared with the Federal government will receive special protections from further disclosure."

Efforts are also called for to carry the cybersecurity effort into American and foreign universities. The bill instructs the National Science Foundation to establish cybersecurity research centers at "institutions of higher learning or other entities. It also orders the new cybersecurity director and the Secretary of Defense "to establish Centers of Excellence in cybersecurity for the protection of critical infrastructure in conjunction with academic and professional partners from countries that may include allies of the United States."

The bill also establishes "cybersecurity exchanges" basically for monitoring the Internet for cybersecurity threats. They would be under the combined responsibility of DHS, the Defense Department, the Justice Department, and the National Intelligence Agency.

# Why Ecuador REALLY Gave Assange Asylum
**Roger Armbrust,** August 16, 2012

Ecuador's President Rafael Correa's granting journalist Julian Assange asylum is no real surprise. You could have seen it coming as far back as 2005 when Correa was Ecuador's rebellious finance minister. And it would have been even more predictable if you watched the evolution of his presidency and his aim toward becoming Latin America's "most enigmatic leader."

A child of poverty who worked his way to a Ph.D. in economics at the University of Illinois-trained there in the philosophy of the conservatives' economic sweetheart Milton Friedman-Correa rebelled even then, leaning instead toward socialism. He believes he understands the world economic and social order, particularly the United States' and multinational corporations' desire to control it, and he has consistently rebelled against that, too.

An intellectual who has proved to be a savvy politician, Correa connects the dots of economics and politics, and his dots don't align with the western powers. He knows South America needs a charismatic leader to follow his good friend, cancer-battling Venezuela President Hugo Chavez. And Correa's moving into a position to do that.

Political leaders, to expand power, know they need an enemy

## The Vital Realities for 2020 and Beyond

so they can unite the populace at home. And Correa has found one in the U.S., the International Monetary Fund(IMF) and the World Bank.

As finance minister in 2005, he opposed a free-trade agreement with the U.S. He also bucked the IMF by heavier cooperation with other Latin American countries. When the World Bank then withheld a loan, Correa resigned his minister's post. The next year he ran for president, proposing that Ecuador rewrite its constitution, increase petroleum-revenues spending on social programs, and reform the petroleum industry and the financial sector. He obviously loved walking among the people, and communicated with the indigenous population in their own language. He won a runoff election with 56 percent of the vote.

As president, he hit the west with a heavy economic shot: In December 2008, he declared that Ecuador would not pay its national debt. He accused the IMF, World Bank, and CIA of manipulating Ecuador's earlier unelected military dictators, saying he would not honor the loans. He defaulted on billions of dollars, sending a clear sign he would not back down to the U.S. or anyone else.

As for the current case of Assange, Correa had shown clear signs of empathy with the Wikileaks whistleblower's plight. He agreed to a half-hour interview on Assange's international TV news program aired on *RT*, the U.S. Russian television network, in May. He flatly told Assange his efforts at creating transparency among governments was a benefit to the world. They laughed and traded quips, including Assange's closing with the smiling comment, "Don't get shot." Correa responded with a nod and gallows smile.

Both knew it was a bitter ironic joke.

Correa has challenged nearly every authority since taking office, including the country's congress, press, and police. He stalked out into a national police strike's protest in 2010 and bared his chest, challenging them to kill him. Reports are it was close, but he went unharmed.

John Perkins, in his 2004 book *Confessions of an Economic Hitman* and subsequent books, notes that some Latin American elected leaders usually don't survive, but it's not because of local opposition. It's because the U.S. and multinational corporations remove them if they don't play ball.

Perkins claims that-when he operated as an economic hitman for the National Security Agency (NSA) in the 1970s-his failed efforts to convince Ecuadorian President Jaime Roldos Aguilera and Panamanian leader Omar Torrijos to cooperate led to their fatal plane crashes. A former CIA agent backed Perkins' claim in a documentary film based on Perkins' *Confessions*. Perkins and the CIA operative also spoke about Saddam Hussein's demise in Iraq.

Perkins describes a three-tiered process for ingraining multinational businesses into Latin American economies:

1. The economic hitman like Perkins visits the newly elected president. He says he has a million dollars with him to start the payoff process. In return, the president will get loans from the IMF and World Bank. Those loans will really go to multinational corporations who will come into the country, build oil refineries, electric generating plants, and other major capital improvements to give the multinationals an economic base in the country. When the nation can't pay back the loans, the president is asked to do "favors" for the U.S., like help out in a foreign war, or sell the country's oil cheap to the multinationals. If the leader agrees, on they go.

2. If the leader doesn't agree, the process moves to Tier 2: The CIA comes in, attempts to create a coup d'etat, or assassinates the leader, providing a change in government, and an effort to pay off the next president.

3. If that doesn't work, then Tier 3: the American military moves

## The Vital Realities for 2020 and Beyond

in. Perkins claims the three-tiered process took total effect in Iraq, where Saddam Hussein had moved into power with U.S. support. But he lost it when he refused to let Bechtel Corp. build a port refinery in Aqaba for the Iraq-Jordan pipeline. That was in 1983. The CIA's attempts to form a coup or kill Saddam never succeeded, which led to George W. Bush's military invasion.

Perkins' thesis has its critics, including the U.S. government and *The New York Times*. But Correa, no doubt, has his own opinion about whether efforts might rise to forcibly oust him, particularly now that he has directly opposed Great Britain and the U.S. by granting Assange asylum.

Just how that unfolds in the days to come could affect the world economy. Should England and America push the case with Ecuador, who do you think Venezuela and the other South American countries will support? And Correa's friend Chavez and Venezuela hold a big hand in the oil game, touting some of the largest oil and natural gas reserves on the globe.

Also, since 2008, Russia has increased its ties with Venezuela. Where does that tell you this conflict could go?

Correa, of course, realizes all this. You know that when you pay close attention to Correa's terse verbal response to Great Britain's reported threat yesterday to storm the Ecuadorian embassy and take Assange:

"We are not a British colony."

That phrase, no doubt, perked up the ears of every South American country, Africa, India, and others opposed to suffering at the hands of empires. And upsetting international relations, and therefore a world economy already on the ropes, could lead to greater home troubles everywhere.

The economist/politician Correa knows that. He connects the dots. More to come.

# In a Free Country, We Can Protest Conventions
**Roger Armbrust,** August 27, 2012

What gives you the right to protest the Republican and Democratic national conventions, and any other convention? The same First Amendment to the U.S. Constitution that gives the Occupy movement the right to protest, and others the right to protest the protesters.

This journalist wrote about demonstrators' constitutional rights last year during the Occupy movement. What follows is from my November 2011 column "Huddled Masses Yearning to Breathe Free" published in Yahoo!'s *Voices* section–an overview of the evolution of these rights. It's slightly edited.

The First Amendment reads:

> *Congress shall make no law respecting an establishment of religion, or prohibiting the free exercise thereof; or abridging the freedom of speech, or of the press; or the right of the people peaceably to assemble, and to petition the Government for a redress of grievances.*

The federal government's archive website, *The Charters of Freedom*, notes that the Bill of Rights wasn't simply an afterthought to the Constitution. Arguments ensued during the Constitution's forming, questioning the amount of power the national government should garner. That led to the states demanding clear guarantees of individual rights. According to the archives' site:

> *Fresh in their minds was the memory of the British violation of civil rights before and during the Revolution. They demanded a "bill of rights" that would spell out the immunities of individual citizens. Several state conventions in their formal ratification of the Constitution asked for such amendments; others ratified the Constitution with the understanding that the amendments would be offered.*

These rights have also been clarified by a history of court cases, including the U.S. Supreme Court's assuring the right to peacefully assemble. According to the Illinois First Amendment Center–created to educate the public to the amendment's rights and responsibilities–the first Supreme Court case addressing public assembly was *United States v. Cruikshank* (1876). The high court ruled that the "right of the people peaceably to assemble for the purpose of petitioning Congress for a redress of grievances, or for any thing else connected with the powers and duties of the national government, is an attribute of national citizenship, and, as such, under the protection of, and guaranteed by, the United States."

While the *Cruikshank* ruling applied specifically to the individual's relationship with the federal government, by 1929 the Supreme Court had broadened the Bill of Rights and individual freedoms to also cover state and local governments. In *Gitlow v. New York*, the high court simply applied the Fourteenth Amendment's "due process" clause to government at every level. That clause states, "...nor shall any State deprive any person of life, liberty, or property, without due process of law; nor deny to any person within its jurisdiction the equal protection of the laws."

Applying that "due process" clause in *Gitlow*, the Supreme Court's ruling stated that specifically the rights to freedom of speech and of the press were "among the fundamental personal rights and 'liberties' protected by the due process clause of the Fourteenth Amendment from impairment by the states." In other words, the Fourteenth Amendment provides universal protection of individuals under the Constitution. Also, understanding that local governments receive their powers from the states, then freedom to peaceably assemble is included in those protections at every government level.

In *De Jonge v. Oregon*, a 1937 case, the court stressed, "[P]eaceable assembly for lawful discussion cannot be made a crime. The holding of meetings for peaceable political action cannot be proscribed."

The Supreme Court assured the public's right to use streets and sidewalks as public forums in the 1939 case of *Hague v. C.I.O.* The justices concurred that authorities also could not prosecute peaceful demonstrators for "disorderly conduct."

By 1963, during the anti-war, civil rights, and feminist movements, the high court ruled on public assembly in *Edwards v. South Carolina*. Police had arrested black marchers who did not disperse when ordered. The justices ruled that the marchers had assembled on public property, were peaceful, did not block traffic, and could not be guilty of breaching the peace. They had merely stood their ground, singing religious and patriotic songs, including "The Star Spangled Banner." Justice Potter Stewart, writing for the majority, said the marchers had exercised their First Amendment rights "in their most pristine and classic form," adding that a state cannot "make criminal the peaceful expression of unpopular views."

Numerous other cases since these also relate to the freedom of assembly. But here's the basic idea: In the United States we have the legal right to peacefully gather in public, to protest, and to even protest the protesters. And we cannot legally be arrested, hit, or pepper-sprayed for doing so.

# Who Won the Presidential Debate? Edward Bernays!
**Roger Armbrust,** October 4, 2012

> *The conscious and intelligent manipulation of the organized habits and opinions of the masses is an important element in democratic society. Those who manipulate this unseen mechanism of society constitute an invisible government which is the true ruling power of our country...Invisible government, in the shape of rudimentary political parties, arose almost overnight. Ever since then we have agreed, for the sake of simplicity and practicality, that party machines should narrow down the field of choice to two candidates, or at most three or four.*

These are the opening words to Edward Bernays' first chapter of his 1928 classic book *Propaganda*. Bernays, known as the father of public relations, goes on to say:

> *It was, of course, the astounding success of propaganda during the [First World] war that opened the eyes of the intelligent few in all departments of life to the possibilities of regimenting the public mind...the manipulators of patriotic opinion made use of the mental cliches and the emotional habits of the public to produce mass reactions against the alleged atrocities, the terror and the tyranny of the enemy. It was only natural, after the war ended, that intelligent persons should ask themselves*

Roger Armbrust

> *whether it was not possible to apply a similar technique to the problems of peace.*

Last night, during the first of a string of debates for the nation's top political office, you experienced again chunks of propaganda intensely seasoned with Bernays' sauce: spicy words and images meant to subtly, and not so subtly, stir up mind control and crowd control.

When the Chosen Two ignored more than recognized those patent questions on the economy from the Chosen Source (moderator Jim Lehrer), didn't you wonder what our nation's come to?

Mitt Romney, the chirpy kid so excited about having memorized his arithmetic, just couldn't be held back. He spouted out statistics on every issue, as if knowing numbers would grant him power to reason with a mangled Congress mired in gridlock and nearly single-digit approval ratings.

Barack Obama appeared the exhausted executive, having slumped out of his Oval Office chair and slogged to the stage, forcing a smile, slow on responses, and repetitive in arguments.

But aren't they both such nice guys. They sprinkled us with examples of being men of the people, citing their sensitive individual conversations with struggling citizens-images so obviously calculated rather than sympathetic. Obama even tried to woo us with memories of his grandmom. Made you want to call both guys by their first names.

Meanwhile, neither man would tiptoe near specifics about the three main villains of our economic collapse and shadowy future: Wall Street banks, Treasury Secretary Timothy Geithner, and the Federal Reserve Board. Oh, they got their brief mentions, but let's not dwell on the past, right Barack?

Ol' Mitt sounded closer to wanting to help homeowners, savers,

## The Vital Realities for 2020 and Beyond

and the shrinking middle class. But can we really believe that of the former head of Bain Capital and a rich member, in fact now the chosen leader, of the One Percent?

What seemed most clear is this: Romney, having spent months jousting in "debates" with Republican rivals for the nomination, was in shape and prepped for another go at the game. Obama, four years away from his verbal bouts with Hillary Clinton, and with no real propaganda sparring for ages, wasn't in shape.

But the propaganda was plentiful, and if either man truly convinced somebody that his rehearsed lines will lead this country out of endless war and back to economic prosperity, then may Howdy Doody's wooden spirit help us all.

We've fallen a long way from those first TV debates when John Kennedy and Richard Nixon didn't snap at each other but looked into the camera and addressed the American public. It was conducted by a group of TV journalists, with a moderator seated between the two candidates. At times, it was almost like a trial, at one point with Kennedy responding to a question about his experience. When he finished, Nixon was asked for a response, and he said, "I have no response." Nixon then took and responded to the next question, which was directed at him.

It was obvious then, from both candidates' demeanor and tone, it was a serious time, and both men really seemed to take the president's responsibilities seriously and with understanding. Later, of course, we realized they too were feeding us Bernays.

Yet it would be nice to see candidates someday partake in actual, traditional debates, where they take on one issue, state their views at length, then rebut each other directly to the people.

And wouldn't it be nice to move past Bernays and let the American people hear from more than the Chosen Two, and experience views of other political parties too, as they do in Europe? *Democracy Now!* on its TV news program took a shot

Roger Armbrust

at that last night. It would delay the debate broadcast segments long enough so that candidates from the Green Party and Justice Party could spend two minutes each also commenting on issues covered by Obama and Romney.
Americans deserve more of that.

# Big Brother (Homeland Security) Keeps Going Local
**Roger Armbrust,** October 29, 2012

President Obama is looking to further tighten the federal grip on a functioning America for the sake of "security," this time getting more heavily involved in state and local private operations.

Last Friday, he signed an executive order "Establishing the White House Homeland Security Partnership Council." Its purpose according to the order: "to advance the Federal Government's use of local partnerships to address homeland security challenges." Local partnerships would be formed among the Department of Homeland Security (DHS), other federal agencies, and nongovernmental organizations, foundations, and community-based organizations. It's Obama's third major executive order implemented this year regarding national security.

Obama wants Homeland Security to form the local partnerships "to address homeland security priorities, from responding to natural disasters to preventing terrorism, by utilizing diverse perspectives, skills, tools, and resources...'and we will support them through enhanced opportunities for engagement, coordination, transparency, and information sharing,' " according to the order. "This approach recognizes that, given the complexities and range of challenges, we must institutionalize an all-of-Nation effort to address the evolving threats to the United States."

Roger Armbrust

The president is about to get his chance to see how the federal government responds to natural disasters as Hurricane Sandy threatens the entire East Coast.

The executive order comes less than a month after the U.S. Senate issued a scathing report on Homeland Security and its local efforts: "Federal Support for and Involvement in State and Local Fusion Centers" was released Oct. 3 by the U. S. Senate Permanent Subcommittee on Investigations. The report found that Department of Homeland Security efforts to engage state and local intelligence fusion centers "has not yielded significant useful information to support federal counterterrorism intelligence efforts," according to a release from Sen. Carl Levin's (D-Mich.) office. Levin is the subcommittee's chairman. The fusion centers reportedly have combined efforts of federal, state, and local security authorities.

Senator Tom Coburn, the subcommittee's Republican ranking member who initiated the investigation, also stated, "It's troubling that the very 'fusion' centers that were designed to share information in a post-9/11 world have become part of the problem. Instead of strengthening our counterterrorism efforts, they have too often wasted money and stepped on Americans' civil liberties."

The Department of Homeland Security has estimated spending between $289 million and $1.4 billion in public funds to support state and local fusion centers since 2003, "broad estimates that differ by over $1 billion," according to the Senate release. "The investigation raises questions about the value this amount of funding and the nation's more than 70 fusion centers are providing to federal counterterrorism efforts."

Friday's executive order calls for a partnership council chaired by the Assistant to the President for Homeland Security and Counterterrorism, or a designee from the National Security Staff. A steering committee would consist of representatives from 19 different federal departments including State, Treasury,

# The Vital Realities for 2020 and Beyond

Defense and Justice. The steering committee will establish selection criteria for state and local committee members.

**Two Emergency Orders**
Obama's involving major federal departments in the partnership council resembles two other executive orders he issued earlier this year.

In July, he gave the executive branch emergency control of America's communications including the Internet and media outlets, binding more citizens' freedoms under federal government emergency authority. He ordered that emergency control of communications would occur under an executive committee made up of "heads of the Departments of State, Defense, Justice, Commerce, and Homeland Security, the Office of the Director of National Intelligence (DNI), the General Services Administration, and the Federal Communications Commission, as well as such additional agencies as the Executive Committee may designate. The designees of the Secretary of Homeland Security and the Secretary of Defense shall serve as Co-Chairs of the Executive Committee."

Secretary of Homeland Security Janet Napolitano

The Secretary of Homeland Security would oversee communications at every level of government throughout the nation. The secretary's other duties also include power to "maintain a joint industry-Government center that is capable of assisting in the initiation, coordination, restoration, and reconstitution of NS/EP communications services or facilities under all conditions of emerging threats, crisis, or emergency."

Homeland Security also will exercise authority over telecommunications, wireless and "next generation" service.

In May, a Homeland Security attorney indicated that the department was planning to eventually take control of the Internet. Such a move by government logically would end citizens'

Constitutional right to freedom of expression, including limiting them to sharing only government-approved information.

Bruce McConnell, a senior cybersecurity counselor with DHS, reported to a cybersecurity gathering in Washington on May 2 that DHS will establish "institutions" on the Internet to govern it, including working with other nations to determine what content is "proper."

In March, Obama signed an executive order on "National Defense Resources Preparedness."

Edwin Black in *The Huffington Post* says that the order "renews and updates the president's power to take control of all civil energy supplies, including oil and natural gas, control and restrict all civil transportation, which is almost 97 percent dependent upon oil; and even provides the option to re-enable a draft in order to achieve both the military and non-military demands of the country."

The president indicates in the orders that the department functions he outlines are designated by law. Also, Congress has provided the president with vast powers under the National Emergencies Act.

What's the unstated significance of these two orders involving "emergency preparedness?" Obama again placed the nation under a year's limited emergency in September, an extension of yearly limited emergencies begun with President George W. Bush since 2001, based on America's worldwide "war on terror." So, since we're under a state of emergency, it would seem Obama could activate the orders and take emergency control at any time.

# What's Left of Human Rights?
**Roger Armbrust,** December 9, 2012

Talk about a spade calling a spade a spade while both pretend to be hearts:

Congress has approved legislation which "normalizes" trade with Russia, but also will penalize Russian officials involved in human rights violations. Large majorities of the Senate and House said yea to the bill, which is on its way to the president, who is welcoming it.

The human-rights section is called the Magnitsky Actand is attached to the larger trade bill. Sergei Magnitsky was a Russian lawyer and whistleblower who died in a Moscow prison three years ago, and was allegedly tortured.

Russian officials decried the Congressional action, threatening to pass a similar law.

Strange, is it not, to see this legislation coming from a Congress that continues to approve funding for Guantanamo and secret prisons like Bagram, and a president who has waged war against whistleblowers both at home and abroad. Also, neither Congress nor the president appears anxious to prosecute military or CIA officials for torture abuses during the Iraq or Afghanistan invasions.

Meanwhile, last Tuesday, the U.S. Senate voted 98-0, with two abstentions, to approve the 2013 National Defense Authorization Act (NDAA). You may recall that, in the dead of night on Dec. 31, 2011, President Obama signed the 2012 NDAA. It included his added clause allowing the military to arrest anyone in the world, including American citizens, who he deems suspicioned of terrorism, and imprison them without charge or trial.

The new law seems to allow the same practice, only with Sen. Dianne Feinstein's amended yet questionable language, which has brought voiced concerns from the conservative *Washington Times* and the progressive American Civil Liberties Union.

In a Nov. 30 *Washington Times* article headlined "2013 NDAA and Feinstein Amendment Fail Constitutional Test," Blake A. Filippi said, "Congress is now poised to reaffirm the President's ability to prosecute persons within the USA through military tribunals, allow continued indefinite detention without charge or trial, and do nothing to limit the practice of extraordinary rendition."

Chris Anders, the ACLU's senior legislative counsel, a day earlier on the ACLU website, cited three problems with Feinstein's amendment:

- *It would NOT make America off-limits to the military being used to imprison civilians without charge or trial. That's because its focus on protections for citizens and green-card holders implies that non-citizens could be militarily detained. The goal should be to prohibit domestic use of the military entirely. That's the protection provided to everyone in the United States by the Posse Comitatus Act. That principle would be broken if the military can find an opening to operate against civilians here at home, maybe under the guise of going after non-citizens. This is truly an instance where, when some lose their rights, all lose rights — even those who look like they are being protected.*
- *It is inconsistent with the Constitution, which makes*

clear that basic due process rights apply to everyone in the United States. No group of immigrants should be denied the most basic due process right of all — the right to be charged and tried before being imprisoned.
- It would set some dangerous precedents for Congress: that the military may have a role in America itself, that indefinite detention without charge or trial can be contemplated in the United States, and that some immigrants can be easily carved out of the most basic due process protections.

Anders also included a paragraph from the executive director of the Japanese American Citizens League's note to Congress:

*The [Feinstein] amendment is of particular concern to the Japanese American Citizens League because of our historic concern stemming from the Japanese American incarceration experience during World War II. Nearly half of the internees were not United States citizens, and would not have been protected by this amendment. In consideration of due process and the rule of law within the United States, we urge you to oppose the Feinstein amendment, unless revised to protect all persons in the United States from indefinite detention without charge or trial.*

The Senate has sent the bill to the House and called for a conference committee of both houses to finalize the bill. The House approved the unamended bill earlier this year.

Dangers to American human rights aren't limited to the NDAA. We've tracked, through several *Peculiar Progressive* columns, the government's efforts at surveillance of innocent American citizens ranging from phone taps to monitoring the Internet and emails.

In a recent action, a group of state and local police this week asked Congress to have the major phone service providers hold all Americans' text messages for two years, in case police might

Roger Armbrust

need to review them regarding possible future crimes. How's that for securing your freedom?

Russia, of course, has moved forward with its own efforts at both censoring protests-including the notorious jailing of Pussy Riot members-and the Internet.

We'll try to keep you updated on such issues at home and abroad, in hopes you'll get organized, get educated, and get active in having your lawmakers and government stop telling you they're protecting you while abusing your human rights.

# Our Government's Abusive, Selective Rule of Law
**Roger Armbrust,** April 10, 2013

What's wrong with this picture of America's rule of law?

Look at two paragraphs from this *Associated Press* story posted today:

> Osama bin Laden's son-in-law will go on trial in January on charges that he conspired to kill Americans in his role as al-Qaida's chief spokesman, a judge said on Tuesday...

> ...Prosecutors say evidence against [Sulaiman] Abu Ghaith includes a widely circulated video of him in early October 2001 sitting with bin Laden and current al-Qaida leader Ayman al-Zawahri and another in which he calls on every Muslim to join the fight against the United States, declaring that "jihad is a duty."

So far, nothing's wrong. Why? Because Abu Ghaith is receiving what every American has the constitutional right to: a fair trial to prove his innocence or guilt under the law. And he's not even an American.

But here's where we see the picture lethally distort. Check this paragraph from a *New York Times*' Sept. 30, 2011 story:

Roger Armbrust

> The search for Mr. [Anwar al-]Awlaki, the American-born cleric whose fiery sermons made him a larger-than-life figure in the shadowy world of jihad, finally ended on Friday. After several days of surveillance of Mr. Awlaki, armed drones operated by the Central Intelligence Agency took off from a new, secret American base in the Arabian Peninsula, crossed into northern Yemen and unleashed a barrage of Hellfire missiles at a car carrying him and other top operatives from Al Qaeda's branch in Yemen, including another American militant who had run the group's English-language Internet magazine.

Bottom line: The U.S. government will provide a fair trial for a noncitizen *accused* of waging war against America, but will travel across nations' borders to track down and kill American citizens *accused* of waging war against the United States.

We highlight the verb *accused* because it's such a vital part of the constitutional law process.

The same day as the *NYT* article, noted Georgetown constitutional law professor Jonathan Turley wrote this in his blog about Awlaki's killing with the headline "Did Obama Just Assassinate A U.S. Citizen? Aulaqi Killing Raises Questions Over Presidential Powers":

> ...It runs contrary to constitutional guarantees protecting persons accused of crimes. The President can claim that the location of such individuals abroad is the key distinction since courts limit the application of constitutional protections and limitations outside of our border. Yet, we have already seen that the Justice Department argues that other rights can be similarly waived in the country like due process rights and the right to counsel for anyone accused [of] being an enemy combatant. The enemy combatant policy and cases largely eradicated the domestic/foreign distinction used in the past.

Turley wasn't alone in his concern. Constitutional lawyer/journalist Glenn Greenwald also decried Obama's executing American citizens without trial:

> *Remember that there was great controversy when George Bush asserted the power to simply detain American citizens without due process or simply to eavesdrop on their conversation without warrant," he said. "Here you have something much more severe. Not eavesdropping on American citizens, not detaining them without due process, but killing them without due process. And yet many Democrats and progressives because President Obama is doing it have no problem with it and are even in favor of it...*
>
> *...To say that the President has the right to kill citizens without due process is to take the Constitution and to tear it into as many little pieces as you can and burn it and step on it.*

You here in the U.S., far away from the Middle East's daily conflicts, probably aren't concerned about the loss of a couple of *accused* rogue Americans, nor the loss of Awlaki's 16-year-old American-citizen son, who also was blown up by a drone missile.

But you should be concerned, if not because of fellow humans being assassinated without due process, then because it might just occur in your America. Your nation's Attorney General has told you so. Observe this *CNN* report from just last month, March 6:

> *Attorney General Eric Holder is not entirely ruling out a scenario under which a drone strike would be ordered against Americans on U.S. soil, but says it has never been done previously and he could only see it being considered in an extraordinary circumstance.*

Roger Armbrust

> ...But he also said the government has no intention of carrying out drone strikes inside the United States. Echoing what he said in a letter to U.S. Sen. Rand Paul, R-Kentucky, he called the possibility of domestic drone strikes "entirely hypothetical."

Paul, however, didn't buy Holder's efforts to skirt the issue. He responded:

> The U.S. attorney general's refusal to rule out the possibility of drone strikes on American citizens and on American soil is more than frightening. It is an affront to the constitutional due process rights of all Americans.

Consider this struggle over your constitutional right to due process, and whether you care or not. Then consider that Obama had written into the National Defense Authorization Act that the president can order the military to arrest anyone in the world without charge and secretly imprison them without trial, if he considers them a "terror" threat to the U.S. government.

Then consider the column from *Forbes* magazine headlined "1.6 Billion Rounds Of Ammo For Homeland Security? It's Time For A National Conversation."

Then consider this article in the Feb. 24 *Seattle Times*, reprinted from the *Atlanta Journal-Constitution*, headlined, "Police armed with surplus military gear," and the subhead reading, "There is growing concern that donated surplus military equipment is adding to the militarization of law-enforcement agencies nationwide."

*Forbes* based in New York, *Seattle Times*, and *Atlanta Journal-Constitution*: three decades-old respected publications writing about such goings on. Then add to that this *Denver Post* article titled "NRA calls for armed police officer in every school."

## The Vital Realities for 2020 and Beyond

What do you think is really going on?

Do you think it's time for a national conversation?

Do you think it's time to get organized, get educated, and get active?

# Senate Scraps CISPA...But Watch Your Back
**Roger Armbrust,** April 25, 2013

The United States Senate today showed a glimmer of respect for civil liberties. It said "no" to the House-passed cyber-security bill known as CISPA, preferring to draft its own legislation.

The Obama administration, it appears, has proven less respectful. News came yesterday that the Justice Department has secretly authorized intercepting Internet communications on portions of AT&T and other Internet service providers' networks. It also appears such interceptions would prove illegal under federal wiretapping laws.

Yes, it's hard to keep all Congress's Internet-control bills straight. Last year, there was SOPA. There was also PIPA. Two "anti-piracy" bills to iron-fist the Internet. The Internet revolted. The bills failed.

Then, just about this time last year, Congress was looking at another bill: the Cyber Intelligence Sharing and Protection Act (CISPA). Michigan Republican Congressman Michael Rogers introduced it. The House passed it. The Senate didn't.

This year, it barged back for another run. Last week, the House approved basically the same bill again, and it sailed its cyber way over to the Senate.

Basically, the bill would require private technology and manufacturing firms to share with the federal government "Internet traffic information," i.e., what websites Internet users access, and what users publish online and write in their emails. Why? To investigate cyber threats and ensure networks' security against cyber attacks.

Sounds good in general, right? But, in this combative age when conservatives and liberals are even assaulting each other's philosophies at Christmas, guess what? A plethora of both liberal and conservative groups *oppose* CISPA.

They range from the American Civil Liberties Union-the legal organization that defends citizens' Constitutional rights in court-to the American Conservative Union.

What's their problem with the bill? Too few limits on government control: potentially allowing federal agencies to monitor private citizens' Internet browsing, and spying on the public rather than manipulative hackers.

Who favors CISPA? Big Tech Biz: Microsoft, Facebook, AT&T, IBM, Apple and the United States Chamber of Commerce. They trust the government will operate within the law (and protect Big Tech from lawsuits for tapping private citizens' info).

Today, the Senate signaled it had comprehended the naysayers. The question is, what specific language will the upper house compose in its new legislation. Sen. Jay Rockefeller, a Democrat from West Virginia, was quoted in *U.S. News and World Report* today (Thursday) as saying CISPA is "important" but the bill's "privacy protections are insufficient."

So look for the Senate to offer its own bill this year, perhaps soon.

**Obama Sneaks One In**
Meanwhile, Obama has said he would veto CISPA legislation if it doesn't include privacy assurances. At the same time, his Justice

Roger Armbrust

Department officials seem to be avoiding privacy law with their new secret order. According to the tech media site *CNET*:

> *The secret legal authorization from the Justice Department originally applied to a cybersecurity pilot project in which the military monitored defense contractors' Internet links. Since then, however, the program has been expanded by President Obama to cover all critical infrastructure sectors including energy, healthcare, and finance starting June 12.*
>
> *"The Justice Department is helping private companies evade federal wiretap laws," said Marc Rotenberg, executive director of the Electronic Privacy Information Center, which obtained over 1,000 pages of internal government documents and provided them to CNET this week. "Alarm bells should be going off."*
>
> *Those documents show the National Security Agency and the Defense Department were deeply involved in pressing for the secret legal authorization, with NSA director Keith Alexander participating in some of the discussions personally. Despite initial reservations, including from industry participants, Justice Department attorneys eventually signed off on the project.*

You can read the full CNET report *here*.

**Email Privacy Law Updated?**
The Senate is also preparing to update email-privacy legislation. According to *The New York Times*, the Senate Judiciary Committee has "unanimously passed a measure that would require the government to get a search warrant, issued by a judge, to gain access to personal e-mails and all other electronic content held by a third-party service provider. The bill still needs the approval of the full Senate."

Question: With the Senate espousing privacy protection with

its version of CISPA, a Senate panel looking to expand email privacy, and the Obama administration paying lip-service to privacy yet expanding efforts at Internet monitoring, where do you see all this going? Yep, probably to court.

**Wikileaks Beats Valitor/Visa in Court**
Speaking of court and the Internet, neither Obama nor Sen. Dianne Feinstein can be happy with the Iceland Supreme Court. On Wednesday, it ordered Valitor, the international online and e-commerce payment company, to open the payment gateways used by WikiLeaks.

Valitor, formerly Visa Iceland, is Visa and Mastercard's Icelandic partner. According to *News of Iceland*:

> The largest credit card corporations in the World, Visa and Mastercard, told service providers to close down all services to firms that receive payments for WikiLeaks. This was done after the website leaked thousands of mails from US embassies all over the world. DataCell services Wikileaks in Iceland and Valitor, agent for Visa in Iceland, blocked all payments.
> DataCell and WikiLeaks sued Valitor because of this. The district court in Reykjavik ruled that Valitor had to open for the payment gateways. Valitor appealed, but the supreme court reached the same conclusion.

WikiLeaks' founder/editor-in-chief Julian Assange in 2007 published thousands of U.S. government documents and the video of American military aircraft gunning down Iraqi journalists in Baghdad. This garnered the ire of both Obama and Feinstein, chairman of the Senate Intelligence Committee. They have been hoping to try Assange in the U.S. for breaking the federal Espionage Act.

Following the Icelandic high court's ruling, Assange publicly vowed legal action against others who have attempted to shut down WikiLeaks.

# None's Well That's Orwell
**Roger Armbrust,** June 9, 2013

> *It was terribly dangerous to let your thoughts wander when you were in any public place or within range of a telescreen. The smallest thing could give you away. A nervous tic, an unconscious look of anxiety, a habit of muttering to yourself–anything that carried with it the suggestion of abnormality, of having something to hide. In any case, to wear an improper expression on your face...was itself a punishable offense. There was even a word for it in Newspeak: facecrime...*
> **George Orwell, *1984*, Book 1, Chapter 5**

In America now, there is one surveillance camera for every 10 people. With Congress's approval of drones on the U.S. mainland, the Federal Aviation Administration estimates 10,000 drones will be filling America's skies within five years. A recent example of law enforcement's growing use of facial recognition technology: *Slate* magazine reports that the Statue of Liberty is being geared with software called FaceVACS, made by German firm Cognitec:

> *FaceVACS, Cognitec boasts in marketing materials, can guess ethnicity based on a person's skin color, flag suspects on watch lists, estimate the age of a person, detect gender, "track" faces in real time, and help identify suspects if they have tried to evade detection*

## The Vital Realities for 2020 and Beyond

*by putting on glasses, growing a beard, or changing their hairstyle.*

Last year, *Peculiar Progressive* in *CFR* outlined when our country's president, with Congress's concurrence, could become a tyrant, based on the abuse of liberties. You can read that here: *July 4: Our Independence Versus Today's Emergency Powers*.

And now in recent weeks we've seen a rash of reports of Big Brother activity:

London's The Guardian newspaper revealed last week that the Obama administration convinced a secret court to order phone giant Verizon to turn over location, length, duration and phone numbers for *every* call on its system for its millions of customers-a major affront to individual liberty. This is based on the philosophy of guilty until proven innocent, in direct opposition to the U.S. Constitution.

*The Washington Post* reported last week that "the National Security Agency and the FBI are tapping directly into central servers of nine leading U.S. Internet companies, extracting audio and video chats, photographs, e-mails, documents, and connection logs that enable analysts to track foreign targets, according to a top-secret document." But the program, codename PRISM, can also track your information.

In mid-May, *The Associated Press* reported that the Justice Department secretly obtained two months of telephone records of AP's reporters and editors "in what the news cooperative's top executive called a 'massive and unprecedented intrusion' into how news organizations gather the news." This is a blatant attack on the Constitution and freedom of the press.

A secret court. A top-secret document. Secretly confiscating a newspaper's phone records. Those are the latest concrete examples of growing totalitarianism in America. On a broader and deeper scale, here are the four major factors of totalitarianism present in Orwell's novel which show that *1984* is alive and ill in America.

And while, in America, the problem is not just government control over the people-but Wall Street and multinational corporations' control over government and the people-the four major factors in *1984* remain at the basis of our dilemma:

**Nationalism and Endless War**
Merriam-Webster's dictionary defines "nationalism":
*loyalty and devotion to a nation; especially :* a sense of *national* consciousness exalting one nation above all others and placing primary emphasis on promotion of its culture and interests as opposed to those of other *nations* or supranational groups.

*Encyclopedia Britannica* clarifies nationalism's place in our society:

> *Nationalism is a modern movement. Throughout history people have been attached to their native soil, to the traditions of their parents, and to established territorial authorities; but it was not until the end of the 18th century that nationalism began to be a generally recognized sentiment molding public and private life and one of the great, if not the greatest, single determining factors of modern history. Because of its dynamic vitality and its all-pervading character, nationalism is often thought to be very old; sometimes it is mistakenly regarded as a permanent factor in political behaviour.*

In *1984*, the powerful assure nationalism through the societal structure: Big Brother, the Inner Party, Outer Party, and the Proles. Big Brother is the enigmatic leader only seen on the TV screen and posters. The Inner Party consists of the iron-hand top 2% of the population. The Outer Party is the submissive middle class, 13% of the population. The Proles are the massive poor: the remaining 85%.

Where is the U.S. going? Last summer, Pew Research, in its report "The Lost Decade of the Middle Class: Fewer, Poorer, Gloomier," stated:

> *Since 2000, the middle class has shrunk in size, fallen backward in income and wealth, and shed some-but by no means all-of its characteristic faith in the future...*
>
> *...Fully 85% of self-described middle-class adults say it is more difficult now than it was a decade ago for middle-class people to maintain their standard of living. Of those who feel this way, 62% say "a lot" of the blame lies with Congress, while 54% say the same about banks and financial institutions, 47% about large corporations, 44% about the Bush administration, 39% about foreign competition and 34% about the Obama administration. Just 8% blame the middle class itself a lot.*

In *1984*, the powerful assure continued control by instilling fear in the people, and conducting "perpetual war"-a lasting state of global conflict with no clear end in sight.

Today, the United States sees the decaying effects of a decade of invasions of Iraq and Afghanistan, drone invasions into Pakistan, and looking to spread its military aggression possibly into Iran, Syria, Africa, and beyond. All for the sake of an endless war on terror.

**Doublethink**
In *1984*, Doublethink is accepting two mutually contradictory beliefs as correct:

> ***The power of holding two contradictory beliefs in one's mind simultaneously, and accepting both of them...To tell deliberate lies while genuinely***

Roger Armbrust

> ***believing in them, to forget any fact that has become inconvenient, and then, when it becomes necessary again, to draw it back from oblivion for just as long as it is needed, to deny the existence of objective reality and all the while to take account of the reality which one denies – all this is indispensably necessary...***
> **George Orwell, *1984*, Book 1, Chapter 3**

In America today, we tell ourselves we're living in a free society while we're seeing our incomes shrivel, credit card debt expand, our young saddled with lifelong college-loan debt, the Federal Reserve print endless money going to banks and not homeowners or consumers, and we continue to pollute our air, water, and earth in the name of industrial progress. Doublethink.

We noticed on TV recently that Coca Cola airs a commercial of citizens photographed in caring situations by public security cameras, e.g., a young couple kissing on a park bench. The catch line: public security cameras record *good* things, too. Doublethink.

**Censorship and Media**
In *1984*, the Ministry of Truth controls information dissemination in all areas: news, entertainment, education, and the arts. Winston Smith, the novel's protagonist, works for the Ministry of Truth. His job: to edit and revise history to fit the party line according to Big Brother and the Inner Party-the 2%.

> ***Day by day and almost minute by minute the past was brought up to date. In this way every prediction made by the Party could be shown by documentary evidence to have been correct; nor was any item of news, or any expression of opinion, which conflicted with the needs of the moment, ever allowed to remain on record. All history was a palimpsest, scraped clean and reinscribed exactly as often as was necessary.***
> **– George Orwell, *1984*, Book 1, Chapter 3**

# The Vital Realities for 2020 and Beyond

In America today, the majority of news, book publishing and entertainment-once shared by a multitude of independent newspapers, book publishers, radio and TV stations, record companies, film production houses, and the Internet-are financially controlled by five major media conglomerates: the Walt Disney Company, News Corporation, Time Warner, CBS Corporation, and Viacom.

They determine what you're told and not told about your world, and their major concern is making profits, not a more informed public.

**Surveillance, Fear of Expression, and Newspeak**
We gave you a concrete view of the current surveillance situation, at least a part of the growing surveillance, at this column's beginning.

What do you do about taking back your freedoms in a surveillance society? *Peculiar Progressive* constantly urges you to get organized, get educated and get active. Some lawmakers are beginning to respond to the recent public upheaval caused by government wiretapping and Internet control. But that will be for show, unless you hold their feet to the fire, or replace them if they don't protect you. Don't be afraid to express yourself.

Most of all, pay attention to language: Challenge government and business, and yourself, to be specific, not deal in vague generalities...not deal in Newspeak.

In *1984*, Doublethink is a mainstay of Newspeak:

> **Don't you see that the whole aim of Newspeak is to narrow the range of thought?... Has it ever occurred to you, Winston, that by the year 2050, at the very latest, not a single human being will be alive who could understand such a conversation as we are having now?... The whole climate of thought will be different. In fact, there will be**

Roger Armbrust

> *no thought, as we understand it now. Orthodoxy means not thinking-not needing to think. Orthodoxy is unconsciousness.*
> **George Orwell, *1984*, Book 1, Chapter 5**

# American Majority Finally Opposes NSA Surveillance
**Roger Armbrust,** August 13, 2013

It's taken a while for the timid American electorate to speak its mind. But finally a majority of U.S. citizens say they're opposed to the growing massive surveillance conducted by their government, according to a July report of the Pew Research Center for the People & the Press.

The July 26 report states:

> A majority of Americans – 56% – say that federal courts fail to provide adequate limits on the telephone and internet data the government is collecting as part of its anti-terrorism efforts. An even larger percentage (70%) believes that the government uses this data for purposes other than investigating terrorism.
>
> And despite the insistence by the president and other senior officials that only "metadata," such as phone numbers and email addresses, is being collected, 63% think the government is also gathering information about the content of communications – with 27% believing the government has listened to or read **their** phone calls and emails.

However, 50% of those polled still feel that some collection of phone and Internet data are necessary to the anti-terror program the government says its conducting-a sign that half of Americans still believe the federal government's argument that it must combat terror, which allows the U.S. to conduct endless war worldwide.

Still, more of the public is expressing concern about the anti-terror campaign restricting Americans' civil liberties. Pew points out that citizens' growing concerns are affecting Congress's political parties.

> *Overall, 47% say their greater concern about government anti-terrorism policies is that they have gone too far in restricting the average person's civil liberties, while 35% say they are more concerned that policies have not gone far enough to protect the country. This is the first time in Pew Research polling that more have expressed concern over civil liberties than protection from terrorism since the question was first asked in 2004.*
>
> *As concern about civil liberties has grown, the issue now divides members of both parties. Roughly four-in-ten Republicans (43%) and Democrats (42%) say their greater concern over anti-terror policies is that they have gone too far in restricting civil liberties, up sharply from three years ago (25% and 33% in 2010, respectively).*

The politicians also signal who they care more about-the public or the military-industrial-surveillance complex-when asked about transparency. A majority (51%) of each party believes the news media should NOT report information it obtains about the secret methods the government uses to fight terrorism.

**Jimmy Carter Deeply Concerned**
Such reporting, of course, puts these politicians on the spot, making them responsible for responding and protecting the public.

The Vital Realities for 2020 and Beyond

The reality is this: It's very doubtful that a majority of Americans now would oppose the expansive government surveillance if they hadn't heard about the government's tactics from whistleblowers. They certainly haven't heard an outcry from Congress or the White House, who have backed the massive surveillance. It took the likes of Bradley Manning, Julian Assange, and Edward Snowden, to dent the thick walls of secrecy the Bush and Obama administrations had constructed around their elusive wars on terror.

A major voice opposed to surveillance efforts recently arose even from a former president. Jimmy Carter has been highly critical of U.S. intelligence efforts, flatly saying, "America does not at the moment have a functioning democracy." *International Business Times* reported Carter's statement when he spoke in mid-July in Atlanta.

In an earlier interview with *CNN*, Carter said Edward Snowden's revealing information on the NSA's spying was "beneficial" for America. He told the network:

> *...the invasion of human rights and American privacy has gone too far... I think that the secrecy that has been surrounding this invasion of privacy has been excessive, so I think that the bringing of it to the public notice has probably been, in the long term, beneficial.*

Meanwhile, the NSA's battle to remain secret continues. Glenn Greenwald reported in UK's *The Guardian* last week:

> *Members of Congress have been repeatedly thwarted when attempting to learn basic information about the National Security Agency (NSA) and the secret FISA court which authorizes its activities, documents provided by two House members demonstrate.*

On Aug. 1, a former NSA analyst told the *PBS Newshour* that the NSA collects "word for word" every domestic communication.

Roger Armbrust

Russell Tice worked for the NSA for two decades. In his broadcast interview, he told PBS' Judy Woodruff:

> Well, two months ago, I contacted some colleagues at NSA. We had a little meeting, and the question came up, was NSA collecting everything now? Because we kind of figured that was the goal all along. And the answer came back. It was, yes, they are collecting everything, contents word for word, everything of every domestic communication in this country.

On July 31, Bloomberg news reported on "The Public-Private Surveillance Partnership":

> If the National Security Agency required us to notify it whenever we made a new friend, the nation would rebel. Yet we notify Facebook Inc. (FB) If the Federal Bureau of Investigation demanded copies of all our conversations and correspondence, it would be laughed at. Yet we provide copies of our e-mail to Google Inc. (GOOG), Microsoft Corp. (MSFT) or whoever our mail host is; we provide copies of our text messages to Verizon Communications Inc. (VZ), AT&T Inc. (T) and Sprint Corp. (S); and we provide copies of other conversations to Twitter Inc., Facebook, LinkedIn (LNKD) Corp. or whatever other site is hosting them. The primary business model of the Internet is built on mass surveillance, and our government's intelligence-gathering agencies have become addicted to that data. Understanding how we got here is critical to understanding how we undo the damage.

You'll want to read the Bloomberg article if you're concerned at all about the future of your civil liberties, and your children's.

*Peculiar Progressive* has expressed concern in previous columns about the growth of the surveillance state. You can read just two of those ("None's Well That's Orwell") *here* and ("Senate Scraps CISPA...But Watch Your Back") *here*.

Meanwhile, President Obama said last Friday he would work with Congress on reforming the NSA's massive surveillance practices. Good luck with that, America.

# Bradley Manning: Within the Torture, Signs of Victory
**Roger Armbrust,** August 21, 2013

Bradley Manning sent documents to Wikileaks who released them to the world. Surely this, along with other whistleblower actions, helped convince Edward Snowden he needed to inform the public how it's under constant U.S. government surveillance.

This cycle, in turn, seems to have even shaken a cowardly, self-serving Congress into perhaps...perhaps...reigning in a federal policing network gone mad. Time will tell.

But none of it would have occurred if not for the diminutive, 25-year-old record-keeper who compiled recordings of illegal military activity along with other documents and slipped them to Julian Assange's website. The government knows it, and knew that-if they didn't grab him, isolate him, and make an example of him to deter others-revelations of their illicit activities would continue to pour forth.

And, despite their efforts to draw and quarter Manning and his reputation, the dam seems to have broken. Manning could have received up to 90 years in prison for his admitted misdeeds. Prosecutors wanted him to serve 60 years. The military judge today sentenced him to 35 years, subtracting from that his time already served-1,294 days in pre-trial confinement (much in isolation) plus an additional 112 days.

# The Vital Realities for 2020 and Beyond

All that considered, Morris Davis-a former Guantanamo prosecutor who left the military frustrated over the government's abuse of the prisoners' legal rights-tweeted today that Manning's sentence "means he'll likely serve about 8 to 8.5 yrs more in confinement and be out by the time he's 33 or 34."

Despite the government trying to paint him as a traitor, it hasn't been able to scrub away the viral video image of a military helicopter mowing down civilians, including a *Reuters* journalist, on a Baghdad street. An image which Manning slipped to Wikileaks and then to the world. His action has garnered him a following of faithful supporters, even a nomination for the Nobel Peace Prize. And following his sentencing today, rights groups like Amnesty International began calling on President Obama to commute his sentence.

And surely Manning's action has provided a strong catalyst leading to the federal government's cover being blown in other areas: the National Security Agency tapping nearly ALL American phone and email communication and Internet research. And the FBI confiscating phone records of the *Associated Press*, a direct violation of Constitutional freedom of the press.

The government's policing activities, of course, continue. On Tuesday, the *Wall Street Journal* reported:

> *The National Security Agency-which possesses only limited legal authority to spy on U.S. citizens-has built a surveillance network that covers more Americans' Internet communications than officials have publicly disclosed, current and former officials say.*
>
> *The system has the capacity to reach roughly 75% of all U.S. Internet traffic in the hunt for foreign intelligence, including a wide array of communications by foreigners and Americans. In some cases, it retains the written content of emails sent between citizens within the U.S.*

Roger Armbrust

> *and also filters domestic phone calls made with Internet technology, these people say.*

The day before, *The Washington Post* observed:

> *If the police arrest you, do they need a warrant to rifle through your cellphone? Courts have been split on the question. Last week the Obama administration asked the Supreme Court to resolve the issue and rule that the Fourth Amendment allows warrantless cellphone searches.*

But now, thanks to Manning and others, at least we know it's going on. So now, the American public has the option of getting organized, getting educated, and getting active in stopping it. But the public will have to badger Congress to make it happen, because Congress controls the purse strings to all the surveillance activity.

# Whistleblowers, Activists Call on Intelligence Peers to Step Forward
**Roger Armbrust,** December 17, 2013

A powerful letter-a declaration of independence offered for the American and European intelligence community-appeared last week in *The Guardian*, the United Kingdom's newspaper which has stood firm in exposing illegal clandestine activities of the U.S. National Security Agency (NSA).

The open letter was signed by noted government whistleblowers-who felt their government was committing illegal acts and, unable to curtail the activities within the system, took their accusations public-and activists supporting their efforts.

The seven signers are:

Thomas Drake, a former NSA senior executive who in 2006 "leaked information about the NSA's dysfunctional data-gathering Trailblazer Project to the Baltimore Sun. He was prosecuted under the Espionage Act in 2010, but the case collapsed," according to *The Guardian*.

Daniel Ellsberg, a former US military analyst who in 1971 leaked the *Pentagon Papers*, exposing U.S. lies about the Vietnam War.

Katharine Gun, a former British translator for Government

Roger Armbrust

Communications Headquarters(GCHQ), a British intelligence agency. In 2003, she leaked a top-secret email about US plans to spy on the UN, and was charged under the Official Secrets Act.

Peter Kofod, a Danish musician and former participant in the human shield action in Iraq.

Ray McGovern, a political activist and former CIA analyst who served from 1963-1990. He received the Intelligence Commendation Medal, which he returned in protest in 2006 over CIA use of torture.

Jesselyn Radack, national security and human rights director of the Government Accountability Project, which represents whistleblowers.

Coleen Rowley, a retired FBI agent who testified before the U.S. Senate and the 9/11 commission about FBI mishandling of information related to the Sept. 11 attacks.

The missive's headline reads, "Former whistleblowers: open letter to intelligence employees after Snowden."

"Snowden" refers to Edward Snowden, the American computer specialist, former Central Intelligence Agency (CIA) employee, and former NSA contractor who disclosed up to 200,000 classified documents to the press, and continues to present disclosures. Snowden's revelations have opened to the public the U.S. government's worldwide eavesdropping into personal, foreign government, and business activities.

The letter opens with these insiders' view of the extent and seriousness of government clandestine efforts:

> At least since the aftermath of September 2001, western governments and intelligence agencies have been hard at work expanding the scope of their own power, while eroding privacy, civil liberties and public control of

> policy. What used to be viewed as paranoid, Orwellian, tin-foil hat fantasies turned out post-Snowden, to be not even the whole story.
>
> What's really remarkable is that we've been warned for years that these things were going on: wholesale surveillance of entire populations, militarization of the internet, the end of privacy. All is done in the name of "national security", which has more or less become a chant to fence off debate and make sure governments aren't held to account – that they can't be held to account – because everything is being done in the dark. Secret laws, secret interpretations of secret laws by secret courts and no effective parliamentary oversight whatsoever.

The letter notes that the media has paid "scant attention" to this government aggression, which began under the George W. Bush administration and has spread under the tight grip of Barack Obama. It goes on to highlight some of the most telling of the whistleblowers' revelations.

Then the letter makes an appeal to the everyday, dedicated employees in government intelligence:

> Hidden away in offices of various government departments, intelligence agencies, police forces and armed forces are dozens and dozens of people who are very much upset by what our societies are turning into: at the very least, turnkey tyrannies.
>
> One of them is you.
>
> You're thinking:
> ,óè Undermining democracy and eroding civil liberties isn't put explicitly in your job contract.
> ,óè You grew up in a democratic society and want to keep it that way

Roger Armbrust

> *‚óè You were taught to respect ordinary people's right to live a life in privacy*
> *‚óè You don't really want a system of institutionalized strategic surveillance that would make the dreaded Stasi green with envy – do you?*

The letter writers then encourage employees to come forward, emphasizing how "Edward Snowden showed what one person can do." It closes with a more specific call to action:

> *You can be part of the solution; provide trustworthy journalists – either from old media (like this newspaper) or from new media (such as WikiLeaks) with documents that prove what illegal, immoral, wasteful activities are going on where you work.*

It ends with the invitation that "Courage is contagious."
You can read the entire letter here.

This letter seems to be of vital importance as an invitation, not only to intelligence employees, but to the public in general: i.e., become involved in what *Peculiar Progressive* columns have consistently called for: Get organized, get educated, and get active.

The whistleblowers and activists including "new media" in their definition of a free press is also vital to American freedom of expression today. Congress is currently considering legislation that would limit who government would consider as "the press." Those efforts appear to include attempts to quell independent press reporting on the Internet, and may be the beginning of stopping any reporting not under the control of major corporations that own the largest news organizations. The White House has also pushed to limit press freedoms.

This group of courageous whistleblowers and activists address government employees in their letter. But the letter ran in a newspaper, and is shared here via the Internet. It's also vital that you, the general public, be a part of the action to protect press freedom and the free, open distribution of information about government activities worldwide. The question is, are you ready to join them and protect yourself and your children's right to such freedoms?

# National Security Depends on Press Freedom
**Roger Armbrust,** June 9, 2014

The U.S. Supreme Court and U.S. Court of Appeals for the Fourth Circuit have spit on our U.S. Constitution, demanding that a journalist reveal an anonymous source or go to jail.

They're obviously banking on two things: (1) most Americans don't know enough about our own Constitution to notice or care, and (2) we've been beaten down enough by the military-industrial complex and growing surveillance-police state so that we'll remain silent to their actions. (For any of these aggressive phrases that might alarm you, notice we're including links to support our assertions, all of which affect you, the American public.)

The conservative federal judges are hoping you'll think backwards, growing fearful enough to believe that your national security depends on government intelligence and surveillance rather than press freedom. After all, that's what they seem to think. But then again, they get their paychecks from the same Millionaire Congress that the Central Intelligence Agency (CIA) and National Security Agency (NSA) receive their big bucks from, as do the federal prosecutors who answer to the Millionaire President.

But don't think their way. Here's what you should recall:

## The First Amendment
The First Amendment to our Constitution reads:

> *Congress shall make no law respecting an establishment of religion, or prohibiting the free exercise thereof; or abridging the freedom of speech, or of the press; or the right of the people peaceably to assemble, and to petition the Government for a redress of grievances.*

The First Amendment and the rest of the Bill of Rights were adopted by We the People in 1791. No one had even heard of the CIA or NSA then. That's because they didn't exist. Most folks probably knew our nation had spies. We even had spies when we fought the British to become free.

But the press *did* exist. And the Founding Fathers knew that— to keep the federal government in line, from its spying, to its policing, to its use of our tax dollars—we'd require a press with liberty to investigate and report on government, free of its interference. Which is why the First Amendment reads in part: "Congress shall make no law...abridging the freedom...of the press."

That reads "NO LAW." So, what the federal Congress can't do, the federal courts have decided to do. The federal high court and most of the Fourth Circuit judges have recently found it complicit to override the "NO LAW," and to abridge press freedom. They chose to side with the government and its ongoing propagandized argument that release of almost any classified information will endanger national security. And what it deems classified is surely excessive.

This limiting of press freedom goes back to 1972, when the Supreme Court ruled in *Branzburg v. Hayes* that a journalist was not protected by the First Amendment and could be subpoenaed by a grand jury. The decision was 5-4. Writing a concurring opinion for the conservative majority, Justice Lewis F. Powell said that press privilege "should be judged on its facts by the striking of a proper balance between freedom of the press and the obligation of all citizens to give relevant testimony with respect to criminal conduct. The balance of these vital constitutional and societal interests on a case-by-case basis accords with the tried and traditional way of adjudicating such questions."

That's the same Lewis F. Powell who, as a corporate and tobacco lawyer before his appointment to the high court, wrote the infamous "Powell Memorandum"–a year before his Supreme Court opinion on press freedom.  He wrote his telling memo to the U.S. Chamber of Commerce.

Titled "An Attack on the American Free Enterprise System," Powell opened his message to the organization of major corporations by saying, "No thoughtful person can question that the American economic system is under broad attack."

He went on to say later, "The most disquieting voices joining the chorus of criticism came from perfectly respectable elements of society: from the college campus, the pulpit, the media, the intellectual and literary journals, the arts and sciences, and from politicians." He then called for "constant surveillance" and purging of society's left-wing elements.

Get the picture?
Ever since Powell stated his rationale in the Supreme Court case a year later, courts have cited it in opinions on the press, which led to the current case.

**USA v. Jeffrey Alexander Sterling**
Right now, we're speaking specifically of the Fourth Circuit's ordering a *New York Times* Pulitzer Prize-winning reporter, James Risen, to testify in the trial of a former CIA operations officer, Jeffrey Alexander Sterling. In 2010, Sterling was indicted under the Espionage Act of 1917.

It was a sign of the White House's growing effort to quell

transparency in government, to keep secret from the public more and more government activity. Rarely had a federal official been punished under law for alleged contact with a journalist. But the Obama administration has consistently increased efforts to legally harass federal whistleblowers—i.e. government agents who have tried through their agency channels to correct legal wrongs or growing agency errors and, when authorities tried to quiet them, then went to the press to make the damaging activities public.

Sterling is being tried for allegedly revealing details regarding Operation Merlin, a reportedly covert effort under the Clinton administration to supply Iran with flawed nuclear-weapon design information. The government charges that Sterling provided these details to journalist Risen, who revealed them in his book *State of War*. Risen reported the CIA supplied the flawed information to a defected Russian nuclear scientist for him to supply Iran. But the scientist realized the flaws and pointed them out to the Iranians, and may actually have helped them.

Federal prosecutors have demanded that Risen should testify about who his anonymous source is. (Somehow, the CIA and its 21,500+ employees with a $14.7 billion budget evidently haven't been able to find that out.) Risen argues that the First Amendment protects him and his sources, that without that protection federal employees would never come forward to challenge secret government practices. He has said that, rather than reveal his source, he will go to prison.

Obama's prosecutors obviously would love that. Why? Risen is a respected, nationally known journalist—a two-time Pulitzer Prize-winning reporter honored for his stories on (1) President George W. Bush's warrantless wiretapping program, and (2) 9/11 and terrorism. Lately, he's written about the NSA. If prosecutors can get a court to imprison him, that's a powerful, intimidating statement to all American journalists that the federal government will go after them, and probably win with conservative majorities in the higher courts. And if they can get journalists, that surely will put a clamp on critics within the government.

That's one reason why so many news organizations filed as a friend of the defendant in the government's case against Sterling. Those organizations include Newspaper Association of America, the National Association of Broadcasters, Reporters Committee for Freedom of the Press, as well as companies like the *Associated Press*, Gannett News, Hearst Corporation, Reuters America, *The Washington Post*, and more.

If you want to read the legal court filing, that's here. If you want to read a news story summarizing the case, that's here. We will point out that one of the appellant court judges dissented from ordering Risen to testify. Judge Roger Gregory argued:

> *The majority exalts the interests of the government while unduly trampling those of the press, and in doing so, severely impinges on the press and the free flow of information in our society.*

*Peculiar Progressive* concurs with Judge Gregory. If you do too, we suggest you write President Obama and demand he follow our Constitution and instruct the Justice Department to no longer try to intimidate journalists with threats of prison. You can also write your Congressional delegation and demand that it challenge the president on this issue and support freedom of the press. Also, to not allow appointment of federal judges who want to limit press freedom. And let your elected reps know that, if they don't do as you wish, you'll work to find a respecter of our Constitution to replace them.

That's particularly true of the Senate, which is currently trying to form legislation to limit press freedoms. Surely an unconstitutional plot.

It's appearing more and more that it's time for you to protect yourself and your children's future through Peaceful Revolution:

i.e., getting organized, educated and active in defending your Constitutional rights. In this case, the legal right to a free press that can keep you apprised of government's legal and illegal activities. Protecting the press is, in effect, protecting yourself and your national security.

# Oligarchy's Sibling Rivals: the U.S. and Russia
**Roger Armbrust,** December 22, 2014

*The New York Times*, now evidently dedicated to siding with Washington in its sanctions effort against Russia, is publishing a collection of articles under the logo "Putin's Way,"explaining:

> Articles in this series are examining how President Vladimir V. Putin's system of personalized state-sponsored capitalism allows him to wield power at home and abroad.

For example, on Sunday, Nov. 2, the *Times* ran a damning article detailing Putin's manipulation of the Russian school textbook industry. The Russian government has purged "hundreds of textbooks that [14 million] Russian schoolchildren had relied upon for years," basically leading to thought control of the young and endangering the economic lives of small publishers.

But one major book publisher has remained virtually untouched: Enlightenment, chaired by one of Putin's inner circle. The company recently signed a deal with Microsoft "to help it provide Windows-based tablets to Russian schools." This, despite the sanctions, a telling fact in itself of who sanctions help and hurt.

But the *Times* article's most telling paragraph, and not just for Russia, was one summarizing Putin's power over the economy:

> *Enlightenment's story also traces, in miniature, the arc of the Russian economy over the last quarter-century, from Soviet state ownership, to privatization, to what might be called the theater of state-sponsored private enterprise that flourishes today under Mr. Putin. In theory, market competition exists. In reality, the Kremlin and its functionaries have divvied up the nation's strategic industries among a small and malleable circle of allies. They command some of the nation's largest energy companies, control banks and much of the news media, and, increasingly, have a footprint in smaller sectors, like book publishing, that are nonetheless important to Mr. Putin's political control.*

It's that paragraph's section beginning with "In theory..." that's particularly telling, because that description of a small circle controlling energy, banks, news media, and increasingly smaller sectors, happens to mirror the United States. The two major powers, now at odds over who will benefit from the global economy and control of energy sources in Eurasia, are essentially sibling rivals in economic oligarchy.

Indeed, two American political science professors earlier this year released a study determining that the U.S. is no longer a democracy, but an oligarchy. That study, penned by Princeton's Martin Gilens and Northwestern's Benjamin Page, stated:

> *...we believe that if policymaking is dominated by powerful business organizations and a small number of affluent Americans, then America's claims to being a democratic society are seriously threatened...*
>
> *... In the United States, our findings indicate, the majority does not rule—at least not in the causal sense of actually determining policy outcomes. When a majority of citizens disagrees with economic elites and/or with organized interests, they generally lose. Moreover*

Roger Armbrust

> *... even when fairly large majorities of Americans favor policy change, they generally do not get it.*

This is why *Peculiar Progressive* has concentrated columns on the five vital realitiespoliticians won't discuss, but — along with Wall Street and the military-industrial complex — will manipulate. And why we refer to the Millionaire President and Millionaire Congress, because when Big Money controls Washington, then the democracy is dissolved. As it obviously also is in Russia, though both Moscow and Washington claim they continue to grow democracies, while, in fact, they don't.

# Following Paris, Police States Grow as Economies Shrink
**Roger Armbrust,** January 19, 2015

Paris's Charlie Hebdo and supermarket attacks have set the stage for another post-9/11, as countries rev up police/military efforts on terror while hoping that will keep citizens' frightened minds off the shriveling world economy.

France, the U.S., U.K., Germany, and Belgium are examples of nations seeing the Paris attacks as a chance to further instill fear into citizens and plot ways to increase a police-state environment. The effort is in cooperation with major corporate media outlets which are tirelessly repeating news reports of the states' policing efforts.

Last week, French President Francois Hollande oversaw the immediate sending of 10,000 extra military and 5,000 added police to patrol French streets following last week's attack. That was followed Friday by police raids in five Paris suburbs.

In the U.S., President Obama agreed with a visiting U.K. Prime Minister David Cameron to cooperate on growing cybersecurity—i.e., increasing government surveillance control of the citizens' Internet. This following Cameron's call earlier in the week for uniting Brit police and military efforts to fight terrorism, and for eliminating encryption from the Internet.

Roger Armbrust

The Electronic Frontier Foundation (EFF), an international non-profit digital rights group based in the U.S., expressed grave concern, as did others, with Obama's proposal. The EFF issued a statement which, in part, said:

> *The status quo of overweening national security and law enforcement secrecy means that expanded information sharing poses a serious risk of transferring more personal information to intelligence and law enforcement agencies. Given that the White House rightly criticized CISPA in 2013 for potentially facilitating the unnecessary transfer of personal information to the government or other private sector entities when sending cybersecurity threat data, we're concerned that the Administration proposal will unintentionally legitimize the approach taken by these dangerous bills.*

In Germany, a swath of 250 German police united to arrest two "suspected terrorists".

In Belgium, deadly police raids killed two "suspected terrorists" and led to the arrest of a third, while the Belgian prime minister called a press conference to argue there was no terrorist plot.

These are the tips of what will logically be a continuing effort by governments to take control over an increasingly unhappy citizenry.

Meanwhile, independent reports from the right and left are challenging the rising government/media hysteria, calling it propagandized efforts to secure Orwellian military states.

Ron Paul, the former U.S. Congressman and Republican presidential candidate—through his Ron Paul Institute for Peace and Prosperity—has consistently criticized such government/media efforts. He even complained that the nation's policymakers who went before a massive Paris march on freedom of expression were some of the major abusers of that freedom.

He wasn't alone in lashing them. So did journalist Jeremy Scahill, whose latest book, *Dirty Wars: The World is a Battlefield*, was made into an Academy Award-nominated documentary. Appearing on "Democracy Now" last week, Scahill commented:

> ...this is sort of a circus of hypocrisy when it comes to all of those world leaders who were marching at the front of it [the Paris parade]. I mean, every single one of those heads of state or representatives of governments there have waged their own wars against journalists. You know, David Cameron ordered The Guardian to smash with a hammer the hard drives that stored the files of NSA whistleblower Edward Snowden. Blasphemy is considered a crime in Ireland. You had multiple African and Arab leaders whose own countries right now have scores of journalists in prison. Benjamin Netanyahu's government in Israel has targeted for killing numerous journalists who have reported on the Palestinian side, have kidnapped, abducted, jailed journalists. You know, there's this controversy right now: Why didn't President Obama go, or why didn't Joe Biden go?

Obama has had an ongoing battle with government whistleblowers and journalists, the most recent in trying to force *New York Times* Pulitzer Prize-winning reporter James Risen to name a confidential source.

Also, listening to the U.S. government and major media talk about terrorism, you'd think that radical Islamists were the major culprit. But two reports show they're only a small part of anti-government attacks. On Jan. 14, the online news and opinion site *The Daily Beast* published an article headlined "Are All Terrorists Muslims? It's Not Even Close." The article cited statistics from Europol, the FBI, and the University of North Carolina:

> As Europol, the European Union's law-enforcement

> agency, noted in its report released last year, the vast majority of terror attacks in Europe were perpetrated by separatist groups. For example, in 2013, there were 152 terror attacks in Europe. Only two of them were "religiously motivated," while 84 were predicated upon ethno-nationalist or separatist beliefs...

> Back in the United States, the percentage of terror attacks committed by Muslims is almost as miniscule as in Europe. An FBI study looking at terrorism committed on U.S. soil between 1980 and 2005 found that 94 percent of the terror attacks were committed by non-Muslims. In actuality, 42 percent of terror attacks were carried out by Latino-related groups, followed by 24 percent perpetrated by extreme left-wing actors.

> And as a 2014 study by University of North Carolina found, since the 9/11 attacks, Muslim-linked terrorism has claimed the lives of 37 Americans. In that same time period, more than 190,000 Americans were murdered (PDF).

### Failing Economies as Culprit

*Peculiar Progressive*, in a February 27, 2011 column headlined "Solving the Decade of Our Discontent", quoted from a *New York Times* op-ed by a powerful Saudi Prince, Alwaleed bin Talal bin Abdulaziz Al-Saud, a grandson of the founding king of modern Saudi Arabia. He summarized the Arab economic struggle this way, which is actually a portrait of our global dire conditions:

> The majority of the Arab population is under 25, and the unemployment rate for young adults is in most countries 20 percent or more. Unemployment is even higher among women, who are economically and socially marginalized. The middle classes are being pushed down by inflation, which makes a stable standard of living seem an unattainable hope. The gap

*between the haves and the have-nots is widening. The basic needs for housing, health care and education are not being met for millions.*

These conditions surely prove true for Europe and the U.S. We've contended for a while that governments with struggling economies look for an exterior enemy to try to nationalize the citizenry and push them away from revolting against the internal economic conditions. That enemy commonly takes the form of either immigrants—accused of taking citizens' jobs and corrupting the national culture—or a foreign foe threatening the citizenry's safety and freedoms. Or both.

The attack on immigrants is heavy in the U.S. and in Europe, both through legislation and public protests. And the U.S. oligarchy's lead on stirring up enemies continues through the endless war in the Middle East, and now painting Russia's oligarchy as an aggressive foe. All this fascist effort, of course, feeds the ravenous military-industrial complex that drains the public coffers for the war racket. In turn, it's the catalyst for efforts at austerity by governments worldwide, starving electorates from vital services ranging from healthcare to education to infrastructure.

Also, last week, we saw two chief ingredients that can lead to another global economic meltdown, worse than that suffered in 2008. In Switzerland, the government broke its franc away from being pegged to the Euro, bringing hundreds of millions in losses, causing chaos in global financial markets. In the U.S., the new Congress renewed Wall Street-led efforts to weaken more the Dodd-Frank Act which feebly regulates the finance industry.

The Congressional effort encourages more Wall Street activity in derivatives investment. **The gluttonous growth of the nontransparent (as in secret) derivativesinvestment industry, is considered the chief cause for the economic meltdown of 2007-08. International banking analysts**

Roger Armbrust

**are expressing consistent concern that the derivatives racket, at a then-high of over $600 trillion in 2007, is currently over $700 trillion. Analysts are also extremely wary of the growing private debt worldwide.**

Bottom line: If you're going to get the new Millionaire Congress and Millionaire president to serve you rather than Wall Street and the military-industrial complex, you're going to have to get organized, get educated, and get active in communicating with them. If you're afraid to do that, or even worse, indifferent to it, we'll leave you with the words of Dr. Martin Luther King, Jr., whose life and martyrdom the nation is honoring today:

*In the end, we will remember not the words of our enemies, but the silence of our friends.*

# Your Freedoms and the TPP, TTIP, and RCEP
**Roger Armbrust,** October 12, 2015

Last week America's corporate media let you know that representatives from 12 nations including U.S. government officials had agreed on the secret Trans-Pacific Partnership "free trade" deal, much criticized for its being hidden from the public and reportedly controlled by international corporations – which smacks of being detrimental to you, the citizenry.

But TPP is just part of the story of what could affect your freedoms:

Last Saturday in Berlin, at least 150,000 people publicly protested the Transatlantic Trade and Investment Partnership (TTIP), a secretly negotiated proposed pact between Europe and the U.S. As *Reuters* reported this weekend:

> Opposition to the so-called Transatlantic Trade and Investment Partnership (TTIP) has risen over the past year in Germany, with critics fearing the pact will hand too much power to big multinationals at the expense of consumers and workers...
>
> ...The level of resistance has taken Chancellor Angela Merkel's government by surprise and underscores the

> *challenge it faces to turn the tide in favor of the deal which proponents say will create a market of 800 million and serve as a counterweight to China's economic clout.*

You can read details of the TTIP — which the U.S. considers a companion trade deal to the TPP — including criticisms, here.

**TPP and You**
We wrote in detail about the TPP in June of this year in a column, published on *reality: a world of views*, headlined "Washington: 'Trust Us" on Secret TPP. Right.". That's a look at arguments on the TPP from both sides, including a negative argument from Nobel Prize-winning economist Joseph Stiglitz.

Stiglitz has continued criticizing the TPP. Late last month, the Columbia University professor spoke at the University of British Columbia (Canada is a proposed TPP member). The *Vancouver Sun* said Stiglitz "warned Canadians that the 12-nation free-trade deal, which includes Canada, has the potential to damage certain aspects of quality of life for consumers and citizens."

The *Sun* quoted Stiglitz:

> *That's where these agreements are becoming particularly bad. It used to be that trade agreements were negotiated over tariffs ... the consumers gained. The new agreements are about getting rid of regulations. We're talking about regulation over the environment, safety, economy, health. The consumers, who are not at the table, get screwed.*

Thanks to some leaks of the secret TPP, some facts have come forth, as Stiglitz noted:

> *They've been negotiating in secret, so we don't know the exact terms. But we have a pretty good idea. There's one provision which allows any company to*

> sue the government if there's a new regulation. That kind of regulation is being used by (cigarette maker) Philip Morris to sue Uruguay and Australia about cigarette disclosure.
>
> Now imagine if this kind of law had been in place when we discovered asbestos is dangerous to your health. Rather than what did happen — asbestos manufacturers were shut down and used their profits to compensate those who had to re-do their buildings and those who are dying from asbestos — under the new trade agreement, the government would have to pay the companies to not kill anybody ... It takes away the basic right of government to protect its citizens.

Stiglitz also noted how the TPP would favor Big Pharma (drug companies) and other multinationals over nations and citizens.

**China's Non-U.S. Trade Deals**
Did you notice in the *Reuters* quote early in this column: pro-TTIP officials consider the proposed deal "a counter-weight to China's economic clout". *Peculiar Progressive* discussed in a June column how the Obama administration has tried to curtail China's economic growth, including ostracizing it from the TPP. We also discussed how it could lead to military conflict. You can read that column, "China, the U.S. and Looming War", here.

This past week, two articles looked at China's trade moves which offset the TPP. *Reuters* indicated in its article on China's Regional Economic Comprehensive Partnership (RCEP) that Beijing is scurrying to catch up to the U.S.'s TPP efforts. But India's *Economic Times* takes a different view, noting, "observers say the web of bilateral deals Beijing has forged is enough to maintain its global clout."

It's tough to see the Millionaire Congress not favoring the multinationals, military-industrial complex and Wall Street oligarchy

Roger Armbrust

rather than citizens when voting on the TPP and TTIP. It will take a strong citizens' effort to challenge that. Which means, if you want to protect your freedoms, you'll need to get organized, get educated, and get active in challenging the oligarchy.

Why not, for you and your children, see what you can do?

# Time for U.S. "Third" Parties to Rise
**Roger Armbrust,** April 18, 2016

The growing implosions of the Republicans and Democrats, the low voter turnout in major elections, and the increasing dissolution of the global economy — these three realities mark a perfect time for U.S. "Third" parties to finally force themselves into the nation's vital political power structure.

This doesn't mean a third party could win the presidency this year; but — if the Thirds win their federal lawsuit to get admitted to the national TV debates dictatorially controlled by the Democrats and Republicans – surely a percentage of voters would respond in the presidential and congressional races.

And voters shouldn't buy the old lie of a third party vote hurting a Republican or Democrat. The two major parties – assisted by corporate media — for decades have connived and blocked voters' freedoms to hear from third parties, keeping a stranglehold on elections and refusing Americans broader choices they deserve. And Americans have allowed the Dems and Reps to do that by simply deciding to complain and not vote, leading to a federal government now conniving for austerity and limiting constitutional freedoms.

**Republicans, Democrats Rupturing**
Donald Trump's sudden support in Republican primaries has

led the national party's shocked establishment to scurry and find ways to block his presidential nomination. Some big money Republicans are looking at possibly forming a separate political party. This, plus recent successes by U.S. Sen. Ted Cruz, may lead to a raucous Republican national convention this summer that could further separate the fracturing party.

A similar scene appears prevalent with the Democrats. The party establishment is firmly behind Hillary Clinton. But U.S. Sen. Bernie Sanders has leapt from his tiny state of Vermont, welcoming rabid response nationwide to his call for a "revolution" to change America. The Democrats, too, could see a party rupture at its national convention, similar to 1968 with the establishment supporting Vice-President Hubert Humphrey — who got the nomination and later lost to Richard Nixon — and volatile activists who opposed the Vietnam War.

The two majors, by conventions' end, will look to put on a face of unity, but signs are it may only be on the surface.

The key for the third parties, if they are to make significant inroads, is to concentrate on and cultivate the large number of eligible voters turned off by the millionaire Reps and Dems controlling Washington.

**Apathetic Voters**
Only 55% of eligible voters cast ballots in the last presidential election (2012), and nearly 60% of eligibles stayed away from the polls in 2014 Congressional elections. Meanwhile, the Gallup opinion poll showed last week that the public still despises the Millionaire Congress, giving it a miserable approval rating of 17%. President Barak Obama's rating is higher (50%), but still a morbid signal of America's anger with Washington.

It's doubtful either Trump or Sanders will greatly alter their major stances which are dividing the two parties. And, if either or both do somehow find compromise, it will probably only further anger their base of supporters: rabid conservatives for

Trump and liberals for Sanders who are disgusted with endless war, government surveillance, and rule by the rich. Particularly fascinating in Trump's case, since he is a billionaire whose celebrity has captured the hearts of the dissolving white middle class's male population.

**Need for Education**
We covered the "Third" parties' debates the last presidential go-round, recalling how they — as opposed to the Obama-Romney debates — made it appear America was still a democracy. But the major corporate media wouldn't cover the Thirds' debates, blocking most of the public from an education to their platforms. Only *C-SPAN*, *Free Speech TV* and *RT America* covered the minority parties.

Here's what appears, to *Peculiar Progressive,* the Third parties should do now:

1. Win their federal court case to be included in the national TV debates. That will help greatly to broaden their bases in 2016.
2. Whether they win the court case or not, they still need to educate the public to their causes. They can best do that by concentrating on the young, meaning high schools and colleges. They can physically go to campuses to educate them, and file more lawsuits if they're refused access.
3. But their main course must be in flooding social media with their causes. Wherever they can't press flesh and discuss issues with the young, do it online. The Internet has been a major friend to at least four who've sought the presidency: Obama, Sanders, Clinton, and Ron Paul. The Thirds should milk this media avenue and not let up.

**Who Are the Thirds?**
I wrote columns earlier this year when two of the Thirds' front-runners announced: the Green Party's nominee last year, Jill

Roger Armbrust

Stein, the Libertarians' 2012 nominee Gary Johnson. Those two parties will select their 2016 candidates this summer.

The Greens are currently finding a major friend in the world-wide drive to fight global warming. They need to carry that connection to young voters and potential voters. Jill Stein also made free college education an immediate part of her platform when she announced.

The Libertarians, of course, espouse personal freedom, cutting taxes and creating jobs.

But there are a plethora of Thirds which you should know about, and which you should share with any eligible voters you know who plan to avoid the ballot box in November. You can find a list of the Third parties here.

**The Major Draw: Dire Economic Warnings**
What could draw frustrated eligible voters to Thirds more than anything else: the dissolving global economy. Many signs point to another meltdown. We've written about warnings in columns here and here. The first includes concerns about the growing global private and public debt and also central banks' manipulations of interest rates. The second involves unsustainable private debt in the U.S., including student loans and personal credit.

We also complained following the 2014 elections about 11 major economic and social areas where Washington has let the public down. Those problems remain today. You can read that column here: "As U.S. Austerity Deepens, Prepare for Revolution". The rise of the Third parties could be it.

This past week you could see more rising economic warnings in news reports on the International Monetary Fund's fearing that Eurozone banks' £715bn black hole of uncollectible debt is threatening the economy; Saudi Arabia warning the U.S. of pulling $750 billion from the American economy if Washington follows through on a 9/11 liability suit; and oil producers, amid a Saudi-Iran row, refusing to implement an oil production freeze; and the continuing fall in corporate earnings for U.S. banks, energy companies, and other business sectors.

The Thirds need to capitalize on all this in the coming months, shouting their responsible solutions, and asking specifically for votes.

# Why Fascists Fear the Arts... and You
**Roger Armbrust,** March 20, 2017

Let's start with the basics.

First, let's go to the Oxford English Dictionary for two definitions:

Art: "Works produced by human creative skill and imagination."

The Arts: "The various branches of creative activity, such as painting, music, literature, and dance."

Now let's go to the definition of Fascism which we used in our November column about the election of Donald Trump, "Prepare to Fight Fascism: 2017 and Beyond". It's from Merriam-Webster's dictionary:

> ...a political philosophy, movement, or regime (as that of the Fascisti) that exalts nation and often race above the individual and that stands for a centralized autocratic government headed by a dictatorial leader, severe economic and social regimentation, and forcible suppression of opposition.

Honestly comparing and contrasting these definitions should provide us a pretty clear view of why Fascists fear The Arts... and you:

The Arts encourage human creativity and imagination, the free and limitless pursuit of expression in order to expand the body, mind, and spirit, and conceive of the universe's endless connections. Fascism demands a loyalty to a single nation, often a single race, and an authoritarian repression of freedom of thought and expression. Simply stated: The Arts teach us *how* to think. Fascism teaches us *what* to think.

So it's logical why Fascists find the Arts terrifying. A population left free to think and act will begin to understand their suffering from repression, and eventually get organized, educated and active in revolting against it — either peacefully or violently.

This is why, throughout history, when dictators come to power, they immediately go after and corral the free thinkers, primarily the artists, writers, and teachers. Hitler did it. Stalin did it. Today, Turkey's democratically elected president-turned-dictator Recep Tayyip Erdogan is doing it.

In recent years, the US has been caught up in a creeping form of this repression, seen particularly in our handling of higher education. Government and corporations have touted a STEM education. STEM stands for Science, Technology, Engineering and Math — vital pursuits on their own to help make a society sustainable. But without the "A," The Arts, turning STEM to STEAM, you won't have a sustainable society. Because The Arts lead humans' creative thinking to demand free expression, true democracy and respect for human rights.

Fascism can't afford that, including in its recent American form of Oligarchic Capitalism. Here we send money to a few and force slave labor on the many.

In higher education, we've created the racket of more highly paid administrators and fewer adequately paid professors, depending more and more on part-time teachers who've received their advanced degrees but can't find a full-time job with salary and benefits. And when administrations decide to cut college budgets, the first programs to go are in the arts, in the "A," not in the STEM, which they consider big moneymakers. And that's what American higher ed is about today, big money.

This has led teachers, like most other American workers, to try to live on credit, with government allowing Wall Street to seep subprime lending into home loans, credit cards, auto loans and small businesses.

Banks and government have also colluded in placing a generation of college-educated students into long-term debt, with college-loan debt now over $1.3 trillion, larger even than the $779 billion Americans owe for credit cards.

Government, industry and media tout America as the world's exceptional economic leader, but insightful economists are constantly preaching that global private and public debt are the highest in history, and that the unhealthy debt will lead to another global economic meltdown.

All this is the result of government and corporations, especially the major media, encouraging the population to be herded unthinking into debt with delusional promises of future prosperity.

And now we've moved from decades of industrial production and profits for the few to a world experiencing a dangerous climate change that Fascists can't afford to acknowledge. To do so would be admission that the Oligarchic Capitalism is failing not only the people, but the planet.

All this is at the basis of the Trump administration's new budget, introduced last week. It includes eliminating the chief federal agencies involved in encouraging humans HOW to think: a variety of education-grant programs, the National Endowment for the Arts, the National Endowment for the Humanities, the Corporation for Public Broadcasting.

The proposed budget slashes funding for the Environmental Protection Agency; in fact Trump had already erased from the White House website any mention of climate change. And the budget greatly increases the Department of Defense monies, more for Homeland Security, and encourages the development of fossil fuels.

It is a budget which even conservative New York Times columnist David Brooks, an avid espouser of free markets, condemned:

> *They're investing in everything that's hard power... threat and fear. And disinvesting in everything that has to do with compassion, care, thinking and innovation.*

That pretty well summarizes both Fascism and the Trump budget. It will take you getting organized, educated, and active in demanding that the Millionaire Congress oppose both of those destructive forces, which unfortunately the Millionaire Congress is a part of. Some observers believe Congress will oppose such deep budget cuts. But if you want to rely on politicians supporting you without hearing from you, then as legendary broadcast journalist Edward R. Murrow used to say: "Good night, and good luck."

www.ingramcontent.com/pod-product-compliance
Lightning Source LLC
Chambersburg PA
CBHW020238030426
42336CB00010B/533